Gnostic Presences in Ethiopia

Gnostic Presences in Ethiopia

Spiritual Lore and Magic in Ethiopian Christianity

Paolo Cartocci

Translation into English by

Paul Metcalfe

with an introductory essay by

Professor Gianfrancesco Lusini

Gnostic Presences in Ethiopia: Spiritual Lore and Magic in Ethiopian Christianity
Copyright © 2024 by Paolo Cartocci. All rights reserved.

Apart from any fair dealing for the purpose of private study, research, criticism or review, as permitted under the Copyright Act, no part of this publication may be reproduced in any form, stored in a retrieval system or transmitted in any form by any means—electronic, mechanical, photocopy, recording or otherwise—without the prior permission of the publisher. Enquiries should be sent to the undermentioned address.

"The author of the present book has made every effort to obtain permissions for all copyright-protected images. If you have copyright-protected work in this publication and you have not given us permission, please contact the author through the Publisher."

TSEHAI books may be purchased for educational, business, or sales promotional use. For more information, please contact our special sales department.

TSEHAI Publishers
P. O. Box: 90466
Los Angeles, CA 90009

www.tsehaipublishers.com
info@tsehaipublishers.com

ISBN: 978-1-59907-303-3 (Paperback)
ISBN: 978-1-59907-304-0 (Hardcover)
ISBN: 978-1-59907-305-7 (EBook)

Publisher: Elias Wondimu
Cover Illustration: Samson Kebede
Cover Design: Sara Martinez

A catalog record for this book is available from:
Wemezekir Ethiopian National Library, Addis Ababa, Ethiopia.

US Library of Congress Control Number: 2023934372
British Library, London, UK.

10 9 8 7 6 5 4 3 2 1

Printed in the United States of America
Los Angeles | Addis Ababa

CONTENTS

Introduction by the Author — *i*

Introduction About the Religious Past of Eritrea and Ethiopia
by Gianfrancesco Lusini — *vii*

GNOSTIC INFLUENCES IN ETHIOPIA

1. **An Overview of Gnosticism** — 1
   - 1.1 The Definition of Gnosticism — 1
   - 1.2 An Example of a Gnostic Myth — 2
   - 1.3 The General Characteristics of Gnosticism — 5
   - 1.4 Influences: Platonism — 10
   - 1.5 Influences: Judaism — 11
   - 1.6 Influences: Philo of Alexandria — 12
   - 1.7 The Reasons for Condemnation — 14
   - 1.8 Historical and Geographical Outline — 15
   - 1.9 The Sources of Gnostic Thought — 17

2. **Manichaeism** — 19
   - 2.1 Background Information on Mani — 19
   - 2.2 The Manichaean Cosmology — 19
   - 2.3 Historical and Geographical Outline — 21

3. The Debate on Gnostic Influences in Ethiopia   23

3.1 The Debate   23

3.2 Transit and Destruction   26

4. Influences Prior to Christianization   29

4.1 The Possibility of Influences Prior to Christianization   29

4.2 Hermeticism   29

4.3 The "Filter" of Christianity and Undatable Sources   31

5. The First Phase of Gnostic Influences in Ethiopia—Translations from Greek   33

5.1 The Byzantine Empire and Alexandria   33

5.2 *The Book of Enoch*   34

5.3 *The Ascension of Isaiah*   39

5.4 *The Shepherd of Hermas*   43

5.5 A Summary of Gnostic Influences in the Period of Translations from Greek   48

6. The Second Phase of Gnostic Influences In Ethiopia—The Period of Translations from Arabic   51

6.1 Historical Outline: The Circumstances and Reasons for Translation   51

6.2 *The Qäləmənṭos*   54

6.3 *The Testament of Solomon* and Other Works of a Magical Character Devoted to the Biblical King   62

     6.3.1 Solomonic Magical Texts   62

     6.3.2 Sources of Arab Influence?   63

6.4 The *Kəbrä Nägäst*   67

     6.4.1 The Narrative   67

- 6.4.2 The Debate on the Origin and Dating
  of the *Kəbrä Nägäśt* — 69
- 6.4.3 The Historical-Theological Compendium of the
  Kəbrä Nägäśt and Hypostatic Entities — 71
- 6.4.4 The Myth of the "Pearl" — 76
- 6.4.5 Gnosticism or "Thomas Christianity" — 83
- 6.5 *The Book of the Mysteries of Heaven and Earth* — 84
- 6.6 *The Christian Novel of Alexander the Great* — 85
  - 6.6.1 Historical Outline — 85
  - 6.6.2 Gnostic Characteristics? — 86
- 6.7 The *Combat of Adam* — 90
  - 6.7.1 The Genesis of the Work — 90
  - 6.7.2 The Influence of Gnosticism and of Origen — 91
- 6.8 *Barlaam and Josaphat* — 94
  - 6.8.1 The Genesis of the Work — 94
  - 6.8.2 Gnostic Influences and Traces of the Dispute
    on Iconoclasm — 94
- 6.9 The *Ləfafä ṣədəq* and Other Talismanic Works — 96
  - 6.9.1 A "Magical" Christian Literature — 96
  - 6.9.2 The Theme of Names and Egyptian Influences — 103
  - 6.9.3 The Names of God and Jewish Influences — 105
  - 6.9.4 Similarities and Possible Relations: The *Picatrix* — 111
  - 6.9.5 Magic and the New Man — 118
- 6.10 A Summary of Gnostic Influences in the Period
  of Translations from Arabic — 122

7. **The "Mikaelite" Opuscula: A Third Phase of Gnostic Influences?**   **127**

    7.1 Background Information on the Mikaelite Heretics and the Publication of the Opuscula by Enrico Cerulli   127

    7.2 Cerulli's Gnostic Interpretation   131

    7.3 The Debate on the Gnostic Interpretation of the Supposedly Mikaelite Opuscula   134

    7.4 The Limitations of the Above Interpretations   139

    7.5 The Need for a New Interpretation   142

    7.6 The Originality of the Investigation Carried Out in the "Mikaelite" Opuscula   145

    7.7 Doubts as to the Gnostic Interpretation of Opuscula   148

    7.8 A Summary of the Gnostic Elements in the "Mikaelite" Opuscula Published by Cerulli   151

8. **Some Undatable Sources—Talismanic and Thaumaturgical Practices**   **153**

9. **Analysis of the Sources of a Possible Ethiopian Gnosticism**   **165**

    9.1 Components, Transits, and Intermediaries   165

    9.2 Judeo-Christian Influences in the Period of Translations from the Greek   166

    9.3 Gnostic Influences on Egyptian Coptic Christianity   169

    9.4 Thomas Christianity   170

    9.5 The Influence of Origen   171

    9.6 Late Jewish Influences   173

    9.7 Late Gnosticism and Magic   177

10. Conclusions 181

Appendix 185

The "Mikaelite" Opuscula Published by Cerulli and the Suggested Gnostic Influences 185

Background Information on the Mikaelite Heretics and Cerulli's Interpretation of the Opuscula 185

Some Quotations 189

The Debate on the Gnostic Interpretation of Opuscula Published by Cerulli: The Interpretations Put Forward by Cerulli, Father Agostino Tedla and Piovanelli 193

A New Interpretive Hypothesis 208

The Originality of the Investigation Carried out in the "Mikaelite" Opuscula 220

The Provenance of the Sole Manuscript 230

Another Ambiguous Passage 235

Doubts on the Gnostic Interpretation of the Opuscula and a New Dating 237

The Attribution of the Opuscula to Mikaelite Heretics 241

Bibliography of Works Cited 245

Index of Names 249

INTRODUCTION BY THE AUTHOR

This book was born as a secondary shoot, a lateral bud of a larger comparative research concerning the stories of the true cross of Christ circulating in Ethiopia and their similarities and differences with the ones circulating in Europe and other areas around the Mediterranean sea.

This research, not yet completed, has been conducted in Ethiopia and in Italy but while I was writing the first draft of the text I had to stop when confronted with the theme of gnostic presences in Ethiopia, discussed during the last century and consequently nearly forgotten. It is an important theme and it had to be examined carefully to clarify the meaning of the symbol of the cross and of the relics of the true cross in the Ethiopian cultural landscape. To consent or to deny the presence of the said influences can substantially change the meaning to be given to such entities.

For this reason I interrupted the main research concerning the stories of the cross, to give my attention to this other specific theme of the story of Ethiopian Christianity and to the debate that, during the last century, developed about it.

This interruption, which in the beginning should have lasted just a few days and then a few weeks, actually extended to months and then, a bit further on, to some years and my research was entrapped between the difficulties of the theme and some changing circumstances of my life. That chapter which, at that moment, seemed to be the only impediment to finalize, as soon as possible, the book about the cross, became a kind of marsh sticking to my feet, while I went on reading and reading the old documents and watching for new materials. At the same time, the drafts of the text that I was writing crossed one over the other. But with the time going by it became every day clearer that this theme of the gnostic presences in Ethiopia was becoming independent and that the number of pages I was writing and rewriting was no longer compatible with the other chapters already sketched.

These circumstances caused me to transform that chapter, drafted so many times, into one independent book. Apparently it was quite a simple operation and according to my plan I had just to prepare a bezel setting on which to fix the text already written. But very soon this operation revealed to be much more complex than I had supposed. The first sections of this book make direct reference to the periods of penetration in Ethiopia of foreign influences, from areas where Gnosticising models of thought were already present. For this reason the same sections, presenting texts containing such characteristics, make reference to their translation from Greek or from Arabic languages. Most of these texts are well known to the scholars and have been object of deep investigations, so the presentation of these texts in the sections dedicated to the period of translations from Greek or from Arabic is very smooth, a simple popularization of the research already available. For the aims of this book it was sufficient to draw the necessary conclusions from the same studies.

On the contrary, the situation was much more complex for the section dedicated to the so called "mikaelite opuscula" edited by Enrico Cerulli in 1958. These opuscula seem to be original Ethiopian creations and the debate dedicated to them remained limited to just a few scholars who have given very different interpretations of the same. For this reason it was necessary to study a controversial subject and to take a position concerning a very important question: whether these texts are evidence of the presence of gnostic influences in Ethiopia, as Cerulli believed; or if these opuscula have nothing to do with Gnosticism, as other scholars, who have opposed the opinion of Cerulli, have written.

When I was studying this matter, the above question had already received an imposing answer with the acceptance, in the *Encyclopaedia Aethiopica*, of the sceptic opinions expressed by Pierluigi Piovanelli in an essay of 2004. But these opinions are, at least partially, contradictory with the conclusions of this book concerning the periods of the translations from Greek and from Arabic languages.

The above circumstances led me to conduct a deeper examination of these opuscula to understand their meaning and define their collocation in the context of production. But from this analysis was born a chapter, boundless with reference to the others already sketched and much more analytical. So I found myself again in front of a choice. That chapter dedicated to the "mikaelite opuscula" certainly was the most original part of my research about the theme of this book, but was it possible to put it together with the other parts of the book, which certainly were more synthetic and divulging? The final decision, taken to avoid presenting the readers a drastic change of style in the explanation and probably some difficulties in understanding the text, has been that of rewriting that chapter, in a less analytical form, with mostly the aim of exposing the results of the research, while the more complex version, the essay containing the analysis of the texts, has become an appendix to this book, for anybody interested and patient enough to read it.

Once this decision had been taken, it was possible to cope with the aim I had given to myself: to present a synthesis that, even if dedicated to a complex matter, wanted to be divulging; a synthesis of the research that several scholars have conducted over the years, going deeply inside one or another text or tradition useful in contributing to the matter of the present research. These are very important studies and very useful to my aims, but conducted for other purposes or simply for exegetical reasons, without trying to create a synthesis of the theme object of this study, despite the intention expressed by Jean Doresse and Cerulli in the 1960's and the importance attributed to this matter by them and all the scholars studying Ethiopia in those years. On the contrary, over the years this theme has been minimized or even totally ignored, as is evident from the absence of the entry "Gnosticism" in the *Encyclopaedia Aethiopica*. Certainly there is a reason for this and it is not the result of distraction on the part of scholars. The finding of original gnostic manuscripts at Nag Hammadi in 1945 and their publication and translation between 1975 and 1996 have made clear how inaccurate was the information about Gnosticism left by the Fathers of the Church and consequently how incorrect were the detectors of gnostic presences used in the past, for example by Cerulli, during his research on the "mikaelite opuscula" and on other books of Ethiopian literature.

The new availability of original texts pushed the scholars to defer any judgement until the moment when the results of the studies of the new texts would be completely assimilated. But even if many years have already passed since 1996, until now the study of the new texts do not seem to have produced its results with reference to Ethiopia and the theme object of this book. The present study would like to be a first endeavour to sketch this synthesis which is still missing.

But I have also to underline the limits of the present work which does not aim to give a complete picture of the matter. My purpose is to make reference to the essential texts showing the supposed gnostic influences and to draw a guide along the historical path of these presences, for anybody interested in studying such characteristics of the Ethiopian civilization and for anybody who decides to use this book as a starting point to find traces of the same presences in other texts. This guide, drawing its itinerary through a matter at the same time both complex and obscure, tries to give some reference points, some "stations" which are the texts here described, their essential characteristics and their sources of influence. It will be the reader's duty to complete the map here sketched with the help of the information supplied by this book and of other materials, together with their awareness of the dynamics of the historical processes. I believe that this work, despite its limits, can be useful to have a comprehensive vision of the matter and of its problems, in the light of the research conducted during the last 50 years.

I started to write the following pages with the lightness and the arrogance of a person who, without academic competences, decides to rely on his patience, passion and the analytical skill obtained thanks to his juvenile philosophical studies and an in-extinguished passion for the same. Readers will decide if these pages, written probably without modesty, are also without merit. I hope, at least, to have drawn the attention of people who like and study Ethiopia on a theme of its cultural history neglected for so many years.

Before closing these lines, it is my duty to thank the persons who have stimulated, encouraged, helped me and contributed also to give to this book the present final shape. First and foremost Professor Gianfrancesco Lusini who has followed all the phases of my research from the beginning, helping me to find texts, giving suggestions, indicating itineraries of research and supporting me with his deep professional knowledge of Ethiopia and its history and culture. He has read with interest the several drafts of this text offering advice, suggestions and revising when necessary. He has also written the introductory pages to the present edition. Without his help, this book would never have been born. The second person I would like to thank is Luigi Berliocchi, who is no longer with us. He is the first person who spoke to me about the stories of the tree of the cross, from where the present research has taken its first step. Then I have to thank all the scholars and persons who, with their assistance and suggestions, have helped me to overcome some difficulties I have found during my work. My gratitude goes to Alessandro Gori, Alessandro Bausi, Padre Marco Innocenti, Diego Malara, Sara Fani, Milena Batistoni, Gian Paolo Chiari, Eyob Derillo from the British Library, Jacques Mercier, Michele Petrone, Manuela Galaverni, Simone Fabbrini. A warm memory is due to the late Richard Pankhurst and to his wife Rita. A special thanks to Enrico Castelli who accepted to read the entire text after the translation and has given me important suggestions to clarify some parts and to Mirella Daniell who assisted me during the revision of the translation and the selection of the images. Thanks also to the employees of the libraries of the Pontificio Istituto Orientale in Rome and of the Institute of the Ethiopian Studies in Addis Abeba and to the institutions and publishers which authorized the use of their images, giving a substantial contribution to the present work. Their names and references are always indicated. Rosalia Beccarelli helped me to find some very important texts for my research and Emanuele Ragni has given permission to use some of the images printed here. My warm gratitude goes finally to Maria Tewelde Kidane who has patiently accepted the long afternoons, evenings and weekends I have spent behind closed doors, studying and writing about questions which are part of her history and are emotionally moving but for her it is good that they remain mysteries.

All these persons have given a substantial contribution to my research and it is difficult for me to make a selection to thank some of them for their suggestions concerning the stories of the cross and others for their help with reference to the gnostic presences in Ethiopia. The two are one and the same research which has produced this initial partial result. I hope to have time and energy to conclude the main one, from which point everything started. In any case, the help I have received from the persons quoted above and from all the others whom I have probably forgotten, does not exempt me from the full responsibility for any inaccuracy, mistake, omission or hazardous hypothesis which the reader may find in the following pages.

Paolo Cartocci

INTRODUCTION
ABOUT THE RELIGIOUS PAST OF
ERITREA AND ETHIOPIA

Gianfrancesco Lusini

Università di Napoli "L'Orientale"

We must be grateful to Paolo Cartocci for undertaking the intellectual endeavor, which brought about the publication of this book. The issue of the Gnostic presences in Late Antique and Mediaeval Ethiopia requests a tremendous effort of interpreting and understanding ancient sources, together with a certain degree of empathy for the historical and religious studies. Moreover, the cultural background in question is a particularly rich and complex meeting point, characterized by a strong and permanent changing and alternation of material and spiritual cultures. With a little imagination, but not erring from the truth, one may notice that – beyond Egypt and Maghreb – Abyssinia is the only African milieu a scholar can investigate diachronically. This is owed to the obvious fact that written records of remarkable antiquity have been rediscovered on the plateau, and for a great part, they contain fragments of a religious speech.

Since Hiob Ludolf's time, for two hundred years connoisseurs of the Ethiopian-Eritrean cultural complex have pointed out religion as the key factor for the comprehension of the identities that confronted each other for three millennia in this part of the world. Later on, from James Bruce to Carlo Conti Rossini, great scholars have oriented their researches in the wake of the anxiety of defining peoples through the description of their languages (Semitic, Cushitic, Nilotic and so on) and religions (Christian, Islamic, Animistic and so on). They treated peoples as if they were the product of an original self-creation, and as if languages and religions *ab antiquo* were characteristic features of the historical communities. We can consider it a Biblical legacy, a sort of unconfessed psychological subjection to the *Table of Nations* of Genesis as an everlasting representation of ethnic and cultural differences.

In our days, excepting for those who have a political interest in supporting a reactionary mind, we can admit that not only languages and religions, but also every single aspect of the material and spiritual culture of a community is the result of historical processes. Here, we can recognize the effects of a wide spectrum of variables, including conflict and dialogue, misappropriation and exchange, tradition and reception, conservation and transformation of elements. Every attempt to define cultures as monolithic blocs, carved and shaped since immemorial time, is in itself an ideological construction, and therefore, from the point of view of the investigation of the historical truth, an obstacle to remove before starting the research.

Another trivial, but not useless, consideration derives from the geographical and historical map of the region. From the first half of the first millennium BC Abyssinia has been a linguistic border and a cultural frontier, where traditional elements met new cultural trends. Therefore, the Ethio-Semitic languages are the southernmost attested idioms of the Semitic family, and from Late Antiquity to Middle Ages astral religions, Judaism, Christianity and Islam found in Eritrea and Ethiopia a limit to their southward expansion. Yet, along this border, on the plateau, urban civilizations deriving from a Near Eastern background constantly melted with local substrata. Each innovative wave coming from the Eastern Mediterranean world, via the Nile Valley, and from the Arabian Peninsula, via the Red Sea, gave birth to political and social bodies derived in different ways from a common model, but constantly reassembled in a creative form, taking into account the local traditions.

This is verifiable at least from the times of Daʿamat, a cultural complex whose «exogenous elements are like ingredients which are mixed and cooked according to a recipe which is typically local—the syntax—and dressed in a local sauce».[1] As to the same Kingdom of Aksum, some aspects of its culture can be regarded as the southernmost expression both of the Semitic and the Hellenistic world, but the interaction with the

---

[1] A. Manzo, "*Capra nubiana* in *Berbere* sauce? Pre-Aksumite Art and Identity Building," in *African Archaeologcal Review* 26 (2009): 291–303, at 299.

substratum reshaped the whole figure, giving it an enigmatic look. Though we have an incomplete, but sufficient understanding of the Aksumite Gəʿəz used for the great royal inscriptions, some of the epigraphic records in Old Ethiopic still present many problems, «massimamente perché il tessuto lessicale che in essi appare sfugge quasi del tutto a ogni nostra interpretazione sia per il valore dei suoi temi sia per quello delle sue forme».[2]

In the Ancient World, and in Ethiopia as well, in the first half of the first millennium BC the most ancient written records witness the presence of a pluralistic natural credence. Nevertheless, in the commemorative inscriptions connected to the political experience of Daʿamat, dating to 8th-7th century BC and written in ASA (Ancient South-Arabic), we can recognize religious elements specifically Ethiopian. In some inscriptions, original features appear not attested in Yemen, and then not attributable to the South-Arabian model *tout court*, such as the veneration for the deities called *rb* and *s²mn*. When over a libation altar we found the expression *hqny mṭryn lṣdqn* (*RIÉ* 47),[3] everything is out of the South-Arabic norm. The verb *hqny* 'dedicate' is joined to the object through the preposition *l-* (in ASA the same verb is transitive). The noun *mṭry* is derived from a root well known in Gəʿəz (Ancient Ethiopic) in both forms *ṭaraya* and *aṭraya* with the meaning 'possess, take possession, purchase, obtain, acquire' (in ASA the root is unknown). The personal noun *ṣdqⁿ* (*ṣdq* plus the determination *-n*) is unattested in South-Arabia. Put after the verb 'dedicate', *ṣdqⁿ* can't be other than a god name, and the sentence can be interpreted 'he dedicated this property (the altar bearing the inscription) to *ṣdqⁿ*', namely 'the Righteous' or 'the Friend'. Moreover, another god

---

[2] Lanfranco Ricci, "Iscrizioni paleoetiopiche," in *Semitic Studies In honor of Wolf Leslau On the occasion of his eighty-fifth birthday*, ed. A.S. Kaye (Wiesbaden, 1991): 1291-1311, at 1292-1293, translation: "mostly because the lexical fabric which appears in them almost completely eludes our every interpretation, both in the relevance of its themes and of its forms".

[3] *RIÉ* = Etienne Bernard, Abraham Johannes Drewes, Roger Schneider, *Recueil des inscriptions de l'Éthiopie des périodes pré-axoumite et axoumite – Tome I. Les documents – Tome II. Les planches* (Paris, 1991). Etienne Bernard, *Recueil des inscriptions de l'Éthiopie des périodes pré-axoumite et axoumite – Tome III. Traductions et commentaires – A. Les inscriptions grecques* (Paris, 2000). Abraham Johannes Drewes, *Recueil des inscriptions de l'Éthiopie des périodes pré-axoumite et axoumite – Tome III. Traductions et commentaires – B. Les inscriptions sémitiques. Texte révisé et adapté par Manfred Kropp, édité par Manfred Kropp et Harry Stroomer*, Aethiopistische Forschungen 85 (Wiesbaden, 2019).

name unknown in the South-Arabian context surfaces from the construction *ḥqny lšyḫⁿ* (*RIÉ* 51), 'he dedicated to *šyḫⁿ*' (*šyḫ* plus the determination -*n*), possibly 'the Honorable', corroborating that Da'amat deities were the product of an original Ethiopian processing.

Moving on to Aksum, epigraphic documents dating to the reign of 'Ezana allow again appreciating the specific Abyssinian features in matters of religion, so that «se si cerca una testimonianza dell'originalità della cultura etiopica, in sé e dopo la colonizzazione sudarabica dell'VIII-IV sec. a.C., questo costituisce certo uno degli esempi più chiari – ancorché dei meno citati».[4] In spite of the regrettable lack of evidence about liturgy, for a long time now we have realized that the pantheon of Aksum (or at least of that part of its ruling class that left inscriptions) can't be interpreted simply as an imitation of foreign models. The most frequently associated deities are 'Astär, Bəher and Mäḥräm, and as such this triad doesn't trace back to any Sabaic, or generally South-Arabic, model. There is little doubt that 'Astär is a divinization of the Sky, Bəher of the Land, and Mäḥräm is the War-god intimately connected to the royal dynasty, whose members claim to be 'sons of Mäḥräm'. The status of Mədər, the fourth god, a divinization of the Earth appearing once at the place of Bəher (*RIÉ* 185 ii.21: 'Astär, Mədər and Mäḥräm) and once at the place of Mäḥräm (*RIÉ* 188 25-26: 'Astär, Bəher and Mədər), who is mentioned in the same inscription a few lines later (*RIÉ* 188 29-30), remains ambiguous in our eyes.

The role of local sanctuaries and clergies in venerating specific deities can be called into question to explain why 'Ezana in his inscriptions was sometimes fluctuating between more than one solution, including or excluding god names according to momentary political aims. Greek inscriptions somehow confirm this impression. *RIÉ* 270bis contains a dedication to Uranus, Gea and Ares, probably corresponding to the triad 'Astär, Mədər and Mäḥräm (as in *RIÉ* 185 ii.21). Yet, *Adulitana II* contains the divine triad Zeus, Ares and Poseidon, possibly corresponding to 'Astär, Mäḥräm and Bəher and suggesting that Bəher could have been a god

---

[4] Paolo Marrassini, *Storia e leggenda dell'Etiopia tardoantica. Le iscrizioni reali aksumite, con un'appendice di Rodolfo Fattovich e una nota editoriale di Alessandro Bausi* (Brescia, 2014): 49, translation: "if we search for evidence about the originality of the Ethiopian culture, in itself and after the South-Arabic colonization from the 8th-4th century B.C., this certainly constitutes one of the clearest examples – albeit one of the less quoted".

strictly connected to sanctuaries venerated in Adulis. The position of Bəḥer-Poseidon among the four main deities of the Aksumite pantheon points out the importance of the port of trade within the political geography of the Kingdom. The same introduction of Christianity in Ethiopia is one of the consequences of the direct contact of Aksum with the Greco-Roman world, thanks to its tight economic and political relationship with the port of Adulis, the most important harbour of the whole 'Eritrean' Sea in Late Antiquity.

As everybody knows, under the reign of the same 'Ezana, around 340, the Gospel faith was adopted as the official religion of the court and of the ruling class of the Kingdom. Even after that, apparently, the terminology remained uncertain, and this fact goes without a clear explanation, as in the emblematic case of *RIÉ* 189. In this inscription in vocalized Gə'əz, to indicate the unique God the expressions *əgzi'a sämay* 'Lord of the sky', *əgzi'a sämay zäbäsämay wämədr* 'Lord of the sky which is in the sky and on the earth', and *əgzi'a k^wəllu* 'Lord of everything' are used. Independently from its relationship with the two similar inscriptions *RIÉ* 190 in South-Arabic writing and *RIÉ* 271 in Greek, the adoption of a monotheistic speech not specifically Christian is a problem that requires some comments. In a comparative key, the religious events occurring in the same years on the opposite shore of the Red Sea can provide an interpretative way. Actually, in South-Arabia (the Kingdom of Ḥimyar), after 380, the pluralistic invocation is substituted by dedications to Raḥmānān, the most frequent god name, then also to Il or Ilān or Ilahān. Epithets like 'Master' or 'Lord of the sky' (*b'l* or *mr' s¹myⁿ*) and 'Lord of the sky and of the earth' (*mr' s¹myⁿ w-'rḍⁿ*) are used. In this case, we observe again a terminological fluctuation, but this isn't necessarily an evidence of hesitation about the meaning of the religious message.

Actually, in the current language and culture we can become influenced by a dogmatic tradition, taking for granted that whatever Abrahamic belief is regularly associated to a revelation, of which the holy scripture should be the container and the intermediary at the same time. Consequently, we commonly admit that the features of the message and of the following announcement are defined from the very beginning, namely from the moment of their first appearance. On the contrary, we should always recall that the same monotheistic thought is always the product of historical processes, and as such it is susceptible to variations, adaptations and changes, depending on several factors. Moreover, the search for the words more suitable for defining the religious notions, first of all the same divine nature and personality, is one of the most challenging and risky activities for those who are engaged in developing and spreading their own religious message, and in making it efficacious through the God invocation.

Considering this aspect, all the fluctuations of the religious language must be considered as historical events, outcomes of processes, to be interpreted in the most documented and rational way. This applies also to the prodigious survival of the names of Semitic astral divinity, as the well-known 'Aṭtar(-t). In the inscriptions of 'Ezana – as we have seen – it appears in the form 'Astär as the divinization of the sky. The word survives in Tigre, the northernmost Semitic language of Ethiopia, spoken between Eritrea and Sudan, where *astär* still indicates the celestial sphere. Even more remarkably though, in Gəʻəz the same word is used to translate κύριος, the name of Lord in the two passages of the *Book of Ecclesiasticus* (the *Wisdom of Sirach*) 31:8 and 37:21. In his monotheistic inscription 'Ezana not only calls God 'Lord of the sky' and 'Lord of the sky which is in the sky and on the earth', but also declares that he won *bäḥaylä əgziʼa bəḥer* 'through the strength of the Lord of the land' (ll. 33-34). These are all signs of the linguistic effort aimed at indicating the object of the monotheistic cult with the words of a pluralist religious past. In Gəʻəz this linguistic quest will reach its fulfilment with the systematic and definitive adoption of the god name *əgziʼabəḥer* to indicate the Christian God.

Therefore, the Late Antique background of Aksum is complex, exposed to novelties, and receptive. Particularly, sailors and merchants of various origins and linguistic affiliation used to land at the big harbour of Adulis, along the sea route between Alexandria and India. Many of them were representatives of all the great religions of that time, which is why «it is unreasonable to assume that no Jewish, Jewish-Christian, Samaritan, or Manichaean travellers coming from the Roman harbours of Aila and Clysma ever made a stop in Adulis and, eventually, a visit to Aksum».[5] Moreover, though the documentation tracing back directly to the 3rd-7th centuries is scanty, we must recall the amazing capacity of the Ethiopian clergy to retain and transmit parts of the most remote periods. This is the

---

[5] Pierluigi Piovanelli, "Reconstructing the Social and Cultural History of the Aksumite Kingdom: Some Methodological Reflections," in *Inside and Out. Interactions between Rome and the Peoples on the Arabian and Egyptian Frontiers in Late Antiquity*, ed. Jitse H.F. Dijkstra and Greg Fisher (Louvain, 2014), 331–352, at 350–351.

result of the unceasing work done by learned men who rebuilt history on ancient grounds, as in the case of the so-called royal lists «since it is known that the compilers drew on various sources, also including coins and inscriptions, if not also archival documents».[6]

To sum up, we can see in the religious past of Eritrea and Ethiopia the typical traits of a multi-cultural setting, a crossroad where there was room for a large number of influences, encouraging «la conservazione d'antiche 'eresie' in aree periferiche come l'Etiopia (o la Nubia) ed il Yemen, che lungamente han subito l'influsso della civiltà greco-romana [...], ma a differenza di Siria ed Egitto, d'Armenia e Georgia non furono mai provincia di Roma o di Bisanzio».[7] In this context, the circulation of Gnostic ideas can't be excluded, particularly if they can be detected here and there in later texts. By using the book of Paolo Cartocci, the reader will be guided to the discovery of the possible remains of an ancient philosophical teaching, surviving the periodical religious reforms thanks to the initiative of small groups of Christian monks. Imbued with radical ideas of Salvation, probably they transmitted unorthodox ideas from generation to generation, leaving in their works «tracce di idee gnostiche e di concetti dualistici non lontani da quelli manichei».[8] The responsibility of the modern scholar is to track those ideas with close attention, and to recall the memory of their old Ethiopian advocates.

---

[6] Alessandro Bausi, "The recently published Ethiopic inscription of King Ḥafilā (ΑΦΙΛΑC): a few remarks," *Bibliotheca Orientalis* 75, 3-4 (2012): 286–295, at 289.

[7] Gianfranco Fiaccadori, *Teofilo Indiano* (Ravenna, 1992): xxxix, translation: "the conservation of ancient 'heresies' in peripheral areas like Ethiopia (or Nubia) and Yemen, which for a long time underwent the influx of the Greco-Roman civilization [...], but unlike Syria, Egypt, Armenia and Georgia never became provinces of Rome or Byzantium".

[8] Enrico Cerulli, *La letteratura etiopica. Terza edizione ampliata. L'Oriente Cristiano nell'unità delle sue tradizioni* (Firenze-Milano, 1968): 46, translation: "traces of Gnostic ideas and of dualistic concepts not differing much from Manichean ones".

GNOSTIC INFLUENCES
IN ETHIOPIA

AN OVERVIEW OF GNOSTICISM

1.1 The Definition of Gnosticism

Prior to addressing the subject of this study, it will be necessary to establish some basic working tools. At the same time, in order to avoid misunderstanding and confusion, a brief overview of the general characteristics, history, documentary evidence, and other essential features of the philosophical movement, also classified as a heresy, will serve as a useful framework of reference for the work as it develops.

The Greek word *gnosis* means knowledge and it was Christian writers, as from the *Apostolic Letters*, who used it to label an explicitly condemned school of thought. But what kind of knowledge is involved here? One grounded not on human cognitive processes and reason but on revelation and hence an emanation of the divine will, something that transcends human understanding. All this reminds us of Christianity too, however, not least because the two movements began to spread at the same time and some scholars believe that the Simon Magus mentioned in the *Acts of the Apostles* was indeed the first Gnostic. Examination of the writings of both Christian and non-Christian Gnosticism reveals, however, that the basis of the beliefs is not Christian. The cornerstone of all the Gnostic writings is a reinterpretation of Biblical and Jewish traditions, which makes it possible to state that Christianity and Gnosticism were born at the same time out of Judaism and indeed, according to the illuminating suggestions of Birger A. Pearson,[1] as Judaic heresies. It should be pointed out immediately, however, that the Gnostic movement was not monolithic. There were an indeterminate number of sects, many of which catalogued and described by the Fathers of the Church, and recent

---

[1] Birger A. Pearson, *Ancient Gnosticism. Tradition and Literature*, Minneapolis, 2007, p. 11.

Image of the falling from the sky of Simon Magus. According to old Christian traditions Simon Magus challenged St. Peter in a competition to show his skill in the magic arts. During the competition Simon Magus, helped by demons, showed that he was able to fly but suddenly crashed to the ground when the demons let him down, following the intercession of St. Peter to God. (Mosaic from the Dome of Monreale, Sicily, Italy, XII or XIII century. Photographed by the author.)

discoveries of original writings do in fact attest to the existence of a galaxy of philosophical theories, myths, revelations and prophecies, all akin in some respects and all different. It was unquestionably an anarchical movement, open to external influences and prone to proliferation and diversification.

The basic doctrine of Gnosticism consists in the attempt to reveal the nature of God and the true nature of man, which is divine and must be rediscovered as such. The salvation of mankind hinges on recognizing that it too partakes of the divine and taking all the action required to return to its divine place of origin.

1.2 An Example of a Gnostic Myth

In order to avoid remaining in the realms of abstract exposition, let us now consider, albeit briefly, the Gnostic theories, which were couched in the form of myths. Our example will be taken from what is known as the *Apocryphon of John*, a text produced by the non-Christian Sethian sect that has, however, survived in a Christianized version.

The myth is presented as a revelation of the Apostle John, son of Zebedee, a repository of the secret wisdom revealed to him by Christ. It begins with a dissertation on the supreme being as indescribable, ineffable, pure, infinite, and perfect, beyond all human understanding. In the act of knowing or taking cognizance of itself through thought, this primordial entity emanates another entity named Barbelo,[2] thus introducing duality. It should be noted here that according to the logic of hypostasis, divine thought is creative in itself and God, by the pure act of thinking, produces other beings that are also divine but of lower degree. This system of emanations, upon which the Gnostic mythology as a whole is based, is essential to any understanding of all the subsequent developments. With the assent of the supreme divine father, Barbelo, the first emanation, gives birth to the emanations of Foreknowledge, Indestructibility, and Eternal Life as well as Forethought or the Self-Begotten (Autogenes). The latter gives rise to a further series of emanations including some heavenly bodies and the Perfect Man, Geradamas or Adamas, the entity later known in the history of philosophy as the Celestial Adam. The generation of the heavenly bodies also gives birth to the Aeons, entities created to designate temporal periods but personified here as the individualized expression of virtues such as grace, truth, understanding, love, and wisdom (Sophia, the personification of divine wisdom). This list is no more than an outline, as the developments in the Gnostic myth are far broader. The only emanation of importance to be noted here is Seth, son of Geradamas.

The rift in this order of emanations—which is at this stage still a pure and simple spiritual construct set in motion by an act of self-awareness on the part of the supreme divinity—begins when the above-mentioned Sophia decides to beget a being in her likeness without the assent of the supreme spirit. Born according to some texts out of Sophia's desire for the one who generated her, this clearly sinful act is made still more ungodly by the fact

---

[2] Scholars have put forward various possible interpretations of the name of this first emanation, which is also described as the origin of the cosmos and hence the supreme female principle. Based on possible etymologies, these interpretations include "Supreme Boundary" (in that the being above it is unknowable), "Indistinct/Confused Origin," "Great Emanation," "Seed" and "Divinity of the Tetrad" (the mother, according to some Gnostic sects, of the four emanations giving birth to the cosmos).

that it is performed without her counterpart. Sophia is expelled from the divine world and the fruit of her sin is Yaldabaoth, meaning the son of chaos, a horrendous being and the first of the Archons, lords of the lower world of mankind. Yaldabaoth then gives birth to the other Archons and the beings that rule over the heavens. In the Sethian Gnostic model, Yaldabaoth (also known as Saklas and Samael, god of the blind or the blind god) coincides with the god of Judaism, an obtuse god that claims to be unique and superior to all others. Yaldabaoth is the true creator of the cosmos.

On beholding her son's conduct, Sophia realizes the extent of her sin and repents. The supreme spirit accepts her repentance and decides to admit her to the ninth sphere of heaven—which is, however, outside the Pleroma,[3] the home of all the divine entities—until she has rectified the effects of her misguided actions. He also informs her of the arrival of Man and the Son of Man, who will help her to restore the divine order. Yaldabaoth intercepts this message, however, and decides out of jealousy, together with the other Archons, that he too will beget Man. The result is Adam, an earthly being that cannot come to life and remains inanimate for a long time until Sophia finally intervenes and tells Yaldabaoth breathe life into him by blowing on his face. The earthly Adam produced by Yaldabaoth and the Archons thus receives the breath of life, which is also divine light. By means of this stratagem, Sophia hopes to regain her former rank through Adam as well as the divinity lost in the emanations she has produced. On realizing after the fact that he has breathed divinity into Adam, Yaldabaoth is fired with jealousy and takes steps with the Archons to combat Adam and his wisdom. The most important of these is the creation of Eve. The meaning of original sin is reversed in this myth. In order to help Sophia, it is Christ himself (or Barbelo in some non-Christian versions) that induces Adam and Eve to eat the fruit of the tree of knowledge and thus become aware of the divine origin that they must rediscover. After Adam and Eve have committed the original sin and hence acquired knowledge, the Archons decide to expel them from Paradise. Yaldabaoth then seduces Eve, who gives birth to Cain and Abel. After the death of Abel, Seth is born to Adam and Eve and receives the blessings of Sophia and the superior beings.

Yaldabaoth now begins his war against the human race, the progeny of Seth, in an attempt to corrupt it. The non-Christian version ends with the announcement of the descent of Barbelo to secure the salvation of

---

[3] Meaning plenum or fullness.

mankind. The Christianized versions or reworkings instead speak of the descent of Christ, often presented, however, as the son or emanation of Seth, who is in turn evidently an emanation of the Celestial Adam.

This general framework, which is already complex enough, is then developed in very different forms that involve not only Sophia, Seth and Christ but also prophets like Hermes Trismegistus, the mythic founder of pagan wisdom, Zoroaster, the founder of the new Persian religious tradition, Asclepius, the Greek god of medicine, known to the Romans as Aesculapius, and many other figures variously positioned in the system of emanations. An essential element of Gnosticism that emerges here is its ability to incorporate all of the wisdom preceding it. Gnosticism regards itself as the last in a series of divine revelations, the earliest of which are the Egyptian, Persian, Jewish and Greek religions. This process of assimilation involves not only prophets and symbols but also mythologies and mythic narratives, which are taken up in the Gnostic writings without bothering to refer to the original sources.

1.3 The General Characteristics of Gnosticism

As shown by the above considerations, one of the essential features of Gnosticism is a dualistic vision of God, mankind and the world. Some sects, looking forward to the Manichaean conceptions to be discussed below, regard this dualism as primordial and others as an "accident," an unexpected malignant development in the system of emanations. In both cases, however, the God of the Bible is divided into two different entities. One is a supreme divinity, extraneous to the world, unknowable and describable only in the terms of a negative theology.[4] The other is a lesser god that created and rules the world. This simple model becomes complicated in the different Gnostic schools, however, as both the supreme and the lesser divinity undergo multiplication through the system of emanations. For all his apparent oneness, man too is actually divided and twofold. Apart from the figure of Celestial Man, which is an emanation, terrestrial man also possesses a divine nature extraneous to the world, where he is imprisoned in the physicality of the flesh. At the same time, the body and the spirit that gives birth to the emotions—the sensory spirit, the one that interacts with earthly reality—belong instead to the

---

[4] In the sense that it is only possible to say what God is not and wholly impossible to say what God is.

Gnostic Gems (from Birger A. Pearson, *Ancient Gnosticism – Traditions and Literature*, Minneapolis, 2007, pp. 48–49)

world and are in no way divine. For Gnostics, as we have seen, the world is a sort of prison created by a lesser divinity, the realm of chaos and darkness. The cosmos is not eternal and Gnostic salvation means escaping from the prison of the world and returning to the realm of light in which true man (his divine spark) was born.

The way to achieve this is through Gnosis, awareness of one's true nature. Once the process of liberation is completed, i.e. when all of the elect are fully aware of their divine nature, the material world will be annihilated and the spiritual world will be one again. The apocatastasis, etymologically meaning restoration of the original order, is the end of the world, the culminating moment of the Gnostic vision, which will take place when all the divine elements scattered throughout the universe can return to their origin through knowledge of their true nature. This concept of the "divinity" of mankind is essential to any understanding of the substance of Gnosticism. In this connection, attention must be drawn first of all to the difference with respect to Christianity, which sees man as striving to return to God, in the sense of approaching the divine so as to

Magic Gems (above image and lower left: Kassel, Museumslandschaft Hessen Kassel, Antikensammlung. inv. Ge 127 and Ge 137. Lower right image: Aquileia, Museo Archeologico Nazionale, inv. 49542, photo by Elisabetta Gagetti, Archivio MAN Aquileia, copyright by Ministero per i Beni e le Attività Culturali e per il Turismo, Polo Museale del Friuli Venezia Giulia).

delight in its presence, while remaining a creature, however. Man is therefore distinct from God. While there is no uniform formulation in Gnosticism and its offshoots, the following aspects remain constant despite the multiplicity of possible interpretations:

- The "simplicity" of the original divine form has been disturbed, thus giving birth to plurality or to forms that cannot be admitted to the Pleroma because of their lack of harmony. This simplicity must be restored through the return of all the "parts" of the divine to the Pleroma.

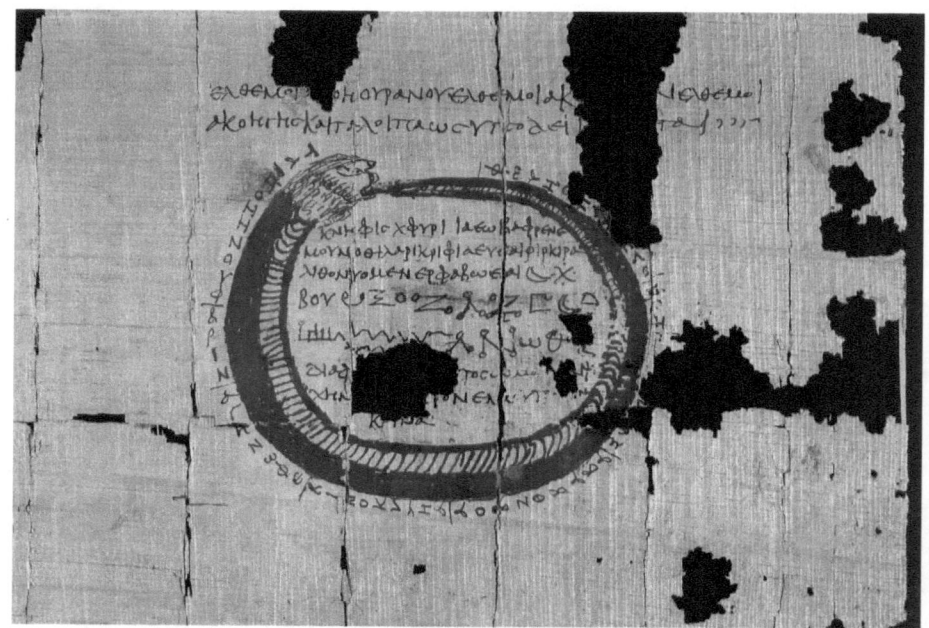

Magic Talisman in the shape of a snake biting it's tail (from a greek magic papyrus, III century a.C. – © The British Library Board, Papyrus 121 [Frame 3]).

- Man is the involuntary custodian of a "fragment" of light or divinity, which yearns to return to its place of origin and become one with it. There is no distinction in the divine and no reason for distinction in the human. It is only a kind of nostalgia that makes the human condition wretched, and this is caused by the mingling of the divine with matter.

At the same time, according to the Valentinian Christian Gnostics, darkness and matter are the product of ignorance, of not knowing one's origin. The triumph of knowledge (Gnosis) therefore means the end of the existence of matter and darkness.[5]

As we have seen, one of the hallmarks of Gnosticism is the formulation of narratives and myths through which the Gnosis is revealed

---

[5] "[I]gnorance of the Father brought about anguish and terror; and the anguish grew solid like a fog, so that no one was able to see. For this reason, error became powerful; it worked on its own matter foolishly, not having known the truth. It set about with a creation, preparing with power and beauty the substitute for the truth." *The Gospel of Truth*, translated by Harold W. Attridge and George W. MacRae, http://gnosis.org/naghamm/gostruth.html.

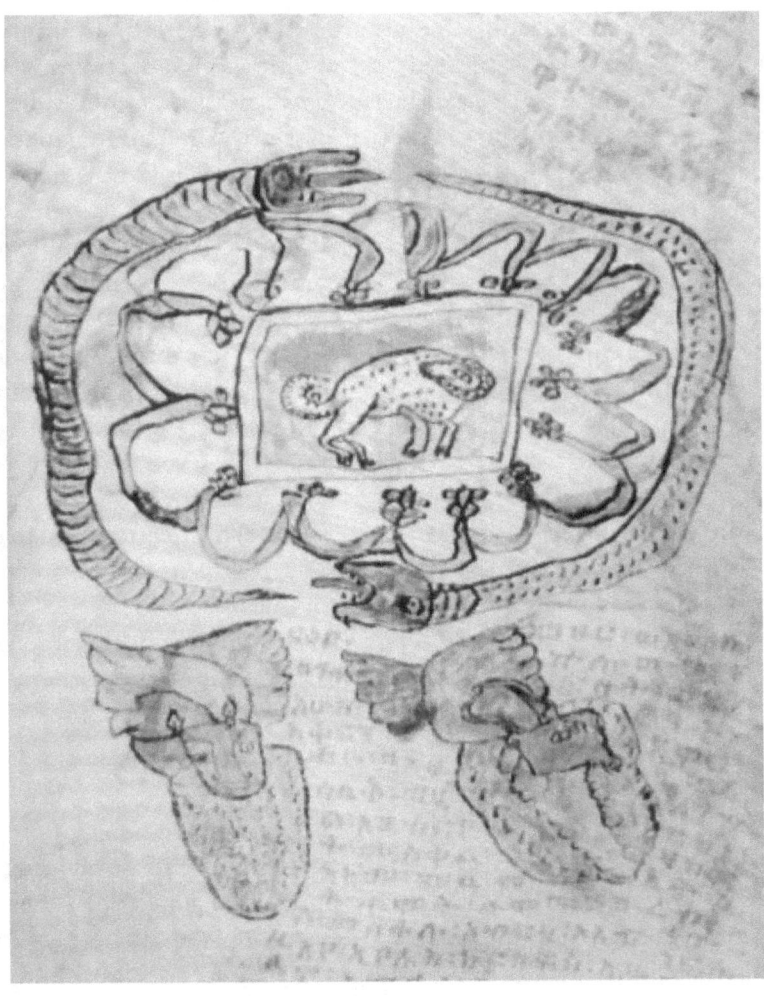

Snakes in an Ethiopian magic scroll (Asmat Prayers [late 19th-early 20th century], British Library, EAP286/1/1/44, https://eap.bl.uk/archive-file/EAP286-1-1-44, copyright Institute of Ethiopian Studies, Addis Abeba. The image is from the Endangered Archives Programme of the British Library, Ethiopian Manuscript Imaging Project [DOI:https://doi.org/10.15130/EAP286])

and made known to the initiated. These narratives take the literary form of dialogues and revelations or apocalypses, and address the following subjects: 1) the true god—not the creator of this world but the one above him—and his world; 2) the birth of the world inhabited by mankind; 3) the origin and imprisonment of man; 4) human salvation. They are generally based on the Bible as well as the *targumim* (plural of *targum*, spoken paraphrases of the Jewish scriptures) and *midrashim* (plural of *midrash*, interpretations and commentaries on the Torah). The reworking to which they were then subjected by the Christian Gnostic movements, especially the Valentinian, was so broad, however, that it should be noted here, for the purposes of our further discussions, that the emanations of the Valentinian system also include the Cross, albeit in a new light as the entity that redeems Sophia when realization of her error, namely seeking to know the Father rather than accept that he is unknowable, plunges her into despair.[6] The Cross, also called the Boundary here, purifies Sophia but not before her anguish has begotten the shapeless being (Yaldabaoth) that disrupts the harmony of the Pleroma. The Cross performs two functions here, one being to redeem Sophia and the other to establish a boundary, hence the name, between the Pleroma and the shapeless, unhappy creature born to Sophia, which disrupts the Pleroma. The Cross thus serves as a boundary,[7] a point both of contact and of separation between the higher world and the lower. It is instead the task of another two emanations, Christ and the Holy Spirit, to restore true serenity to the Pleroma. This concept is expressed in a more obscure form in the Gnostic *Gospel of Philip* in the words *Jesus came to crucify the world*, meaning that he came to join the higher world with the lower by placing himself between them in the center, the point where the two component parts of the Cross meet.

1.4 Influences: Platonism

The two major sources on which the Gnostics drew in developing their ideas were Judaism and Platonic philosophy. One element of Gnosticism taken from Plato is unquestionably dualism, i.e. the dichotomy of the material world, the world of things subject to change and "becoming," and the immaterial world of ideas and the spirit, which always stays the same. According to Plato, material things are copies of eternal, non-material forms found in the world of ideas. Plato is also the source of the Demiurge, the lesser divinity that creates the world by imitating ideas, spiritual reality. The material world is imperfect, however, precisely because it is material. In Gnosticism we find the same distinction between the higher world and the lower, and some Gnostic texts even use the Platonic term *demiurge* to

---

[6] This "knowing" of the Father evidently presents all the ambiguity connected with the use of the verb in the Old Testament, where, for example, "Adam knew Eve" appears in some translations in the sense of carnal knowledge.

[7] As symbolized by its form, the intersecting of a vertical and a horizontal.

designate the god that created the world. But while Plato saw the flaw of our world as the fact of being material and incapable for that very reason of being perfect or even just better, the Demiurge of the Gnostic systems of thought, known as Yaldabaoth in the myth discussed above, is instead ignorant and wicked, a lesser divinity that yearns to be recognized as the supreme god and is intent for this reason on blocking the paths of salvation capable of leading mankind back to its deeper divine nature.

The Gnostic cosmos, like that of the ancient world, was conceived with the Earth in the center, seven planets orbiting round it (the Moon, the Sun, Venus, Mercury, Mars, Jupiter and Saturn), and all the others, the firmament of the fixed stars, outside them. While Plato regarded these celestial bodies as divine beings, the Gnostics saw the planets and stars as occupied by the demonic Archons, rulers of the world below and determined to keep mankind imprisoned there.

The other Platonic idea that influenced Gnosticism is the distinction both between the spirit and the body and, within the former, between the mind (*nous*) and the spirit of the emotions. Plato regarded the mind as immortal and existing prior to its entry into the body. On the death of one body, this spirit migrates to another. In Gnosticism, spirits can be saved through Gnosis (the knowledge of their origins) and recognition of the truth about man, namely that the spirit has the same nature as God, whereas the emotional spirit dies with the body.

1.5 Influences: Judaism

While there are, as we have seen, some similarities clearly revealing the influence of Platonism on Gnosticism, this is not its major source. The real substance of the Gnostic revelation appears instead to be drawn from the post-Biblical Jewish apocalypses of the period from the 3rd century BC to the 1st AD, the most important of which is the *Book of Enoch*. As is known, this text is regarded as canonical in Ethiopia and had a substantial influence on the development of the local religious tradition. The *Book of Enoch*[8] takes the form of a revelation imparted to mankind by the Biblical patriarch of that name, who reveals the truths received from God and the angels during his visits to heaven. It is,

---

[8] To be understood as what scholars refer to as Enoch 1 in order to distinguish it from other texts attributed to the same patriarch.

however, a revelation only for the elect, those endowed with higher understanding, sensibility, and faith.

As is known, apocalyptic Judaism was an expression of the model of philosophical, religious and political thought that characterized many of the communities who resolutely opposed the Roman occupation of Palestine, fighting for political independence as well as the original traditions of the Jews and the purity of their roots and religious and cultural heritage. It must have been one of these communities that was responsible for preserving and handing down the Dead Sea Scrolls discovered at Qumran, where fragments of the *Book of Enoch* in Aramaic were also found. There is, however, one substantial difference between apocalyptic Judaism and Gnosticism, in that the former was expressed through the revelation of God's plans for the people of Israel. In these apocalypses, and the *Book of Enoch* in particular, great importance attaches to the political subject of liberation from the oppressors and their fifth column as well as the revolt against social injustice. This true content is barely masked by its mystical, visionary presentation. Gnosticism instead attaches no importance to the salvation of the chosen people. Its true message is that of individual salvation for all regardless of race or rank through knowledge of one's divine self and the routes enabling it to return to its place of origin. The difference between the two models of thought is probably due to the fact that the Judaic apocalyptic literature reached its peak before the Jewish revolts and the destruction of Jerusalem (in 135 AD), when it still made sense to call for a social uprising. After those events and with the beginning of the Jewish diaspora, the path of collective revolt was no longer possible or perhaps even conceivable. The pursuit of salvation thus became individual, the search for a personal path to reunion with the godhead at the end of time in a palingenesis with no further distinction between the self, others, one's people, the whole of humanity, and God Himself. The way to achieve this was through awareness of one's divine identity and the routes leading back to the place of origin.

1.6 Influences: Philo of Alexandria

It can be stated on the basis of this overview that while Gnosticism unquestionably originated in a Judaic cultural context, the Judaic premises were developed by Jews who had absorbed Greek philosophy. It is no coincidence that one of the major forges of Gnostic thought was

Alexandria, the largest and most dynamic cultural metropolis of the ancient world, home to a strong Jewish community receptive to influences from all over the Mediterranean.

It was in Alexandria that the Greek translation of the Old Testament known as the Septuagint was produced, probably to afford the resident Jewish community, whose long stay in Egypt had caused them to lose their command of Hebrew, access to the primary text on the history of their people. The figure of most importance in this community and this Judaic-Hellenistic culture is Philo of Alexandria, born between 30 and 20 BC into a wealthy Jewish family in the Egyptian metropolis. Having received a complete Greek and Jewish education, he devoted himself to philosophical and theological studies all his life, towards the end of which he was also sent on a diplomatic mission to the Roman emperor Caligula. He left many works in Greek on his death around the year 50 AD.

Philo was not a systematic philosopher. He regarded truth as the fruit of divine revelation and human intelligence as no more than a tool to understand it more fully. The Greek science and philosophy he understood and admired so deeply, especially Platonism, never caused him to lose faith in Biblical revelation. On the contrary, it was in the Greek philosophers and the wisdom attained by them with the tools of human knowledge that he endeavored to rediscover the truths revealed in the Bible. Allegorical interpretation was his key to this arduous synthesis of Biblical revelation and Greek philosophy, Platonism in particular.

Numerous elements later typical of Gnosticism can be found in Philo, above all speculation on the essence of the divine. God has no human form or attributes but is indefinable and inaccessible to our intelligence. Intermediate figures are therefore needed to fill the boundless distance generated by this conception of divinity with respect to mankind and the world. Logos, understood as the personification of divine intelligence, the word of God, is the first such figure, encompassing also the Platonic world of ideas. It is Logos that imparts order to the world by drawing on ideas.

Like Plato, Philo has a completely dualistic conception of the world. The idea of man, the Celestial Man present in Logos, is perfect and divine. Earthly man is material and imperfect, prone to evil. Celestial Man has virtues that make him similar to God, whereas earthly man aspires to those virtues and feels their attraction but is encumbered by the mortal body he inhabits and finds it hard to attain them. The body is therefore the prison of the soul and the purification of earthly man entails liberation from material pleasures. This is the path enabling the higher spirit (*nous*) to return to God.

While Philo cannot be considered a Gnostic, he is obviously an important figure of transition in the construction of the model of Gnostic thought as the first to embark on the synthesis of Jewish theology and philosophy with Greek philosophy.

1.7 The Reasons for Condemnation

The following section will give a historical outline of the conflict between the nascent Christianity and the host of Gnostic sects to be found throughout the Mediterranean area. But what were the reasons for this conflict? Why did Christianity and Gnosticism immediately clash? While some of these reasons have already emerged in the course of our investigations, a more schematic summary is given below.

- While the absolute truths of Christianity, first and foremost the divinity of Christ, are not denied by Gnosticism, they become part of a broader whole that undermines the Christian system of values. Christ becomes one of the many emanations, sometimes a new manifestation of Seth, and Christianity itself becomes the latest in a series of revelations, the earliest of which date back to ancient Egypt and the ancient Persian religion.
- In this complex framework of revelations, where Satan himself (or satanic personifications) does everything possible to conceal the truth to be attained, "figures" or interpretations sometimes emerge that are wholly unacceptable to Christianity. One example is the assertion in the *Gospel of Judas*[9] that Judas Iscariot served as an instrument to bring the bodily manifestation of Christ to an end and therefore acted in accordance with the wishes of God the Father.
- At the same time, all the Gnostic schools adopt a Docetist view of Christ as having no physical body and therefore being a sort of semblance or apparition. The incarnation is not in fact necessary in the Gnostic cosmology. Christ served as a beacon and a point of reference, not as a human sacrifice.

---

[9] See W. Barnstone, M. Meyer (ed.), *Essential Gnostic Scriptures*, Boston & London, 2010, pp. 56-74.

- In name of Gnosis, the Gnostic schools attach a positive value to the sin of Eve, namely appropriation of the fruit of the tree of the knowledge of good and evil. According to the Gnostics, knowledge confers divinity, knowing means "becoming God".
- The other aspect that Christianity clearly cannot tolerate is the libertarian element of Gnostic mysticism. Gnostic salvation can be obtained immediately. There is no need to wait until you are dead. For this reason, the role of the Church as an institution and the priesthood loses a great deal of importance. The way to salvation is an individual path that may require guidance at the beginning but then breaks free of all constraint. The enlightened can then easily serve in turn as guides.

All this immediately came into collision with a religion that aspired to be universal and exclusive, and was seeking of develop the organizational structure required to become an institution. Moreover, as we shall see, Gnosticism was extraordinarily widespread and popular.

1.8 Historical and Geographical Outline

Gnosticism flourished in Egypt, Syria, Arabia, Persia, Cyprus, the whole of North Africa, and Rome in the 2nd and 3rd centuries AD. Christianity immediately saw the danger of this school of thought, which was condemned specifically by Paul in the *First Epistle to Timothy*[10] and then in the *Acts of the Apostles*.[11] Despite this, Gnosticism continued to exist for a long time in different forms. The condemnation of the Christian Church was expressed in more precisely defined terms halfway through the 2nd century, but was designed more than anything else to halt the spread of Christian Gnosticism. It should, however, be recalled that the Christian Church was still clandestine in that period and its denunciations were therefore subject to voluntary acceptance and of limited effect.

The adaptability of Gnosticism soon became evident both in the multitude of sects and communities that drew upon it while maintaining complete doctrinal and organizational autonomy, and in the spread during the third century of Manichaeism, which can be regarded as a more

---

[10] 1 Timothy (6. 20–21). The epistle contains various references to "false doctors" and false doctrines but "gnosis" is explicitly mentioned only in 6.20 and 6.21.

[11] Acts of the Apostles: 8, 9–25.

structured and less anarchical kind of Gnosticism in terms of doctrine and organization. At the same time, the ineffectiveness of the Christian condemnation in the mid-2nd century is shown by the fact that Valentinian communities, i.e. groups of Christian Gnostics inspired by the teachings of the philosopher Valentinus, still existed in the 4th century in Egypt and were indeed mentioned in the documents of the Quinisext Council held in Constantinople in 692.

More precise dating of the presence of Gnosticism in Egypt is made possible by a number of elements. Bishop Athanasius of Alexandria (328-73) sought to combat it by establishing the canon of sacred books because he knew that numerous texts he regarded as heretical were circulating and being used together with the Bible, above all in Upper Egypt. Moreover, as we shall see in a later section, an Egyptian bishop (possibly Theonas of Alexandria) sent the faithful of his diocese a pastoral epistle against the Manichaeans as early as 280. Bishop Theophilus of Alexandria fought doggedly at the end of the 4th century against the followers of Origen (185-254), a Christian philosopher regarded as deeply influenced by Gnosticism and condemned for his theories by the emperor Justinian in an edict of 543. The reign of Theophilus (385–412) fell in the period during which Christianity was gradually being established as the official religion of the Roman Empire. The Edict of Thessalonica prohibited all forms of pagan worship in 392 at the end of a process that began in 313 with Constantine's Edict of Milan, giving Christianity the same freedom as all the other religions practiced in the Roman Empire and putting an end to the persecutions. The promulgation of these legislative measures gave the Christians of the time the strength to combat their opponents. In 391 Theophilus ordered the destruction of the Serapeum of Alexandria, an ancient pagan temple housing the greatest library of antiquity (probably as many as 700,000 papyruses). The bishop Cyril, his nephew, expelled the Jews from Alexandria a few years later and ordered the stoning of Hypatia, daughter of the philosopher and mathematician Theon, in 415. The last Platonist in Alexandria, she was regarded as a representative of the ancient pagan religion.

To conclude this section, we shall recall a number of important points that will certainly prove useful in the course of our subsequent investigations.

- In the early Christianity prior to Constantine, a clandestine religion subjected periodically to persecution, little distinction was drawn between Christian texts and Gnostic texts, which were regarded as offering other revelations and often circulated in Christian communities.
- When the obvious difference between the two schools of thought did emerge, the large-scale Gnosticization of Christian texts on the one hand and Christianization of Gnostic texts on the other necessarily led to doctrinal confusion.
- Until the 20th century, after the attack launched by Christianity and the systematic destruction of Gnostic writings in the 4th century, the only source of information about Gnosticism was the testimony of the Fathers of the Church who had criticized and condemned it.

1.9 The Sources of Gnostic Thought

The situation described in the above four points necessarily resulted in extraordinary confusion and never-ending doubt as to the true nature of Gnosticism until 1945, when thirteen papyrus manuscripts of the 4th century written in Coptic Egyptian, comprising a total of fifty-two texts, were discovered at Nag Hammadi in Upper Egypt. As some of these texts were duplications, they have been winnowed down to a total of forty-four treatises. Three other manuscripts had been discovered at the end of the 19th century and published in 1851, 1891 and 1955,[12] but none of them is comparable in importance with the Nag Hammadi library. The lack of original sources on Gnosticism, the period during which the few surviving testimonies were nearly all Christian and framed so as to elicit condemnation and rejection, thus came to an end. The recent discoveries now offer a reliable overview of Gnosticism based on material from within the movement. Hence the possibility of undertaking an authentic comparative study. If this is to be meaningful, however, it must also harness the historical tool of concrete appraisal of the possibility of transit towards Ethiopia as well as any evidence of this.

---

[12] The Askew Codex was published in 1851, the Bruce Codex in 1891, and the Berlin Gnostic Codex in 1955. The latter contains two works also found at Nag Hammadi. The other two codices contain texts that represent a late stage of Egyptian Christian Gnosticism.

2

MANICHAEISM

2.1 Background Information on Mani

Our brief overview of Gnosticism is now followed by a presentation of the Manichaean heresy. This is prompted by the fact that scholars writing about Gnostic influences in Ethiopian literature often note that they may actually be Manichaean rather than Gnostic or refer to them as Gnostic-Manichaean, implicitly encapsulating the similarity between the two heresies that appears to have led many Gnostics to join Manichaean communities after the condemnation of their beliefs.

Manichaeism takes its name from Mani, the founder of this religion. Born in Babylon in 216 AD, he spent his childhood and youth until the age of 24 in a Jewish-Christian baptismal community. His thinking was deeply influenced by Paul of Tarsus and what is known as Thomas Christianity, a subject to be addressed here at a later stage. He knew the *Gospel of Thomas*, the *Hymn of the Pearl*, and the *Book of Enoch* by heart. He set off on the travels through India, Iran, Media, Parthia, and the Caucasus during which he absorbed many of his doctrines in 241. His preaching won many followers until a ruler contrary to his teachings came to the throne in Persia. He died, supposedly by crucifixion, in 277.

2.2 The Manichaean Cosmology

Mani's vision is a simplified form of Gnosticism grounded on the dualism of the principles of good and evil, light and darkness. The two realms are not simple, however, but present from the outset attributes and powers that manifest themselves also as Aeons, independent entities emanated by each of the two principles with their own autonomy and specific powers and faculties.

The world we know was born out of the yearning felt by the Lord of Darkness for the light he saw high above him. His attempt to possess it gave rise to the war between the two worlds. The First Man, one of the emanations of light, was defeated in battle, dismembered, and devoured by the demonic forces, thus initiating the scattering of light (fragments of light) in the darkness of evil. The cosmos was born out of this initial defeat in order to restore the unity of the world of light. The Manichaean cosmogony is a complex and perfect system of distillation of the particles of light, which seek to return to their place of origin with the aid of a series of emanations including the Cross of Light, which is in turn Jesus Patibilis, Suffering Jesus. The sun and moon are also involved in this cosmology as vessels whose task it is to carry the light that has freed itself from darkness back to the heavens, whereas the other heavenly bodies are evil beings (like the Gnostic Archons) that seek to block the upward path of light.

Adam and Eve, the union of spirit and material body, were also created during the battle between good and evil. At the same time, the injunction of the Jewish god—regarded by the Manichaeans as an evil being—to "go forth and multiply" is designed to increase the dispersion of the light contained in matter, i.e. in darkness, to infinity. The Manichaean prophets, a series that includes Enoch, Shem, Buddha, Zoroaster, Jesus and Paul of Tarsus, have the task of revealing the "truth" to man, which is essentially that the order to "go forth and multiply" was given by a demonic entity and that the true purpose of the world is to enable the particles of light to return to their place of origin and reunite. Manichaeism therefore seeks to halt the dispersion of light and its revelation is also the path of mankind's salvation.

The foregoing gave rise to a deeply sexophobic morality and a vision of the flesh and matter as evil. Hence the idea that the figure of Christ was a spiritual entity and his body a complete illusion, pure appearance. Manichaeans therefore regarded Christ's suffering too as not real but apparent, whereas Mani was thought to have been really crucified and experienced actual pain.

This very rigid conception was tempered in the reality of communal life with its division into the elect and the catechumens responsible for feeding and taking care of them. While the latter could only hope to have children accepted as members of the elect or for reincarnation as such themselves, the former had to follow special rules of conduct and a strictly vegetarian diet so as to become vessels of liberated light. The life of the community was also marked by days of fasting and the celebration of canonical feast days, including the crucifixion of Mani.

2.3 Historical and Geographical Outline

Manichaeism had the great gift of adaptation to the various contexts it penetrated, which enabled it to win followers in the Buddhist world and China, where it arrived via the Silk Roads. The spiritual center of Manichaeism, the see of Mani's successor, moved from Babylon to Samarkand in present-day Uzbekistan in the tenth century.

The period 280–300 saw the first Christian refutations of Manichaeism, which continued, however, to spread in North Africa. The first edict against it, issued by Diocletian in 302, did not prevent it from gaining ground in Syria, Asia Minor, Greece, the Balkans, and Italy.

Unquestionably present in Rome between 311 and 314, Manichaeism then spread into Spain and Gaul. St Augustine of Hippo, born in Algeria in 354, was a Manichaean before his conversion to Christianity in 386. The first edict of a Christian emperor against Manichaeism was issued in 372 by Valentinian I. While the introduction of the death penalty for Manichaeans in the 6th century soon led to the movement's extinction in the West, it survived in the Far East, as stated above, until the 17th century.

It will also be useful at this point to provide a chronological framework for the presence of Manichaeism in Egypt. Disciples of Mani appear to have reached Alexandria around 270 and continued from there as far as Armenia. They were in any case already present in Licopolis in Upper Egypt around 260. As mentioned above, the pastoral letter of an Egyptian bishop against the Manichaeans appears to date from 280, and the opposition of the Coptic Church became increasingly resolute as from 370.

The characteristics listed above, including solid communitarian organization, rigid moral discipline, and the fact that Manichaeans presented themselves in Christian areas as the true Christians, the true followers of Christ, have led scholars to suggest that Manichaean influences played some part in the birth of the Pachomian monasticism. The elements for this development were indeed already all in place in geographical and chronological terms. Like the Gnostics, the Manichaeans were great translators, above all from Greek and Syriac, another characteristic shared with the Pachomian communities, whose rule included study, prayer and work.

As previously stated, many Gnostics entered the Manichaean movement, which continued to grow and spread until the 6th century. Its apparent disappearance at that point is probably due only to a lack of sources, given the strong and evident Manichaean influence on the Cathars during the European Middle Ages and the continued existence of Manichaean communities in the Far East in the 17th century.

3

THE DEBATE ON GNOSTIC INFLUENCES IN ETHIOPIA

3.1 The Debate

After this brief overview of the general characteristics of Gnosticism and Manichaeism in terms of history and the history of ideas and religions, we shall go on to examine the Ethiopian texts that appear to be indicative of Gnostic influences. Before we do so, however, it should be pointed out the existence of Gnostic elements or influences in Ethiopia is not unanimously recognized, as attested in particular by the absence on an entry on Gnosticism in the *Encyclopaedia Aethiopica*.[13] The index does contain references to Gnosticism but only in relation to other entries and in any case only about a dozen. This is quite surprising in view of the statement made by Enrico Cerulli in the introduction to the first volume of his edition of texts attributed by him to followers of the Mikaelite heretics in 1958:

> Where do these Gnostic tendencies in Ethiopia come from and how are they related to the history of eastern Gnosis? Have they ever been linked to some form of medieval Manichaeism? While I believe it useful to draw attention to this question here, it can hardly be answered prior to the complete examination of the Gnostic literature mentioned above. This cannot be undertaken in the present volume but certainly deserves to be carried out, which I shall do separately at a later stage.[14]

In other words, the question existed and it was his intention to devote specific attention to it.

---

[13] Siegbert Uhlig (ed.), *Encyclopaedia Aethiopica*, Wiesbaden, 2003-14.

[14] Enrico Cerulli, *Scritti Teologici Etiopici dei secoli XVI-XVII—Tre opuscoli dei Mikaeliti*, Vatican City, 1958, p. XVI.

Nor was Cerulli the only scholar to hold these views. In 1966, at the Third International Conference of Ethiopian Studies in the Institute of Ethiopian Studies in Addis Abeba, Jean Doresse and Father Agostino Tedla challenged his Gnostic interpretation of the above texts and made the following statements:

> The editors of certain Ge'ez texts such as the *Book of Mysteries* [...] and the recently published Mikaelite writings have suggested the presence here and there of echoes of old eastern Gnostic heresies. They are generally mistaken on this point. This does not mean, however, that there are no vestiges of Gnostic myths or quotations from the writings of heretical sects in the Ge'ez literature. It is only that these vestiges have so far remained unidentified, paradoxical though this may appear. We are currently preparing a detailed work on these unknown remnants in which we shall also specify the apocryphal texts that served as models for certain passages in Ethiopian writings.[15]

While Doresse thus confirmed his intention of addressing the question, Father Agostino made this observation:

> [T]he fact that traces of Gnostic doctrines should have survived until the 17th century in Ethiopia is in itself hardly surprising given that this country, which clings so stubbornly to the ancient traditions, has preserved with the utmost care and religious piety manuscripts of works and doctrines of Christian antiquity that are seldom or indeed never to be found elsewhere. Count (*sic*) Rossini admits this possibility and Cerulli himself speaks of it specifically at length in various works in which the hypothesis formulated on the basis of these writings reappears. [...] no particular difficulty is encountered in admitting, in principle, the possibility of the occasional and more or less limited and vigorous reappearance of ancient Gnostic infiltrations [...][16]

---

[15] Jean Doresse, "Survivance d'Ecrits Gnostiques dans la Litterature Gueze," in *Proceedings of the Third International Conference of Ethiopian Studies*, Addis Abeba, 1970, vol. II, p. 213.

[16] Agostino Tedla, "A proposito di alcuni passi oscuri negli Scritti teologici etiopici pubblicati da E. Cerulli," in *Proceedings of the Third International Conference of Ethiopian Studies*, Addis Abeba, 1970, p. 217. The passage quoted then goes on to present the reasons for disagreeing with the Gnostic interpretation of the documents in question.

In the light of the above, the absence of an entry on Gnosticism in the *Encyclopaedia Aethiopica* gives rise to certain doubts.

Examination of the references made in other entries in the encyclopedia, and especially to the one on the *Fəkkare mäläkot* or *Interpretation of the Godhead*, the first of the writings published by Cerulli in the above-mentioned volume, reveals that the most important interpretive reference is to an essay of 2004 by Pierluigi Piovanelli.[17]

While seeking, like Doresse and Father Agostino, to refute the Gnostic interpretation of the supposedly Mikaelite writings, Piovanelli did so by taking the extreme stance of denying not only the existence of a Mikaelite movement, the Mikaelite character of the documents published by Cerulli, and the Gnostic character of Mikaelite thought but also the very existence of Gnostic influences in Ethiopia. While the latter denial is never explicitly stated, it can certainly be deduced from a reading of the beginning of the essay[18] and the section on the "Gnostic Interpretation,"[19] which contains in particular very short quotations from the above-mentioned texts by Doresse and Father Agostino designed to suggest assertions that are not completely faithful to the spirit of the originals.

What happened between 1966, the date of the Third International Conference of Ethiopian Studies, and 2004, when Piovanelli's essay was published? How is it that the views stated so directly, explicitly, and unanimously[20] by Cerulli, Doresse and Father Agostino in the 1950s and '60s came to be so flatly denied some thirty years later? The period between 1966 and 2004 did in fact see something that substantially altered the approach of scholars to this subject, namely the first appearance in the 1970s of facsimile editions and translations of the texts discovered at Nag Hammadi and the other codices mentioned above. This is a crucial factor and one that could not fail, in certain respects, to halt the debate on this subject for a long time. It meant that original Gnostic writings were finally available for the first time and no longer only partisan sources specifically designed to discredit and condemn Gnosticism.

---

[17] Pierluigi Piovanelli, "Connaissance de Dieu et Sagenne Humaine en Ethiopie," in *Le Museon*, 117 (2004), pp. 193-227.

[18] Ibid., pp. 193-94.

[19] Ibid., pp. 202-05.

[20] Apart, of course, from the Gnostic interpretation of the three texts published in 1958.

With the more complete and accurate vision of the movement thus provided, certain elements previously regarded as essential lost their importance. For example, Cerulli's assumption that the presence of references to the *Pearl* constituted a clear proof of Gnostic influences is not borne out by the original documents. As Birger A. Pearson points out,[21] these references bear witness rather to the influence of Thomas Christianity.[22] Other elements regarded as touchstones by Cerulli—including references to "Wisdom," severe condemnation of the flesh, allusions to the fact that the doctrines set forth in the texts in question are to be kept secret, and the idea of being wholly reabsorbed into the godhead after death with no preservation of individuality[23]—are unquestionably present in Gnosticism and Manichaeism but not exclusive to those schools of thought.

The accessibility of the newly discovered texts shed light on many aspects of the Gnostic movement and also provided further tools for the analysis of its presence in Ethiopia. While Piovanelli drew in some respects on these new studies in his contribution to the debate on the supposedly Mikaelite opuscula, he appears to have extended their results also to the periods prior to these writings and drawn conclusions that appear open to serious doubt. We shall endeavor in the following pages to define some tools of inquiry making it possible to cast light on this question.

3.2 Transit and Destruction

Before ending this section, however, we must draw attention to an important aspect also addressed by Piovanelli in another work.[24] Like the rest of the Christian world, Ethiopia was periodically subject to the wholesale destruction of manuscripts regarded as unorthodox. Some of these campaigns are also recorded in history. Zär'a Ya'əqob (1434-68) is

---

[21] Birger A. Pearson, *Ancient Gnosticism*, op. cit., pp. 256-61.

[22] We apologise to the reader for briefly mentioning here some subjects that will be examined at length below in a way that will be clearer and more comprehensible to those not already conversant with them.

[23] This subject will be discussed below as "nebular" divinity.

[24] Pierluigi Piovanelli, "Les Aventures des Apocryphes en Ethiopie," in *Apocrypha. Revue Internationale des Littératures Apocryphes*, 4 (1993), pp. 197-224.

to be regarded as responsible for launching at least one and the destruction of heretical texts circulating in Upper Egypt by order of the Egyptian Patriarch has already been mentioned above. This is the reason why a text in the Ethiopian literature is sometimes found to contain references or similarities to other texts not discovered in Ethiopia. The other important fact is that the Ethiopian Patriarch came from Egypt with his retinue, bringing not only manuscripts and painted images but also oral testimonies of writings not to be found in Ethiopia. These circumstances must be recalled in order to make sense of some otherwise incomprehensible transits.

4

INFLUENCES PRIOR TO CHRISTIANIZATION

4.1 The Possibility of Influences Prior to Christianization

While the Christianization of Ethiopia took place in the 4th century, the fact that the Aksumite port of Adulis was already long established as an important center of trade on the Red Sea means that prior contact with Egypt can be assumed as well as the possible penetration of Gnostic texts or influences. Though plausible, the latter possibility is as yet wholly unsupported by textual evidence. Moreover, the established view among scholars is that the earliest texts in the Ethiopian literature were not translations from Coptic originals, whereas the most ancient Gnostic texts found in Egypt are all in that language.[25]

It is obviously possible to suggest that such texts did exist but were lost in the above-mentioned campaigns of destruction. In that case, however, they could have left an imprint on other later texts, as often happens, and traces of the myths, narratives, and philosophical conceptions outlined above should be found in Ethiopian literature. These could be of Gnostic, Manichaean or Hermetic origin, as Hermetic writings in Coptic have also been found in Egypt.

---

[25] It should be remembered that Arabic did not become the official language of Egypt until 706 and that this did not in any case mean the complete elimination of Coptic, which is indeed still used today in the rites of the monophysite Egyptian Church.

4.2 Hermeticism

It will be useful at this point to provide a brief outline of this other philosophical and religious tradition, which appeared at roughly the same time as Christianity and Gnosticism, and presents some affinities with the latter. Hermeticism was unquestionably born out of the combination of Graeco-Roman and ancient Egyptian religious conceptions. Once again, it is a religion revealed to man by a semi-divine figure, in this case the mythical Hermes Trismegistus ("Thrice Great"), a representation of the syncretic combination of the Greek god Hermes and the Egyptian Toth, the guide of spirits after death. Hermeticism displays numerous similarities with Gnosticism and was also influenced, according to some scholars, by early Christianity, especially the Christian Gnosis of Valentinus.[26] It involved an esoteric path in stages of ritual approach to a revelation that was probably a combination of ancient mystery religions and Platonism. The ideas of the divinity of man, of the ascent of spirits through the heavens after death as a process of gradual purification and the shedding of earthly attributes, of revelation as prompting the rediscovery of oneself and one's true divine nature, of the superiority of mankind over gods, which it can create as idols, of special enlightenment to be obtained through contact with the divine by repeating sequences of mystical words, and of the judgment of spirits after death are all to be found together with magical and astrological beliefs in Hermeticism.

There are also substantial differences, however, especially with respect to Christianity, in that Hermeticism was a fundamentally pagan and pantheistic philosophy that regarded sexuality and the ability to give birth as expressions of the divine and had no place whatsoever for a savior, as it did not regard the world as inherently evil.

The idea of the ascent of spirits through the heavens is to be found in the Ethiopian texts of the period of translations from Greek during the Aksumite Empire, albeit with characteristics different from those outlined above. Moreover, those of the later period of translations from Arabic (13th–15th century) contain the ideas of the divinity of man, of spirits shedding their earthly determinations after death, and of special powers to be obtained through the knowledge of magical names (possibly in connection with the verbal repetition of sequences) as well as magical and

---

[26] For an in-depth examination of the elements influencing Hermetic mysticism, see the extensive introduction to Alberto Camplani (ed.), *Scritti Ermetici in Copto*, Brescia, 2000.

astrological beliefs. As we shall see, however, all of these were based during those periods on Greek and Arabic sources. While these may of course have drawn on earlier influences and derivations dating from before the Christianization of Ethiopia, this is no more than a hypothesis.

4.3 The "Filter" of Christianity and Undatable Sources

In the light of the foregoing, we shall now take a different tack and acknowledge that the hypothesis of Gnostic influences prior to Christianization finds no support whatsoever in the sphere of exegesis. On the contrary, as will be shown at a later stage, all of the traces of Gnosticism or Manichaeism to be found in the texts during this study emerge as though filtered through Christianity. There is, however, also a different sphere of research, not mentioned here so far, to which a specific section will be devoted below, namely the area of what we shall call talismanic or thaumaturgical practices. As attested by research into popular beliefs, the production of talismans, exorcism, and esoteric practices with sometimes Christian and sometimes other characteristics, similarities are unquestionably to be found not only with Gnosticism and probably Hermeticism but also, according to some scholars, with the ancient Egyptian religion and the talismanic use of the *Book of the Dead*. The fact that these similarities and influences are undatable makes it necessary to address them in a separate section.

THE FIRST PHASE OF GNOSTIC INFLUENCES IN ETHIOPIA—TRANSLATIONS FROM GREEK

5.1 The Byzantine Empire and Alexandria

Scholars believe that the conversion of Ethiopia to Christianity was a result of political and commercial agreements reached between the Aksumite and Byzantine empires in the 4th century. Christianization was immediately followed by the arrival of texts, first of all the Bible, which were translated into Ge'ez from Greek. It should be recalled here that Egypt was part of the Byzantine Empire at the time and that Greek was normally used both as the official language and as a lingua franca throughout imperial territory. Moreover, Coptic itself was born out of a combination of the ancient Egyptian language and Greek, which was introduced after the Roman conquest.

Egyptian Christianity was deeply influenced by the schools of philosophy developed and promoted in Alexandria, which was unquestionably the major center for the dissemination of Gnosticism. Cerulli repeatedly asserts this in his works and the recent discoveries give us no reason to reject his views. Pearson thus refers, for example, to *On the Origin of the World* and *Hypostasis of the Archons*, works belonging respectively to the 2nd and 3rd century, as originating in Alexandria and influenced both by Valentinian Christianity and by Manichaeism.[27] The former[28] presents some of the essential elements seen above and in particular the attribution of particular importance to Eve. In the revision

---

[27] See Birger A. Pearson, Ancient Gnosticism, op. cit., pp. 221-22.

[28] See *On the Origin of the World*, in W. Barnstone, M. Meyer (eds.), *Essential Gnostic Scriptures*, op. cit., pp. 90-98.

of Genesis found there, it is Eve who gives life to Adam as the agent of Sophia when the "lords of the world" fail, and the serpent that persuades Eve to eat the fruit of the tree of knowledge is "the wisest of creatures."[29] She is, however, raped by the lords of the world in an attempt to rob her of her divine nature.

Examination of the translations from Greek produced during this period in Ethiopia immediately reveals that they include the *Book of Enoch*, identified by Pearson as one of the most important sources of the Judaic apocalyptic literature. While this is not a Gnostic text, Gnosticism was born out of the same socio-cultural context, as noted above. Gnostic influence can instead certainly be found in the *Shepherd of Hermas* and the *Ascension of Isaiah*. This set of works can be described as marking the first datable period of penetration of Gnostic influences.

5.2 The Book of Enoch

As stated above, the *Book of Enoch* is a Jewish apocalyptic work written between the 4th century BC and the 1st century AD that contains the revelations imparted to the Patriarch Enoch during his ascent to heaven. The only surviving version, through which the work is known today, is the Ethiopian one. The original was probably written in Aramaic and then translated into Greek. Some Fathers of the Church regarded it as part of the Biblical canon and it is still a canonical text in Ethiopia. This complex work relates the fall of the angels who coupled with mortal women and the ensuing destruction of the human race in the Flood. The revelations received by Enoch in heaven from angels and from God regard the mysteries of creation and the future of mankind as well as the disasters that will befall humanity for its sins. Many of them are couched in complex symbolic terms and the text includes recurrent references to the astronomical order of the heavens.

A number of quotations will provide a clearer understanding of the text in question. It is Enoch himself that speaks in the first:

> And a terrible thing I saw there – seven stars like great burning mountains. And like a spirit questioning me the Angel said: "This is the place of the end of heaven and earth; this is the prison for the stars of heaven and the host of heaven. And the stars

---
[29] Ibid., p. 96.

which roll over the fire, these are the ones which transgressed the command of the Lord from the beginning of their rising because they did not come out at their proper times. And he was angry with them and bound them until the time of the consummation of their sin in the year of mystery."[30]

This evidently looks forward to the Gnostic idea of the Archons that rule the heavenly bodies and their demonic ranks.

Enoch is again the speaker in the second:

Wisdom found no place where she could dwell, and her dwelling was in heaven. Wisdom went out in order to dwell among the sons of men, but did not find a dwelling; wisdom returned to her place and took her seat in the midst of the angels. And iniquity came out from her chambers; those whom she did not seek she found, and dwelt among them, like rain in the desert, and like dew on parched ground.[31]

Even though it is uncertain whether the author is speaking of Wisdom here as an emanation or as an angelic personification, the theme is again typically Gnostic and explicitly stated together with those of distance, condemnation of the historical period and the sense of not belonging in the world, which proves irrational or perhaps simply alien and incomprehensible (the dwelling place of "iniquity" which appears to be another personification or emanation despite the lack of a capital letter).

Enoch speaks again:

And there I saw one who had a head of days, and his head (was) white like wool; and with him (there was) another, whose face had the appearance of a man, and his face (was) full of grace, like one of the holy angels. And I asked one of the holy angels who went with me, and showed me all the secrets, about that Son of Man, who he was, and whence he was, (and) why he went with the Head of Days. And he answered me and said

---

[30] Michael A. Knibb, *The Ethiopic Book of Enoch*, Oxford, 1978, XVIII, 13–16 p. 106.

[31] Ibid., XLII, 1–3, p. 130. It should be noted that while wisdom is also a theme in the Bible, it takes on different meanings and overtones in Gnosticism, acquiring its own personification and absolute predominance over other themes.

to me: "This is the Son of Man who has righteousness, and with whom righteousness dwells; he will reveal all the treasures of that which is secret, for the Lord of Spirits has chosen him, and through uprightness his lot has surpassed all before the Lord of Spirits for ever. And this Son of Man whom you have seen will rouse the kings and the powerful from their resting-places, and the strong from their thrones, and will loose the reins of the strong, and will break the teeth of the sinners. And he will cast down the kings from their thrones and from their kingdoms, for they do not exalt him, and do not praise him, and do not humbly acknowledge whence (their) kingdom was given to them. And he will cast down the faces of the strong, and shame will fill them, and darkness will be their dwelling, and worms will be their resting-place; and they will have no hope of rising from their resting-places, for they do not exalt the name of the Lord of Spirits. And these are they who judge the stars of heaven, and raise their hands against the Most High, and trample upon the dry ground, and dwell upon it; and all their deeds show iniquity ... and their power (rests) on their riches, and their faith is in the gods which they have made with their hands and they deny the name of the Lord of Spirits. And they will be driven from the houses of his congregation, and of the faithful who depend on the name of the Lord of Spirits."[32]

This quotation is very important because it presents some of the key themes of the *Book of Enoch*, first and foremost explicit condemnation of the mighty and unrighteousness but also messianic belief in the "Son of Man"[33] and the palingenesis that will restore dignity to the righteous. The subject is continued in the following quotation:

And I looked and turned to another part of the earth and I saw there a deep valley with burning fire. And they brought the kings and the powerful and threw them into that valley. And there my eyes saw how they made instruments for them – iron chains of immeasurable weight. And I asked the angel of peace

---

[32] Ibid., XLVI, 1–8 pp. 131–32.

[33] As seen above, the Son of Man is an emanation in some Gnostic sects.

who went with me, saying; "These chain-instruments – for whom are they being prepared?" And he said to me: "These are being prepared for the hosts of Azazel, that they may take them and throw them into the lowest part of Hell; and they will cover their jaws with rough stones, as the Lord of Spirits commanded. And Michael and Gabriel, Raphael and Phanuel – these will take hold of them on that great day, and throw them on that day into the furnace of burning fire, that the Lord of Spirits may take vengeance on them for their iniquity, in that they became servants of Satan and led astray those who dwell upon the dry ground. And in those days the punishment of the Lord of Spirits will go out, and all the storehouses of the waters which (are) above the heavens ... and under the earth will be opened, and all the waters will be joined *with* the waters which (are) above the heavens. The water which (is) above heaven is male, and the water which (is) under the earth is female. And all those who dwell upon the dry ground and those who dwell under the ends of heaven will be wiped out. And because of this they will acknowledge their iniquity which they have committed on the earth, and *through this* they will be destroyed.[34]

Here we also find the idea of the male and female waters.

Another quotation:

And the spirit of the sea is male and strong, and according to the power of its strength (the spirit) turns it back with a rein, and likewise it is driven forward and scattered amongst all the mountains of the earth. And the spirit of the hoar-frost is its (own) angel; and the spirit of the hail is a good angel. And the spirit of the snow has withdrawn because of its power, and it has a special spirit; and that which rises from it is like smoke, and its name (is) frost. And the spirit of the mist is not associated with them in their storehouses, but has a special storehouse; for its course (is) glorious both in light and in darkness, and in winter and in summer, *and in its storehouse is an angel*. The spirit of the dew (has) its dwelling at the ends of heaven, and it is

---

[34] *The Ethiopic Book of Enoch*, op. cit., LIV, 1–10, pp. 138–39.

> connected with the storehouses of the rain; and its course (is) in winter and in summer, and its clouds and the clouds of the mist are associated, and one gives to the other.³⁵

Here we find the idea of the spirits that give life to nature, corresponding in the microcosm to the role of the Archons (or fallen angels) in the heavens. It also follows implicitly, however, that natural catastrophes are controlled by these spirits and can therefore be avoided by means of prayer or, if the spirits are evil, by the actions required to placate them.

The following passage instead speaks of one of the angels responsible for the downfall of man:

> And the name of the fourth (is) Penemue: this one showed the sons of men the bitter and the sweet, and showed them all the secrets of their wisdom. He taught men the art of writing with ink and paper, and through this many have gone astray from eternity to eternity, and to this day. For men were not created for this, that they should confirm their faith like this with pen and ink. For men were created no differently from the angels, that they might remain righteous and pure, and death, which destroys everything, would not have touched them; but through this knowledge of theirs they are being destroyed, and through this power it (death) is consuming me.³⁶

This passage is very interesting because of its explicit condemnation of wisdom and those who write down their knowledge on paper in ink. A clear distinction is thus drawn between those who have the right to do this, including the author of the *Book of Enoch*, and those who do not, namely the uninitiated and the possessors of false wisdom, thus also establishing the hierarchy between initiates and disciples to be found in Gnosticism. The last succinct quotation is on the rich and mighty, the true central subject of this book:

> Woe to you who build your houses with the toil of others, and all their building materials (are) the bricks and stones of sin; I say to you: "You will not have peace."³⁷

---

³⁵ Ibid., LX, 16–20, pp. 146–147.

³⁶ Ibid., LXIX, 8–11, p. 161.

³⁷ Ibid., XCIX, 13, p. 234.

Apart from the apocalyptic accents and atmosphere of these quotations, presented here for the benefit of readers unacquainted with the work, the subjects looking forward to Gnosticism are not a call for social revolt but in any case strong enough to suggest that the *Book of Enoch* and the other two texts discussed below may have contributed to the Gnostic influence in Ethiopia, at least during the initial period. These subjects comprise Wisdom and its inability to find a dwelling place on earth, the war between the forces of good and evil, the presence of evil spirits in the heavens and on earth, astrology connected to demonology, the sense of alienation, the expectation of a social and spiritual upheaval whereby the righteous will regain their dignity, and the idea of an esoteric revelation that must be concealed from the ungodly and unworthy. The differences in tone and emphasis with respect to Gnosis have already been mentioned.

5.3 *The Ascension of Isaiah*

The second text to be addressed is the *Ascension of Isaiah*, which presents evident Christian elements. It is dated to the 2nd century AD by some scholars and thought to have originated in Syria, but may have been written prior to Christianization. Like the *Book of Enoch*, it has survived in complete form only in Ethiopia in the Ge'ez version. It is divided into two parts, the first of which presents the martyrdom of the prophet Isaiah, cut in half with a wooden saw by order of the king Manasseh for refusing to bow down to the power of evil. The second recounts his ascension, guided by an angel through the seven heavens until he beholds God and Jesus, and ends with a vision of the life of Christ. The first part, an account of the martyrdom is based on Jewish traditions, but the *Ascension* as a whole, previously regarded as the result of a simple sequential combination of different texts, is now recognized as a complex work of unification.

The Ethiopian translation was probably produced in the 5th century. Piovanelli's study of the Ethiopian apocrypha states that it was eliminated from the canon in the period of Zär'a Ya'əqob on account of the unorthodox doctrines it contains.[38]

---

[38] Pierluigi Piovanelli, "Les Aventures des Apocryphes en Ethiopie," op. cit., p. 206.

The signs of Gnostic influence are stronger here. An example is provided in chapter 4, which presents the prophecies of Isaiah on the age of the Antichrist:

> Now, therefore, Hezekiah and Josab my son, [these are the days of the completion of the world]. And after it has been brought to completion, Beliar will descend, the great angel, the king of this world, which he has ruled ever since it existed. He will descend from his firmament in the form of a man, a king of iniquity, a murderer of his mother – this is the king of this world – and will persecute the plant which the twelve apostles of the beloved will have planted; some of the twelve will be given into his hand. This angel, Beliar, will come in the form of that king, and with him will come all the powers of this world, and they will obey him in every wish. By his word he will cause the sun to rise by night, and the moon also he will make to appear at the sixth hour. And he will do everything he wishes in the world; he will act and speak like the Beloved, and will say, "I am the Lord, and before me there was no one." And all men in the world will believe in him. They will sacrifice to him and will serve him, saying, "This is the Lord, and besides him there is no other." And the majority of those who have associated together to receive the Beloved he will turn aside after him. And the the power of his miracles will be in every city and district, and he will set up his image before him in every city.[39]

Beliar, king of this world as from the creation, is thus attributed with the words spoken by the God of the Jews in Genesis and he also claims to be the creator and is hence equivalent to the Demiurge, the lesser god of the Gnostics. Other references to lesser, demonic divinities that govern the world are to be found at the beginning of chapter IX, where Isaiah, on ascending to the seventh heaven, hears a voice that seeks to prevent him from taking this celestial route. On the other hand, verses 13-16 of the same chapter read as follows:

> The Lord will indeed descend into the world in the last days, (he) who is to be called Christ after he has descended and

---

[39] James H. Charlesworth, *The Old Testament Pseudepigrapha*, 2 vols., New York, 1985, IV, 1–11, vol. 2, pp. 161–62.

become like you in form, and they will think that he is flesh and a man. And the god of that world will stretch out [his hand against the Son], and they will lay their hands upon him and hang him upon a tree, not knowing who he is. And thus his descent, as you will see, will be concealed even from the heavens so that it will not be known who he is. And when he has plundered the angel of death, he will rise on the third day and will remain in that world for five hundred and forty-five days.[40]

The reference to Christ is direct and explicit but Christ must beware the "god of that world," who will hang him on a tree in their ignorance, and for this reason His descent "will be concealed from the heavens," i.e. from the Archons that rule them. The references to Manichaeism are evident.

The last part of the *Ascension* of interest to us here is found in the last two chapters, X and XI:

And I heard the voice of the Most High, the Father of my Lord, as he said to my Lord Christ, who will be called Jesus, "Go out and descend through all the heavens. You shall descend through the firmament and through that world as far as the angel which (is) in Sheol, but you shall not go as far as Perdition. And you shall make your likeness like that of all who (are) in the five heavens, and you shall take care to make your form like that of the angels of the firmament and also (like that) of the angels who (are) in Sheol. And none of the angels of that world shall know that you (are) Lord with me of the seven heavens and of their angels.[41]

The need for disguise, to take the form of the angels of the heaven one is passing through, is a constant in Gnostic ascensions and it was normal praxis in Gnostic communities to bury the dead with talismans that would protect them from the Archons, and to teach initiates formulas to be recited to any Archons seeking prevent them from ascending to the heavens. In this text, even Christ is warned by God, His master, of the risks inherent in His descent from heaven to become a man, which will instead no longer exist when He returns there in glory as the true God accompanied by the ranks of angels, His army. In the course of His descent

---

[40] Ibid., IV, 13–16, vol. 2, p. 170.

[41] Ibid., X, 7–11, vol. 2, p. 173.

through the lower heavens, however, Christ must exhibit the document or talisman serving as a sort of passport enabling him to continue his journey. Then comes the most important moment, the birth of Christ:

> And I saw a woman of the family of David the prophet whose name (was) Mary, an she (was) a virgin and was betrothed to a man whose name (was) Joseph, a carpenter, and he also (was) of the seed and family of the righteous David of Bethlehem in Judah. And he came into his lot. And when she was betrothed, she was found to be pregnant, and Joseph the carpenter wished to divorce her. But the angel of the Spirit appeared in this world, and after this Joseph did not divorce Mary, but he did not reveal this matter to anyone. And he did not approach Mary, but kept her as a holy virgin, although she was pregnant. And he did not live with her for two months. And after two months of days, while Joseph was in his house, and Mary his wife, but both alone, it came about, when they were alone, that Mary then looked with her eyes and saw a small infant, and she was astounded. And after her astonishment had worn off, her womb was found as (it was) at first, before she had conceived. And when her husband, Joseph, said to her, "What has made you astounded?" his eyes were opened, and he saw the infant and praised the Lord, because the Lord had come in his lot. And a voice came to them, "Do not tell this vision to anyone." But the story about the infant was spread abroad in Bethlehem. Some said, "The virgin Mary has given birth before she has been married two months." But many said, "She did not give birth; the midwife did not go up (to her), and we did not hear (any) cries of pain." And they were all blinded concerning him; they all knew about him, but they did not know from where he was.[42]

There is evidently nothing carnal about this birth and Christ's childhood is fictitious, serving only to bring Him to the moment when He will commence his preaching and His mission of salvation.

This conception of a spiritual Christ devoid of carnality is another essential element of the Christian Gnostic and Manichaean beliefs, in

---
[42] Ibid., XI, 2–14, vol. 2, pp. 174-75.

which Christ is often conceived, in line with Platonic philosophy, as an emanation, an abstract entity, often the reincarnation of Seth, with the function of descending on earth to impart His message of salvation. There is, however, no need in Gnosticism of a God who becomes man (through incarnation) in order to atone for original sin, but only for a beacon-like God, a divinity showing the way to return to Him, because the sin, if it exists, is not of man but of a divine entity (often Sophia) that abandoned or became estranged from the Father. In this story of a battle between light and darkness, between higher and lower divinities, mankind is never anything other than incidental, the involuntary vessel of a spark of light that seeks to return to its origin.

The other noteworthy features of this text comprise the need for Christ to disguise Himself during his journey to the earth, the fact that a demon asks for His "passport" during his descent, and the attribution to the demon Beliar of the words spoken in Genesis by the God of the Jews. In this case, the dualistic vision is so strong that the *Ascension* later became the canonical book of the Albigensians during the European Middle Ages.

5.4 *The Shepherd of Hermas*

The *Shepherd of Hermas* is an apocalyptic or perhaps simply visionary text produced in Rome probably between 140 and 155 AD, possibly in the sphere of a Jewish-Christian community. It was written in a form of Greek with Judaic overtones.

It can be described as a series of visions, parables and teachings in which Hermas, the author, relates the revelations of a "shepherd," a prophetic figure who denounces the decay of the Church and Christian institutions and failure to announce the imminent reign of Christ. Through Hermas, the Shepherd urges Christians to repent and return to the prophetic spirit of the early Church.

While the number of fragments found in different languages, including Latin, Coptic and Persian Median, attests to the broad circulation of the *Shepherd*, the Ethiopian version is the only complete one discovered so far.

This text displays evident Gnostic influences and was translated into Ge'ez in the 6th century, a period in which it was rejected in Europe and condemned by Pope Gelasius I as apocryphal and fit only for heretics and schismatics. Its primary features are listed below.

- The idea of being in exile in the world is a recurrent theme. Despite its clearly Christian inspiration, however, the work makes no explicit reference either to Christ or to Christianity.
- The Son of God is mentioned but indicated as a incarnation of the Holy Spirit.
- The hierarchical ranks of angels are a strong presence but evil angels also exist.
- There is a radical dualism of good and evil, and a bitter struggle between the entities representing them.
- The rich are again attacked but less violently than in the *Book of Enoch*.

Let us now examine some extracts that reveal probable connections with Gnosticism. In the first, the Shepherd tells Hermas a parable:

"Hear the parable which I shall tell thee relating to fasting.

A certain man had an estate, and many slaves, and a portion of his estate he planted as a vineyard; and choosing out a certain slave who was trusty and well-pleasing (and) held in honor, he called him to him and saith unto him; "Take this vineyard [which I have planted], and fence it [till I come], but do nothing else to the vineyard. Now keep this my commandment, and thou shalt be free." Then the master of the servant went away to travel abroad.

When then he had gone away, the servant took and fenced the vineyard; and having finished the fencing of the vineyard, he noticed that the vineyard was full of weeds.

So he reasoned within himself, saying, "This command of my lord I have carried out I will next dig this vineyard, and it shall be neater when it is digged; and when it hath no weeds it will yield more fruit, because not choked by the weeds." He took and digged the vineyard, and all the weeds that were in the vineyard he plucked up. And that vineyard became very neat and flourishing, when it had no weeds to choke it.

After a time the master of the servant [and of the estate] came, and he went into the vineyard. And seeing the vineyard fenced neatly, and digged as well, and [all] the weeds plucked up, and the vines flourishing, he rejoiced [exceedingly] at what his servant had done.

So he called his beloved son, who was his heir, and the friends who were his advisers, and told them what he had commanded his servant, and how much he had found done. And they rejoiced with the servant at the testimony which his master had borne to him.

And he saith to them; "I promised this servant his freedom if he should keep the commandment I gave him, which he did, as well as doing good in my vineyard, and pleased me greatly. For this work therefore which he has done, I desire to make him joint-heir with my son, because, when the good thought struck him, he did not neglect it, but fulfilled it."

In this purpose the son of the master agreed with him, that the servant should be made joint-heir with the son.

After some few days, his master made a feast, and sent to him many dainties from the feast. But when the servant received [the dainties sent to him by the master], he took what was sufficient for him, and distributed the rest to his fellow servants.

And his fellow-servants, when they received the dainties, rejoiced, and began to pray for him, that he might find greater favor with the master, because he had treated them so handsomely.

All these things which had taken place his master heard, and again rejoiced greatly at his deed. So the master called together again his friends and his son, and announced to them the deed that he had done with regard to his dainties which he had received; and they still more approved of his resolve, that his servant should be made joint-heir with his son."[43]

The Shepherd now explains its meaning:

"I told thee just now," saith he, "that thou art unscrupulous and importunate, in enquiring for the interpretations of the parables.

---

[43] Maria Beatrice Durante Mangoni (ed.), *Erma – Il Pastore, Bologna, 2003*, Parable V, 2, pp. 145–146.

But since thou art so obstinate, I will interpret to thee the parable of the estate and all the accompaniments thereof, that thou mayest make them known unto all. Hear now," saith he, "and understand them.

The estate is this world, and the lord of the estate is He that created all things, and set them in order, and endowed them with power; the son is the Holy Spirit; the servant is the Son of God, and the vines are this people whom He Himself planted; and the fences are the [holy] angels of the Lord who keep together His people; and the weeds, which are plucked up from the vineyard, are the transgressions of the servants of God; and the dainties which He sent to him from the feast are the commandments which He gave to His people through His Son; and the friends and advisers are the holy angels which were first created; and the absence of the master is the time which remaineth over until His coming."

I say to him; "Sir, great and marvelous are all things and all things are glorious; was it likely then," say I, "that I could have apprehended them?" "Nay, nor can any other man, though he be full of understanding, apprehend them." "Yet again, Sir," say I, "explain to me what I am about to enquire of thee."

"Say on," he saith, "if thou desirest anything." "Wherefore, Sir," say I, "is the Son of God represented in the parable in the guise of a servant?"[44]

The Shepherd replies:

"Listen," said he; "the Son of God is not represented in the guise of a servant, but is represented in great power and lordship." "How, Sir?" say I; "I comprehend not."

"Because," saith he, "God planted the vineyard, that is, He created the people, and delivered them over to His Son. And the Son placed the angels in charge of them, to watch over them; and the Son Himself cleansed their sins, by laboring much and enduring many toils; for no one can dig without toil or labor.

---

[44] Ibid., V, 5, p. 150.

Having Himself then cleansed the sins of His people, He showed them the paths of life, giving them the law which He received from His Father. Thou seest," saith he, "that He is Himself Lord of the people, having received all power from His Father.

But how that the lord took his son and the glorious angels as advisers concerning the inheritance of the servant, listen.

The Holy Pre-existent Spirit. Which created the whole creation, God made to dwell in flesh that He desired. This flesh, therefore, in which the Holy Spirit dwelt, was subject unto the Spirit, walking honorably in holiness and purity, without in any way defiling the Spirit.

When then it had lived honorably in chastity, and had labored with the Spirit, and had cooperated with it in everything, behaving itself boldly and bravely, He chose it as a partner with the Holy Spirit; for the career of this flesh pleased [the Lord], seeing that, as possessing the Holy Spirit, it was not defiled upon the earth.

He therefore took the son as adviser and the glorious angels also, that this flesh too, having served the Spirit unblamably, might have some place of sojourn, and might not seem to have lost the reward for its service; for all flesh, which is found undefiled and unspotted, wherein the Holy Spirit dwelt, shall receive a reward.

Now thou hast the interpretation of this parable also."[45]

The presentation of the Son of God as a servant chosen as joint heir with the master's son by virtue of his fidelity is evidently at variance with the figure as subsequently established. In particular, it appears to suggest a human birth and divine "adoption" of Christ, a conception that was unquestionably current in the early days of Christianity, especially among the Jewish-Christian communities. At the same time, the Holy Spirit is not God in this parable but the Creator. Christ is "the flesh in which the Holy Spirit dwelt," which Christ kept "in holiness and purity." The model of the Trinity is clearly

---

[45] Ibid., V, 6, p. 151.

subverted, as also happens in other texts from Judaic spheres. Another example of this is the *Book of Baruch*,[46] to be understood not as the prophetic book of the Bible but as the Gnostic text mentioned by Hippolytus of Rome in his *Refutation of All Heresies*. According to this book, the universe is governed by three principles, two male and one female, but none of these is the creator, the creation of man being the work of the angels.

What we might call the meaning of the incarnation makes no appearance whatsoever in the *Shepherd of Hermas* or indeed in any of the Gnostic literature. The flesh is an accident with which we must live and of which we must beware so as to preserve our purity. Moreover, the *Shepherd* makes no mention of the crucifixion or the cross. It is therefore certainly no coincidence that the only two manuscripts of this text discovered in Ethiopia were found in the monastery of Gunda Gunde, the center of the Stephanite heresy. It is also possible that none were found anywhere else because this work, like the *Apocalypse of Isaiah*, was subjected to systematic destruction for its unorthodox character. It should be noted in passing that the Gnostic elements appear more marked in the previous texts than in the *Shepherd*, which nevertheless presents numerous anomalous features.

5.5 A Summary of Gnostic Influences in the Period of Translations from Greek

By way of partial conclusions to be drawn from this brief examination of three texts translated into Ge'ez from Greek, it can be stated that traces of Gnostic influence are clearly evident in the aspects listed below.

- The solid and well-structured demonology, the presence of hierarchical ranks of demons with specific powers, who control the celestial spheres and natural phenomena to the point of constituting an authentic "second kingdom" or "sphere of power" of which even Christ must beware. It is the existence of these malignant powers that justifies the need for special talismans to enable spirits to escape the clutches of demons and enter paradise. In the *Apocalypse of Isaiah* a demon is identified as the God of the Bible. Attention should also be drawn in passing to the great importance attached in Gnosticism to Satan, the "lord of this world" and in certain contexts even its

---

[46] *The Book of Baruch*, in W. Barnstone, M. Meyer (eds.), *Essential Gnostic Scriptures*, op.cit., pp. 132–142.

creator. Satan has a kingdom of his own that comprises all the reality of the cosmos, both natural and human. What is above the firmament of the fixed stars is instead the realm of God. Even Christ must hide when he descends into the realm of Satan or be escorted by his armies of angels.

- The corresponding existence of hierarchical ranks of angels that perform the function of protecting those who side with good. This is combined in some works with the social fight against injustice. The "mighty" are condemned and the advent of the kingdom of heaven is awaited also as the time of punishment for those who have made themselves rich with the sweat of the poor and humble.
- The reference to Wisdom, the sense of being in exile in the world, the messianic expectation of social upheaval, and the idea that all this must be the object of an esoteric revelation uniting those who feel this alienation and await the kingdom of heaven all constitute a single theme that encapsulates the will to react against the present condition of unhappiness.
- The other thing that emerges in all the texts examined above is the distortion of the model of the Trinity. This sometimes involves a shifting of roles with respect to the subsequently established framework and sometimes denial of the real incarnation of Christ and hence the attachment of little importance to the crucifixion, the cross and the "death" of Christ. This also gives rise to contempt for the flesh, seen as no more than an accident against which purity must be maintained, something to be triumphed over only with death and requiring rigid codes of conduct aimed at avoiding reproduction.

These subjects will be addressed at greater length below in our examination of their developments in the period of translations from Arabic and in the section presenting the conclusions of the study.

6

THE SECOND PHASE OF GNOSTIC INFLUENCES IN ETHIOPIA— THE PERIOD OF TRANSLATIONS FROM ARABIC

6.1 Historical Outline: The Circumstances and Reasons for Translation

The logical premise for the beginning of the period of translations from Arabic was the Arab conquest of Egypt (639–42) followed by the gradual abandonment of Greek when Arabic became the country's official language (706). The Coptic language survived this process solely for Christian religious functions and Arabic was indeed used as from the 9th century even by Christian theologians of different faiths in their polemical writings with respect to Islam and to one another.[47]

Even though these reasons for translations from Arabic into Ge'ez were in existence from at least the 9th or 10th century, however, there is in fact no trace of any until the 13th or 14th. This is probably due to the fact that the end of the Aksumite Empire, which coincided with the Arab conquests in the Red Sea and Egypt, led in Ethiopia to a period of weak authority unable to ensure the economic power, continuity, and solidity constituting the prerequisite for any serious cultural initiatives.[48] This period ended with the rise to power of the Zagwe dynasty (c. 1140), which

---

[47] Helen C. Evans with Brandie Ratliff, *Byzantium and Islam. Age of Transition 7th–9th Century*, New York, 2012, p. 39; see also E.J. Van Donzel, 'Ǝnbaqom — *Anqäṣä amin — La Porte de la Foi*, Leiden, 1969, pp. 151–52.

[48] In actual fact, the authority of the Aksumite Empire itself was weakened in the 6th century by military and commercial initiatives on the part of the Persian Empire in the Red Sea.

unquestionably left a major imprint on the history of Ethiopian art but is not regarded unanimously by historians as being marked by the beginning of translation or the production of original texts. As works celebrating the Zagwe were, however, certainly produced during the Solomonic dynasty, which took over in 1270, they may well have actually been reworkings of texts produced before its rise to power.

Translations from Arabic were commissioned by both the imperial and the ecclesiastical authorities, accompanied by the composition of original works that will be discussed below.[49] The translators were often Ethiopian monks living in Coptic monasteries or Ethiopian monastic communities in Egypt.

A particularly important part was played in this production of translations by Abuna Sälama, significantly referred to as "the Translator," *abuna* or metropolitan of Ethiopia from 1348 (or perhaps 1350) to 1388 (or perhaps 1390). How are we to understand his commitment to the translation of Coptic Christian works from Arabic into Ge'ez, carried out partly in person and partly through other translators? Sälama arrived in Ethiopia as the successor to Abuna Ya'əqob, who had been expelled in 1344 over conflict with the Ethiopian authorities. This fact, together with the aim of consolidating contact also in doctrinal terms between the Egyptian Coptic church and the monks of Debre Libanos, who had become the guardians of Ethiopian orthodoxy with the advent of the Solomonic dynasty, may well have prompted Abuna Sälama to increase the production of translations to the utmost. He must therefore have seen this as a way of bringing the Ethiopian and Alexandrian faiths into harmony as regards doctrine.

The question arises, however, of whether there were also other reasons for this. According to Taddesse Tamrat, even though Ethiopia had now been Christian for at least seven centuries, large pockets of paganism still survived. The priests made no effort to convert the people and were in any case not enough to cover all of the territory, where even converts were in the habit of practicing magical or pagan rites. Moreover, large areas of Ethiopian territory were now under Muslim rule and their inhabitants had been converted to Islam. Abuna Ya'əqob himself had endeavored to organize the monastic

---

[49] Even though this period in the penetration of Gnostic influence is defined with reference to the existence of translations from Arabic, the texts discussed below comprise not only translations but also what are regarded as original Ethiopian works, which attest in turn, however, to the influence of other works translated from Arabic.

clergy of the Šäwa to undertake the conversion of pagans, the reconversion of renegades, and control over the practices of Christians.[50]

Finally, the possibility exists that this production of translations was also designed to combat the dissemination of other writings that are now lost but attested both by other Christian works, as discussed below, and by beliefs that are still current. We refer to the circulation in the Islamized areas of the Mediterranean as from the 11th century of magical works, which we shall address below, as well as still earlier astrological conceptions attested also in Ethiopian texts. The information provided by Taddesse Tamrat on the cults persecuted in Ethiopia during the period from 'Amdä Ṣəyon to Zär'a Ya'əqob[51] gives the impression that in Ethiopia, as in Europe, the same centuries saw a fusion of old pagan cults surviving in rural areas with new beliefs based on astrology and magic, devil worship and alchemy, the science of names, and the power of letters and numbers. In other words, it can be suggested that Abuna Sälama's translations were actually intended to combat the new expressions of Gnosticism and Manichaeism that were resurfacing, like new forms of paganism, both in Europe and on the other side of the Mediterranean, whence they may have found their way to Ethiopia.

Finally, it should be recalled that this flow of texts from Egypt into Ethiopia included not only rigorously orthodox works but also others of a "deviant" character, including some drawing on the legacy of Jewish religion and tradition. Scholars now believe that what were once regarded as very ancient Jewish influences (prior to Christianization, according to some) actually date back to Zär'a Ya'əqob, the ruler who did his utmost to endow the Solomonic dynasty with the legitimacy of Israelite derivation, a point to be discussed at a later stage.

The works of the period of translations from Arabic that appear to display traces of Gnostic influence are the *Qälemənṭos*, the *Testament of Solomon*, the *Kəbrä nägäst*, the *Book of Mysteries of Heaven and Earth*, the *Christian Romance of Alexander*, the *Combat of Adam, Barlaam and Josaphat* and others with specific talismanic characteristics like the *Ləfafä ṣədəq* or *Bandlet of Righteousness*.

---

[50] Taddesse Tamrat, *Church and State in Ethiopia 1270-1527*, Oxford, 1972, pp. 175-82.

[51] Ibid., pp. 175-82 and 233-40. It should be noted that the reference in this case is not to the repression of the Stephanite or Mikaelite heretical movements but to the intervention in rural areas of priests, often accompanied by troops, who immediately inflicted corporal punishment and even carried out executions without trial wherever evidence was found of the practice of magic, paganism or heretical beliefs.

6.2 The Qälemǝnṭos

The *Qälemǝnṭos* is a canonical text of the Ethiopian church thought to date from 13th or 14th century. Currently known by its Ethiopian name, the work supposedly contains the revelations of the apostle Peter to Clement, regarded as his successor on the papal throne, and had a highly complex genesis. It combines a number of different traditions within a single framework, including the apocryphal Greek text known as the *Apocalypse of Peter*, which reached Ethiopia through an Arabic work,[52] two texts for which no other foreign sources and originals are known (*The Second Coming of Christ and the Resurrection of the Dead* and *The Mystery of the Judgment of Sinners*[53]), and other writings that appear to have been the work of an Ethiopian compiler drawing on different sources.[54]

The narrative framework is the revelation to Clement by Peter of secret teachings imparted to him by Christ on the Mount of Olives. These regard the creation of the world, the history of man and his sin, cosmology, angels, paradise, the fall of Satan, the judgment of sinners, the advent of the Antichrist, and stories about devils. Books 3–7 focus in particular on moral questions and precepts of ecclesiastical discipline.

The following quotation, in which the apostle Peter addresses Clement, is taken from the first part of the above-mentioned text *On the Judgment of Sinners*:

> And now write this revelation, that it may give hope to the children of men. And understand too that the Lord did not create Adam for punishment or corruption but for happiness and delight. When he transgressed the (Lord's) command, death followed Adam's life as light follows darkness. So it was

---

[52] Paolo Marrassini, "L'Apocalisse di Pietro," in *Etiopia e oltre. Studi in onore di Lanfranco Ricci*, Naples, 1994, pp. 171–232.

[53] These three sources, which make up the first two books of the *Qälemǝnṭos*, have been translated and published in S. Grébaut, "Littérature éthiopienne pseudo-clémentine. Texte et traduction du mystère du jugement des pécheurs," in *Revue de l'Orient Chrétien* 12 (1907), pp. 285–97, 380–92, and 13 (1908), pp. 166–80 and 314–20, and in "Littérature éthiopienne pseudo-clémentine. Texte et traduction du traité La seconde venue du Christ et la résurrections des morts," in *Revue de l'Orient Chrétien* 15 (1910), pp. 198–214, 307–23, 425–39.

[54] Books III-VII, published in Alessandro Bausi, *Il Qälemǝnṭos Etiopico. La rivelazione di Pietro a Clemente. I libri 3-7*, Naples, 1992.

Image of the temptation of Adam and Eve (from the church of Maryam Teamina in Tembien (Tigray) – Photographed by Emanuele Ragni

that the reward (of Adam) was destroyed by death. Moreover, after (Adam) atoned, did (the Lord) say again that he would be sent back into destruction and corruption? Far from that, (nothing) of the kind came again, as the punishment of the first (man took place) because he had betrayed His trust. Thus spake (the Lord) to Adam: "I created you for honour and glory but you did not understand. You became like the beasts with no intelligence. You heard my word and disobeyed my command. This is why I will pass judgment on you, which is death." He said to him: "Dust you are. Return to your dust where many

Image of the temptation of Adam and Eve (from the church of Yohannes Maequddi in Gheralta (Tigray) – Photographed by Emanuele Ragni

> sins lie." After bringing him back to life, will He destroy him again by death and Scheol? After retribution in accordance with his sin, (will) the Lord (destroy him again)? Penetrate and understand this, that He will not make him die a second time. Let this become a mystery for all men, like the first revelation.[55]

The text then continues:

> Thus will you know the greatness of the Lord's mercy to Adam, His creation: (You will know) how (Adam) once sought

---

[55] S. Grébaut, "Littérature éthiopienne pseudo-clémentine," op. cit., 13 (1908), pp. 177-78.

to make himself God and (how) wanted to become God himself when he was beguiled by the snake, (he) and his wife. The serpent said to the woman: "O woman, why has the Lord forbidden you to eat (the fruit) of the tree?" The woman answered: "So that we shall not die." The serpent said to the woman: "It is certainly not (so that) you shall not die but so that you do not become God that he has forbidden you the tree." It is in the hope of becoming God that (Adam) disobeyed the Lord's command. The (first) parents were as children who walked in the garden. Their Father had planted in the garden a beautiful (and splendid tree). Its fruit was delicious. It was good for the soul and the body. If (the first parents) had been patient, (the fruit) would have ripened. They were the children of the Lord of the garden. Their Father sent them to watch over the garden and ordered to them to cultivate it. They ate (fruits) of all colors from the garden. Their flavor was that of fig and excellent. When they saw (the forbidden tree), so that they should make no mistake, (the Lord) took them at once and showed them (the tree) with the fruit of excellent taste that He had planted in the garden. He said to them: "Do not touch this tree. Do not approach this tree, otherwise death will befall you."

Again he told them and said: "Take care not to touch it lest I strike you in my wrath." Again he spoke to them, taught them, and told them not to touch it and not to approach. "If you raise your hands to this tree before I myself give you (of its fruit) to your teeth to eat, as it is unripe, your bellies will be tortured and (this unripe fruit) will rot your eyes, break your bones, shatter your limbs, will make ashes of your body and putrefaction of your strength, which will harm you to the hair of your head and the nails of your feet. Until (these fruits) have grown and ripened, I myself will come to you, I will gather them, I will clean (the tree), I will keep every being away from it so that your tongue does not fester in your throat and your teeth are not shattered. (Keep) in (all) the strength of your vigilance. Take care not to covet (the forbidden fruit) and to taste it, because it is unripe fruit." This is what he taught them. He permitted them to feed on the other fruits that were in the garden. It so happened, however, that when they were hungry, they ate (the fruit) of the (forbidden) tree. But (in truth it was) in the hope of becoming God that they disobeyed their Father's command. When they ate (the fruit) of the tree, it was unripe, they did not wait until it had grown and ripened. The unripe fruit corrupted (them). The children's teeth were blunted. They brought it (punishment) upon themselves in the hope of becoming God. The Enemy had made them insane. The Father knew that the unripe fruit had corrupted (them), (as He had told them), and that they had eaten (the fruit) that was harmful to them before the time had come of ripeness, harvesting, and goodness (of the fruit, the time when) He would have given (it to them). This is why He was angered against these children and drove them out of the garden that He had made for their joy and pleasure. He drove them out into a land of thorns and brambles that they would cultivate in heat and sweat (during their) lives. The Father of these children knew that the Enemy had led them astray. He Himself knew the temptation of the Adversary (and knew) how he had confounded the children by hiding in the body of a serpent (and) whispering in their ears. The Father of the children who knew not evil (acted in the same way towards the Enemy), He confounded him that had confounded the children, He partook of the flesh and the blood of these children, and He partook of their death in order to give them His own life. With mysterious wisdom, He joined their flesh, which he took, with His own divinity. Moreover, He joined His own beauty to our corruption and (our) death. The weight of our corruption was absorbed by the beauty of the divinity, by the glorious godhead. Our death was absorbed by His sublime life. He thus became similar (to man) except only for sin. He bore our burden, our sufferings and our weakness so as to confound the Enemy who had confounded the children, corrupted by the unripe fruit. Just as (the Enemy) had hidden in the body of a serpent, so did Our Savior hide in the body of Adam. Not immediately did he confound (the Enemy) and partake of our flesh but after waiting until he who had confounded the children had forgotten, so that he did not know. When (the Enemy) approached Him. (Our Savior) killed him with the staff of his cross. When (the Enemy) confounded (the children), the unripe fruit (corrupted them). He too, (Our Savior), when he confounded the evil one, He corrupted (him) entirely and bound him in dreadful Scheol, in the outer darkness, in weeping and the gnashing of teeth. On returning to life, (the Savior) brought His children back to life, made them gods like Him, gave them of His own life, made them equal to Him, for He gave them of His flesh and His blood so that they became equal to him.[56]

The points listed below are of evident interest here.

- The Lord created man not for punishment or corruption but for happiness and pleasure.
- Salvation awaits everyone, including sinners.
- This truth must remain a secret and must not be revealed to everyone.
- The sin of Adam and Eve arose from their desire to become God. It is, however, clear from the context that the author of the apocryphal text regards this as neither reprehensible nor blasphemous.
- Adam and Eve behaved like children unable to wait for a promise to be kept.
- The fruit was not really forbidden by God, who told Adam and Eve not to eat it because it was still unripe but would have given it to them in due course.
- Satan's temptation was not based on a falsehood, as the fruit will actually enable man to become God. As stated above, the time was not yet ripe. Divinity is the destiny of man, however, as clearly emerges in the last lines of the quotation.
- Even though the text does not dwell on this point, it follows the Satan's own sin is not so very great. It is a sin of failure to obey the rules laid down by God but not based on falsehood.
- The text quoted refers repeatedly to the fact that God became man and experienced human suffering but Christ is never

---

[56] Ibid., pp. 178-79.

mentioned. The reference is always to Our Lord, Our Father or the divinity. While it is true that the narrative as a whole is presented as the revelation by Peter to Clement of truths received from Christ, the fact that Christ is not mentioned suggests that this part may be an interpolation from another non-orthodox source into the Christian narrative framework Christ is visible to man because he was made flesh but God is not. There is also a quotation on this point: "When the sinners see that I intercede with my Father for them, they too will beg me. I will entreat my Father for them. They will see no one but me, who bore their flesh. But I will see my Father, because I am one with my Father in divinity, because I departed from His essence and His love by His will to do as He wished. This is why (my) Father will give them all everlasting life, glory and kingdom."[57] The question of whether God can be seen by man is obviously closely related to that of whether He can be known.

A completely new vision both of the original sin and of Satan's part in it follows from all this. The text appears to have been translated from Arabic, even though the sources have been lost.[58]

The contents expressed have marked Gnostic connotations, the subversive impact of which is attenuated only by Peter's warning that this "different" truth must remain a "mystery," meaning that it must only be revealed to those in possession of higher knowledge and wisdom, probably monks or perhaps the members of some religious congregations or monastic communities in which the theories circulated. This idea of truths to be imparted solely to the initiated is, however, itself typical of the Gnostic model of thought, and the question therefore arises of whether Peter's injunction was only to maintain two levels of revelation (as practiced by Gnostics in general) or to keep secret and thus protect the adherence to doctrines evidently verging on heresy. Moreover, both might well have been considered valid.

As Gianfrancesco Lusini points out in the essay cited above in footnote 58, it is possible to suggest the existence in medieval Ethiopia of a theological school influenced by Origen or perhaps other Gnostic

---

[57] S. Grébaut, "Littérature éthiopienne pseudo-clémentine," op. cit., 15 (1910), p. 434.

[58] G. Lusini, "Naufragio e conservazione di testi cristiani antichi: il contributo della tradizione etiopica," in *Annali dell'Università di Napoli "L'Orientale"* 69 (2009), pp. 69-83.

thinkers. This must have been based in the monasteries on the shores and islands of the Lake Tana, given the historical evidence connected with the discovery of the manuscripts containing this text. As stated above, however, no works by Origen appear to have been translated into Ge'ez. We thus have one of those cases in which there has unquestionably been a transit but the channels are unknown and it is therefore necessary to assume that already translated works by Origen or other intermediaries were destroyed, that the transit took place orally or that the texts contained in the first two books of the *Qälemənṭos* were themselves the agents of the transit and subsequently inserted into the framework known today.

There is something new here with respect to the relations of Gnostic derivation found in the period of translations from Greek. The only themes to recur in both periods are the idea that these revelations are a "mystery" to be kept secret, which is also to be found in Enoch, and the "revision" of Genesis, even though this is a generic reference, as the texts of Greek origin are very brief and allusive, whereas the references in the *Qälemənṭos* are more specific and sometimes constitute authentic reversals of values with respect to the traditional interpretation of Genesis.

In the seventh book of the *Qälemənṭos*, which has been translated into Italian and published by Alessandro Bausi, we find a clear and explicit condemnation of dualism, i.e. of any formulation of Manichaean belief (albeit never named as such) involving a dualism of good and evil powers:

> Whoever says that the pure spirit is of the Lord and the impure spirit of the Devil is wrong. Pure and impure are of the Lord. Who created the Devil? Was it not perhaps the Lord to His Glory? As for as the Devil, it is the wickedness of his mind that gave it birth in his heart, wishing to become God. Through pride he became impure and was repudiated by the holy angels. Let the foolish not believe in their hearts that everything impure is created by the Devil and everything pure by Lord. Whoever says this makes the creation equal to the creator and the Devil like his God for pure and impure creation, making what the Lord created pure and what the Devil created impure. This is a falsehood. It is the Lord that created the pure and the

impure to His Glory, wishing them to be pure, not impure. It is they themselves that have become impure.[59]

It remains to be understood whether this condemnation is aimed explicitly at certain representatives of this school of thought.

6.3 *The Testament of Solomon* and Other Works of a Magical Character Devoted to the Biblical King

6.3.1 Solomonic Magical Texts

Ethiopia has numerous traditions that regard the Biblical King Solomon, recounting his deeds with a particular focus on his renown as a wizard, mastery of demons, and boundless wisdom, due not least to the possession of a magical ring enabling him to talk to animals. Being therefore somewhat marginal in character and often verging on magic, this literature has still to be studied in depth and indeed to be thoroughly catalogued. It is, however, of great importance for those interested in the subjects addressed here.

The best-known text is the *Testament of Solomon*, derived from a Greek original of the 1st–3rd century, which probably arrived in Ethiopia through Egypt at some unknown date.[60] The brief narrative framework consists of Solomon's efforts to free a worker from a demon that robs him and sucks his blood by meeting and questioning all of the demons in order. The work thus becomes a long and detailed demonology. In response to Solomon's questions, each demon lists its powers and the ways in which it can kill and wound people or cause them to fall ill. The demons' answers also provide information about the angels able to protect man from their powers.

This set framework also includes narratives clarifying the existence of solid links between demons and heavenly bodies,[61] the function of demons in causing illnesses,[62] and their ability to know the future. Moreover, some of these are apocryphal stories referred to also in the Quran and Quranic

---

[59] Bausi, *Il Qālemǝntos Etiopico*, op. cit., p. 172.

[60] Steven Kaplan, "Solomon," in Siegbert Uhlig (ed.), *Encyclopaedia Aethiopica*, op. cit., IV vol., pp. 687–88.

[61] Solomon asks the demon in one case to which sign of the Zodiac he is subject.

[62] From which it follows logically that every cure must also serve as an exorcism.

exegesis[63] as well as in ancient Jewish traditions. This ancient text therefore contains traditions of Jewish origin turned into common sources through transit in both Christian and Islamic contexts.[64]

Another important work among the Ethiopian Solomonic writings is the *Net of Solomon* (*Märbäbtä Sälomon*), which is similar in structure to the *Testament*. In addition to narratives and written information, however, this literature also offers the reader magic squares, to be copied as talismanic seals onto scrolls carried by those desiring protection, and other designs understood as copies or drawings of the seal of Solomon, perhaps his ring itself, which had magical powers. These figures also performed talismanic functions and are often found in the magic scrolls studied by Jacques Mercier, as discussed below.[65]

In addition to these two works, the tradition of Solomonic magical texts in Ethiopia includes the *Seal of Solomon* and other writings, the different versions of which often display such dissimilarities that they can hardly be recognized as the same document. Some of the texts in question were short and accompanied by verses and images to be copied onto scrolls for use as talismans, which accounts for the numerous differences from one copy to another.[66]

---

[63] Jacques-Paul Migne (ed.), *Dictionnaire des Apocryphes: Ou, Collection de tous le livres Apocryphes relatives à l'Ancien et au Nouveau Testament*, Paris, 1858, vol. II, pp. 847-71. This dictionary draws in turn on the German *Biblische Legenden der Muselmanner*, G. Weil, Frankfurt, 1845. The present author has been unable to see this original source first-hand.

[64] Some of these sources, for example, were to be used in the compilation of the *Kəbrä nägäst*, which is discussed in the following section.

[65] The author has unfortunately been unable to obtain access to these texts (apart from the *Testament of Solomon*, but in the Greek version). For this reason, no quotations are given in this section.

[66] The variety and richness of the Solomonic literature, not only in Ethiopia but in the Middle East as a whole and the Arabian peninsula, is also attested by Anne Regourd, "Le Kitab al-Mandal al-Sulaymani, un ouvrage d'exorcisme yéménite postérieur au Ve/XIe s.?" in R. Gyselen (ed.) *Démons et merveilles d'Orient*, Res Orientales 13, Bures sur Yvette: Groupe pour l'étude de la civilization du Moyen-Orient, 2001, pp. 123-38. The essays clearly demonstrates both the transit of traditions regarding the biblical king from Jewish to Christian and Muslim contexts and the close connection between the narrative components, the descriptions of the demons' functions and the hierarchical relations between them, and the talismanic function of these texts, which always included a pharmacopea (as in the case of the *Kitab al-Mandal al-Sulaymani*) or a list of instructions or symbols with talismanic functions. I am grateful to Sara Fani of Copenhagen University for bringing this work to my attention.

Two pages from the Arabic manuscript *Seal of Solomon* (pp. 10-11 of the manuscript edited by Rosanna Budelli, Il Sigillo di Salomone. In tre manoscritti di magia copta in lingua araba, Milan, 2014 - Archivio FCCOS della Custodia di Terra Santa, Muski, Cairo.)

6.3.2 Sources of Arab Influence?

The immediate points of reference of the above-mentioned texts appear to be two works in Arabic, published from modern texts in 2014,[67] circulating in Egypt but apparently bearing witness to more ancient traditions. We refer to the *Guide to the Guide* and the *Seal of Solomon*,[68] Christian works that display traces of earlier versions used by Muslims and contain magic squares of numbers with instructions for calculation related to the Psalms

---

[67] Rosanna Budelli (ed.), *Il Sigillo di Salomone in tre manoscritti di magia copta in lingua araba*, Milan, 2014.

[68] The author does not know whether this *Seal of Solomon* bears any similarity to the Ethiopian *Seal of Solomon* mentioned a few lines above.

and the specific characteristics of the person using the talisman.[69] They also contain instructions on purification for those required to perform the exorcistic or talismanic rites involved (the "Work"). There are constant references to the power of the name or names of God or the angels and to the hour and the position of the heavenly bodies at the moment of performing the Work so as to obtain the fulfillment of all desires. There are also magical figures related to the different heavenly bodies, the names of the higher angels, the perfumes to be used during rituals, lists of the psalms to be used in relation to the different illnesses to be cured or desires to be satisfied, and finally the following admonition:

> The Work rests on this. Take care to do no evil, otherwise you will be lost and obtain no benefit from your wicked actions, as the All-Highest and Almighty created his angels like spirits ... and his servants ... like burning fire ... They are forced ... to serve whereas you are the one responsible and deserving punishment. This is the description of the three seals that perform all the works.[70]

This is followed by images of three magic squares.

In other words, these are magical texts in all respects and point out, while recommending that this wisdom be used for good, that in any case the spirits are forced to obey whoever performs the Work. They were also texts used both by Christians and by Muslims.

Even though the Ethiopian texts mentioned above appear simpler and less structured than those in Arabic, the similarities are surprising: demonology, astrology, the protection provided by angels against the different demons, the use of magic scrolls or other talismans, the powers of demons, their ability to know the future and therefore their status, in a certain sense, as minor divinities and in any case as useful if agreement can be reached with them, and, still more importantly, the magical practices common to different religions, the talismans, whose magical powers do not depend on religious persuasion. These are essential

---

[69] The numbers are represented by letters of the alphabet in Hebrew. It is therefore possible, by means of a simple procedure, to calculate the numerical value of words, entire phrases or quotations from the Scriptures, such as the Psalms.

[70] Rosanna Budelli (ed), *Il Sigillo di Salomone in tre manoscritti di magia copta in lingua araba*, op. cit., p. 121.

characteristics that will prove useful in the further development of our investigation.

As mentioned above, however, these texts circulated in Egypt. Is there any evidence at all of a transit to Ethiopia? The Arabic manuscript MS IES 272 of the Institute of Ethiopian Studies in Addis Ababa, copied in 1796, includes three works containing instructions and indications regarding magical practices: the *Kitab bahga al-tarf fi 'ilm al-harf* ("The book of the joy of the glance into the science of the letters") by Nasr al-Din Muhammad b. 'Abdallah Ibn Qurqmas (d. 1477), the *Kitab fi 'ilm al-arqam wa-l-awfaq* ("The book on the science of number and of the magic squares") by an unknown author, and the *Al-Nur al-asna fi sarh al-asma' al-husna* ("The most brilliant light on the explanation of the most beautiful Names of God") by Ahmad al-Buni (d. 1225).[71] Despite their Islamic context of origin, these writings display surprising similarities to the above-mentioned Egyptian manuscripts, which do in any case, as stated, present traces of earlier Muslim versions. Suffice it to point out, for example, that the third text contained in the manuscript—identified above as "The most brilliant light on the explanation of the most beautiful Names of God"—is attributed to Ahmad al-Buni, the author whose *Sams al-ma'arif al-Kubra* ("The big sun of knowledge") expresses the idea that the universe is made up of numbers and that numbers are the language of God and the expression of the energy of the creator and the organization of the cosmos. The nature of numbers is expressed in the letters of the alphabet and especially in the letters of the word of God, and therefore the Holy Scriptures, in accordance with their numerical value[72] and in correspondence with other codes (e.g. those of an astrological nature). According to al-Buni, the wise and compassionate can understand this language to some extent and use it to alter both natural events and

---

[71] The reference to the manuscript and to the three works mentioned above is taken from Sara Fani, "Magic, traditional medicine and theurgy in Arabo-Islamic manuscripts of the Horn of Africa: a brief note on their description," in *Essays in Ethiopian Manuscript Studies - Proceedings of the International Conference Manuscripts and Texts, Languages and Contexts: The Transmission of Knowledge in the Horn of Africa*, Hamburg, 17-19 July 2014, ed. Alessandro Bausi, Alessandro Gori and Denis Nosnitsin, Wiesbaden, 2015. The author thanks Prof. Alessandro Gori and Sara Fani for their helpfulness in responding to his request for information and to Sara Fani for making her essay available to him at a time when it was impossible for him to consult it in the library.

[72] See note 69 above.

psychological states, which does not constitute manipulation of divine powers but rather cooperation with divine action on the part of persons initiated into this esoteric wisdom.

Evident and surprising similarities in content can also be found in manuscript MS IES 272, including numerous squares similar to those present in the Egyptian manuscripts.[73]

One last important point emerging from Sara Fani's essay regards the classification of different types of magic (*sihr*) in the Muslim sphere. While the models of classification are various and do not always overlap or coincide,[74] they always contain a branch corresponding to what would be identified in the European tradition as black magic, which involves mediation on the part of demons and spirits that must be summoned and forced to obey. This type of magic is prohibited by both the Islamic and the Christian religion. At the same time, both spheres contain other forms of magic, identified in the Islamic for example as theurgy or natural magic, which instead make use of different instruments such as the divine names, numbers, some spells, amulets, talismans, enchantments, potions, and medicinal plants as well as what we would now call conjuring. This distinction will prove useful in the following chapters and should be remembered.

6.4 The *Kəbrä Nägäśt*

6.4.1 The Narrative

The *Kəbrä nägäśt*, translated by Wallis Budge as *The Glory of the Kings*, performs the function of an epic poem relating the mythic origins of the Ethiopian nation, its reigning dynasty, and the conversion of its people to the God of the Bible, thus creating the ideal unity with which traditional Ethiopia identifies. It tells the story of the meeting of King Solomon and the Queen of Sheba, the two leading figures in the legend underpinning the birth of the Ethiopian state, and of the fruit of that encounter, King Mənilək I, the source of the Solomonic dynasty's claim to Jewish ancestry.

---

[73] The manuscript, identification code EAP/286/1/1/393, is accessible online through the site of the British Library: http://eap.bl.uk/database/results.a4d?projID=EAP286.

[74] Sara Fani, "Magic, traditional medicine and theurgy in Arabo-Islamic manuscripts of the Horn of Africa: a brief note on their description," op. cit., pp. 134-36.

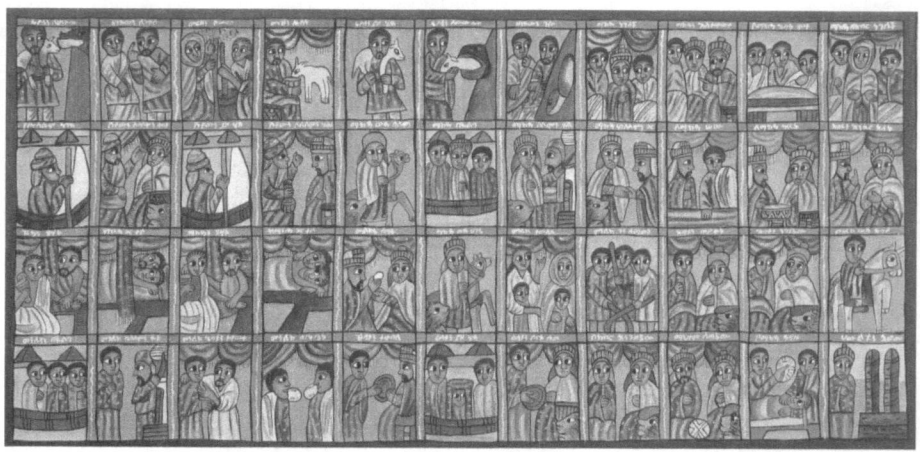

Traditional Ethiopian painting of the narrative of the *Kəbrä nägäśt* (Painting by Solomon – Asella)

The narrative of the events leading to the birth of Mənilək is very simple. Makədda, Queen of Ethiopia, hears of Solomon's wisdom and the splendor of his court from a merchant named Tamrin. She decides to visit him and delight in his wisdom. Solomon welcomes her joyfully and marvels in turn at the beauty and wisdom of Makədda, who finally converts to the God of Israel and abandons the worship of the sun. She decides to return to Ethiopia six months later but Solomon tricks her into sleeping with him before her departure. He requests that any son born as a result be sent to Israel so that they may know one another. After returning to Ethiopia, Makədda gives birth to a son, who then decides in his twenty-second year to go and meet his father. Solomon recognizes him and offers him the throne of Israel but the young man wishes to return to Ethiopia. Solomon grants him permission to depart but sends the first-born sons of the elders of Israel to accompany him, so as to turn Ethiopia too into a Jewish kingdom. Before their departure, the young men decide to steal the Ark of the Covenant, unbeknown to Mənilək, and take it with them to Ethiopia.

Every attempt made by Solomon and the elders to regain possession of the Ark proves unsuccessful. After a dialogue with the Angel of God, who reveals the future to him, Solomon decides to have his son Jeroboam anointed king of Israel, at which point there is a lengthy digression that lists all of the world's reigning dynasties and shows that they are all Israelite, albeit of lesser dignity than the Ethiopian. The narrative then resumes with Mənilək's return to Ethiopia, the ceremony to confer the kingly title upon him, and above all the discovery of the arrival of the Ark on Ethiopian soil, which gives rise to a sort of apotheosis. The closing pages of the *Kəbrä nägäśt* take on apocalyptic overtones and prophesy a war against the people of Israel, an attempt to destroy the race of Judah through an alliance formed against them by the kings of Byzantium and Ethiopia. The kingdom of Christ will then be established until the coming of the false messiah, which will be followed by the Last Judgment.

6.4.2 The Debate on the Origin and Dating of the *Kəbrä Nägäśt*

According to scholarly studies, the *Kəbrä nägäśt* was composed between 1314 and 1321 during the reign of 'Amdä Ṣəyon (1314-44).[75] The traditional interpretation of this work emphasizes its ideological aim of asserting the legitimacy of the new Solomonic dynasty with respect to the Zagwe and regards it in this light as a work produced at the court of 'Amdä Ṣəyon. Other points are, however, stressed by various scholars, including Lanfranco Ricci, as listed below.

- When the new Solomonic dynasty was born and the political center of the Ethiopian empire shifted southwards, the clergy of Aksum probably thought it advisable to draw the new rulers' attention to their city's historical and religious primacy. It is therefore no coincidence that the *Kəbrä nägäśt* should underscore this pre-eminence in the religious sphere by tracing the origins of the Christian empire back to Solomon and the Queen of Sheba.

- Other scholars, cited by Marrassini,[76] instead argue that the retelling of the Aksumite legend was probably designed to justify the movement for independence emerging in northern Ethiopia with respect to the new center of political power in the Shewa region. As evidence of this, Marrassini points out that, according to the colophon, the work was written at the behest of Ya'əbikä Egzi', governor of Enderta. As the

---

[75] See "Kəbrä Nägäśt," in Siegbert Uhlig (ed), *Encyclopaedia Aethiopica* 3, op. cit., pp. 364a-368a. The entry is the work of the late Paolo Marrassini.

[76] Ibid.

governor had, however, rebelled against ʿAmdä Ṣəyon, the present consensus is that the *Kəbrä nägäśt* was written to justify an attempt to create a new and independent dynasty in the north of Ethiopia and only later adopted by the Solomonic dynasty.

- According to the colophon, the work constitutes the translation of an original in Arabic and the date given there corresponds to the year 1225. Robert Beylot has endeavored to solve the problem of the difference of nearly a century between the date in the colophon and the one arrived at by scholars with the suggestion that 1225 is instead the date of an Arabic compilation of a collection of legends about Ethiopia undertaken by Egyptian ecclesiastics. This compilation would not be the *Kəbrä nägäśt* we know today but a collection of materials out of which it was subsequently composed. Beylot also suggests that the *Kəbrä nägäśt* as known today is instead the result of a further reworking carried out between the 13th and 15th centuries, possibly during the reign of Zärʾa Yaʿəqob (1434-68), when there was an attempt to restore the historical and religious importance of Aksum and the Tigray region.

According to Enrico Cerulli, while the work was unquestionably composed out of heterogeneous materials from different sources and cultural traditions, among which the Arab certainly played an essential role, there is no evidence whatsoever of any Arabic original of which the *Kəbrä nägäśt* could be a translation.

At the same time, one of the primary sources of reference—which are Syriac and Egyptian in the Christian sphere as well as Jewish and Muslim—cited by Ernest A. Wallis Budge in his English edition of 1922 and published in the introduction, is the translation of an Arabic text already published by Carl Bezold in his German edition of the *Kəbrä nägäśt*.[77] Structural analysis of this text, one of the ancient narratives of the Coptic church of Egypt presented as "Describing How the Kingdom of David was Transferred from Jerusalem to Ethiopia," reveals that the part regarding Solomon and the Queen of Sheba corresponds in all respects to the narrative of the *Kəbrä nägäśt*. The Arabic version is, however, unquestionably far more concise and gives only the bare bones of the story without lingering over descriptions or long quotations from

---

[77] One similar source had already been summarized by Edouard Amélineau from a manuscript discovered in Cairo but now lost (and therefore undatable) and others were found later.

the Scriptures. Moreover, it is completely devoid of references to the Council of Nicaea, which are instead legion in the *Kəbrä nägäśt* known today. This text could be one of the sources suggested by Beylot as part of the above-mentioned compilation of 1225. As matters now stand, however, there is no documentary evidence to support this hypothesis, as the narrative itself is not dated. We can therefore say with Marrassini: "Whether the Copto-Arabic text derives from the Ethiopic ... or vice versa, or whether they depend on a common source ... is exactly the core of the problem."[78]

To conclude, there is, as Cerulli says, certainly no evidence of an Arabic original of which the *Kəbrä nägäśt* known today could be a translation. It follows that, as things now stand, the work is to be regarded as a product of Ethiopian culture that may draw on previously existing narratives but constitutes an original and harmonious synthesis of the same.

6.4.3 The Historical-Theological Compendium of the *Kəbrä Nägäśt* and Hypostatic Entities

The following quotation is an exposition of the "regime of truth"[79] and narratives on which the historical-theological compendium of the *Kəbrä nägäśt* is grounded. The words are uttered by the Angel of the Lord, who speaks to Solomon before his death and announces the salvation to be brought by the Redeemer:

> "And again, there shall be unto thee a sign that the Saviour shall come from thy seed, and that He shall deliver thee with thy fathers and thy seed after thee by His coming. Your salvation was created in the belly of ADAM in the form of a Pearl before EVE. And when He created EVE out of the rib He brought her to ADAM, and said unto them, 'Multiply you from

---

[78] Marrassini, "Kəbrä Nägäśt," in Siegbert Uhlig (ed.), *Encyclopaedia Aethiopica* 3, op. cit., p. 367.

[79] We draw here in simplified terms on Michel Foucault's concept of the *régime de vérité*, defined as the set of ideas and assumptions combined in a given historical period into an organic whole to provide the foundation or justification of a claim to hegemony, an already established power structure or common practices. As an example, Foucault gives the sets of assertions used at various times to define the concept of "madness" on the basis of radically differing parameters that were, however, considered certain and absolute in the periods during which those specific parameters were in use. See Michel Foucault, *Histoire de la folie à l'âge classique*, Gallimard, 1972.

the belly of ADAM.' The Pearl did not go out into CAIN or ABEL, but into the third that went forth from the belly of ADAM, and it entered into the belly of SETH. And then passing from him that Pearl went into those who were the firstborn, and came to ABRAHAM. And it did not go from ABRAHAM into his firstborn ISHMAEL, but it tarried and came into ISAAC the pure. And it did not go into his firstborn, the arrogant ESAU, but it went into JACOB the lowly one. And it did not enter from him into his firstborn, the erring REUBEN, but into JUDAH, the innocent one. And it did not go forth from JUDAH until four sinners had been born, but it came to FÂRÊS (PEREZ), the patient one, And from him this Pearl went to the firstborn until it came into the belly of JESSE, the father of thy father. And then it waited until six men of wrath had been born, and after that it came to the seventh, DAVID, thy innocent and humble father; for God hateth the arrogant and proud, and loveth the innocent and humble. And then it waited in the loins of thy father until five erring fools had been born, when it came into thy loins because of thy wisdom and understanding. And then the Pearl waited, and it did not go forth into thy firstborn. For those good men of his country neither denied Him nor crucified Him, like ISRAEL thy people; when they saw Him Who wrought miracles, Who was to be born from the Pearl, they believed on Him when they heard the report of Him. And the Pearl did not go forth into thy youngest son 'ADRÂMÎ. For those good men neither crucified Him nor denied Him when they saw the working of miracles, and wonders by Him that was to be born from the Pearl, and afterwards they believed in Him through His disciples.

"Now the Pearl, which is to be your salvation, went forth from thy belly and entered into the belly of 'ÎYÔRBĔ'ÂM (REHOBOAM) thy son, because of the wickedness of ISRAEL thy people, who in their denial and in their wickedness crucified Him. But if He had not been crucified He could not have been your salvation. For He was crucified without sin, and He rose [again] without corruption. And for the sake of this He went down to you into SHEÔL, and tore down its walls, that He might deliver you and bring you out, and show mercy upon all of you. Ye in whose bellies the Pearl shall be carried shall be saved with your wives, and none of you shall be destroyed, from your father ADAM unto him that shall come, thy kinsman 'ÊYÂḴÊM (JOACHIM), and from EVE thy mother, the wife of ADAM, to NOAH and his wife TARMÎZÂ [...]⁸⁰

The angel continues:

"None of you who shall have carried the Pearl shall be destroyed, and whether it be your men or your women, those who shall have carried the Pearl shall not be destroyed. For the Pearl shall be carried by the men who shall be righteous, and the women who have carried the Pearl shall not be destroyed, for they shall become pure through that Pearl, for it is holy and pure, and by it they shall be made holy and pure; and for its sake and for the sake of ZION He hath created the whole world. ZION hath taken up her abode with thy firstborn and she shall be the salvation of the people of ETHIOPIA for ever; and the Pearl shall be carried in the belly of 'AYÔRBĔ'ÂM (REHOBOAM) thy son, and shall be the saviour of all the world. And when the appointed time hath come this Pearl shall be born of thy seed, for it is exceedingly pure, seven times purer than the sun. And the Redeemer shall come from the seat of His Godhead, and shall dwell upon her, and shall put on her flesh, and straightway thou thyself shalt announce to her what my Lord and thy Lord speaketh to me.

"I am GABRIEL the Angel, the protector of those who shall carry the Pearl from the body of ADAM even to the belly of ḤANNÂ, so that I may keep from servitude and pollution you wherein the Pearl shall dwell. And MICHAEL hath been commanded to direct and keep ZION wheresoever she goeth, and URIEL shall direct and keep the wood of the thicket which shall be the Cross of the Saviour. And when thy people in their

---

[80] *The Kəbrä nägäśt*, translated by E.A. Wallis Budge, 1932, sec. 68, *Concerning* MARY, *Our Lady of Salvation*, pp. 95-96.

envy have crucified Him, they shall rush upon His Cross because of the multitude of miracles that shall take place through it, and they shall be put to shame when they see its wonders. And in the last times a descendant of thy son 'ADRÂMÎS shall take the wood of the Cross, the third [means of] salvation that shall be sent upon the earth. The Angel MICHAEL is with ZION, with DAVID thy firstborn, who hath taken the throne of DAVID thy father. And I am with the pure Pearl for him that shall reign for ever, with REHOBOAM thy second son; and the Angel URIEL is with thy youngest son 'ADRÂMÎ[S]. This have I told thee, and thou shalt not make thy heart to be sad because of thine own salvation and that of thy son."[81]

The historical-theological conception emerging from this passage is crystal clear. There are three phenomenologically concrete historical entities, namely the Ark of the Covenant (Zion),[82] the Virgin Mary (the Pearl) and the wood of the True Cross. These entities are, however, endowed with identities of their own that precede their phenomenal manifestation, i.e. their presence in human and natural history, because their essence was created before history and outside the natural world. The entities that then manifested themselves historically are only the materialization or development of essential forms born before the creation, which we shall refer to as hypostatic from now on.

In this text, the subject that appears most indicative of Gnostic influences regards the hypostatic entities of the Ark, the Pearl and the Cross, which are indeed written with capital letters precisely because, as we have seen, they are personified entities created before the creation of the world in order to act upon the world from the moment of the creation for precise purposes established by God.[83]

---

[81] Ibid.

[82] The Ark of the Covenant, described in Exodus as containing the Tables of the Law, is still preserved in Aksum according to Ethiopian tradition.

[83] It is clearly stated in the *Kəbrä Nägäśt* that the Ark has a will of its own and that the sons of the elders of Israel could not have stolen it against its will.

The meaning of these entities is clearly comprehensible. The Ark is the dwelling place of the Glory of the Trinity[84] but also of its Law, as it contains the tablets of the Ten Commandments. The Pearl is the instrument or intermediary making possible the birth or incarnation of Christ, the manifestation of God in the cosmos. The Cross is the instrument of the death of Christ (in the sense of a return to His origin in the Father) but also the symbol of His power, the instrument of the greatest miracle, the redemption of original sin. These three entities (the birth, dwelling, and death of the godhead) are therefore the instruments of the manifestation of God on earth, in the cosmos. As regards the point of interest to us here, however, the Ark, the Pearl, and the Cross, together with the Glory and the Covenant between God and Noah, all become "personifications." Stated in terms that probably display little respect for tradition, they are objects (like the Cross) and circumstances (the making of a covenant or the granting of particular honour and glory) that transcend their ascertainable, empirical, earthly existence and become entities existing as divine creations and preceding the rest of creation by God's will.

It should also be noted that the subject of hypostatic entities was nothing new in the history of Christianity and had already been widely discussed, albeit usually with reference to the three persons of the Trinity. The anomaly that suggests a possible Gnostic influence is therefore not the presence of hypostatic entities in the *Kəbrä nägäśt* but rather the fact that these are not the three persons of the Trinity but other figures born as emanations to perform a precise role assigned to them by the Trinity as instruments of the manifestation of the godhead in human history and man's salvation. As in the Gnostic models, albeit on a smaller scale, we thus have a proliferation of divine manifestations through personified entities that, while performing God's will, are detached from God and thus give rise to a sort of intermediate hierarchy between Him and the cosmos inhabited by mankind.

This is a model that originated in western philosophy with Plato (our world, created by the Demiurge, is a world of "copies" of the world of ideas) and reached its peak over two thousand years later with Georg Wilhelm Friedrich Hegel, for whom human history and institutions follow a logical development based on general, abstract, and apparently

---

[84] The "Indwelling place of their Glory," which must also be written with an uppercase G if, like a human being, it requires somewhere to live.

simple entities from which, in a wholly spiritual process, more complex entities are "deduced" to form a ramified system offering a logical justification and description of the reality of the world we know. The model has evidently been turned upside-down, as it is no longer human experience and cognitive processes that slowly work, as happens in history, to construct abstract knowledge and human institutions in their concrete reality. On the contrary, it is the world of the spirit that constructs the reality of our world through a model of logical development and construction that is not so very different from the emanations of Gnosticism.

This model is evidently based not only on Platonism but also on Jewish philosophy, according to which the pure act of thought on the part of God is itself an act of creation. According to some Gnostics, the very birth of the Word, and therefore of Christ, is nothing other than this. In thinking Himself, God is detached from Himself. In this detachment from Himself, He gives Himself a name (the first word, the Word) and the Word is Christ but also the name of God (as clearly indicated in the *Gospel of Truth*, another Gnostic text), which is miracle-working by definition. In the Jewish tradition, it is the name of God that gives birth to the Golem but also to Adam. The Word and Christ cannot of course coincide in the Jewish world, however, as it does not believe in the divinity of Christ, and these conceptions belong instead to Christian Gnosticism, even though, as we shall see, some Gnosticizing schools of Judaism did attribute the creation to Logos, i.e. the Word.

The system of emanations of Valentinian Gnosticism is an exemplary model of the sequence of personifications described above, which also includes Christ, the Church and the Cross. It should be recalled here that the Ark created prior to creation, the dwelling place of the Glory of the Trinity, is the heavenly Ark, the spiritual counterpart of the earthly Ark subsequently stolen by Mənilək. The same therefore holds for the Pearl and the Cross. The correspondence with Platonism and the system of Gnostic emanations exemplified above is evident.

6.4.4 The Myth of the "Pearl"

This is, however, not the only thing in the *Kəbrä nägäśt* to reveal traces of Gnostic influence. Another has already been mentioned here and discussed repeatedly in the literature. We refer to the myth of the Pearl, which some scholars consider indicative of unquestionable Gnostic influence. Its original source is found in the *Acts of Thomas*, a Syriac narrative probably composed in Edessa (in the southeast of present-day Turkey) at the beginning of the 3rd century. Didymos Judas Thomas is regarded as the founder of the church among the Parthians (Mesopotamia). The text, which was written in Syriac and translated into Greek soon after, tells of the apostle's preaching and miracles in India. Thomas was thought to be the "brother" of Christ and hence the depositary of special revelations imparted directly by Him. When the *Acts of Thomas* had just begun to circulate, the beautiful song now known as the *Hymn of the Pearl*, composed before the year 165 in Edessa, was interpolated into it. In the description of the apostle's imprisonment in India, it is related that the other prisoners asked him to pray for them and in response he sang this hymn, which is actually a Christianized version of a popular Parthian story. The text of the hymn is given below.

> When I was a child and lived in the kingdom of my father's house and delighted in the wealth and splendor of those who raised me, my parents sent me from the East, our homeland, with provisions for the journey. From the riches of our house, they made a bundle for me that was large but light, so that I could carry it myself [...] They took the raiment of glory that they had made for me in their love and the purple mantle, woven in such a way as to fit me perfectly, and made a pact with me and wrote it in my heart so that I might not forget it: "When you have been to Egypt and brought back the Unique Pearl that lies in the midst of the sea, encircled by the hissing serpent, you shall again wear your raiment of glory and your mantle over it, and with your brother, next to us in dignity, you shall be heir to our kingdom."
>
> I left the East and set off accompanied by two royal couriers, as the way was hard and dangerous, and I was too young for such a journey. I crossed the border of Maishan, where the merchants of the East gather, reached the land of Babel and entered the walls of Sarbug. I went down into Egypt and my companions left me. I went resolutely to the serpent and waited near his abode for him to rest and sleep so that I might take the Pearl from him. As I was alone and aloof, I was a stranger to the

inhabitants of the inn. There I saw one of my race, a lovely, handsome youth, the son of kings. He approached me and I greeted him with familiarity and trust, and told him of my mission. I warned him to beware of the Egyptians and to avoid contact with the unclean. I wore their dress, however, so that they might not suspect me of coming from afar to take the Pearl and arouse the serpent against me. They somehow realized that I was not one of them, however, and sought to ingratiate themselves. In their cunning, they poured me drink and gave me their meat to eat, and I forgot that I was a son of kings and I served their king. I forgot the Pearl, for which my parents had sent me. The richness of their food caused me to fall into a deep sleep.

My parents were aware of everything that was happening and grieved for me. A proclamation was made in our kingdom that everyone should come to our doors. The kings and princes of Parthia and all the nobles of the East devised a plan so that I might not be left in Egypt, and they wrote me a letter signed with the names of all the highest.

"Greetings from your father, the king of kings, and your mother, mistress of the East, and your brother, our next in rank. Wake up, rise from your slumber, and understand the words of our letter. Remember that you are the son of kings and see whom you have served in slavery. Remember the Pearl, for which you departed to Egypt. Remember your raiment of glory and your splendid mantle to wear and adorn yourself with, so that your name may be read in book of heroes and you may become with your brother, our viceroy, heir to our kingdom."

Like a messenger was the letter, which the king had sealed with his right hand against the wicked, the children of Babel, and the rebel demons of Sarbug. It soared in the likeness of an eagle, king of all winged creatures, and flew until it alighted by my side and became entirely word. At the sound of its voice I awoke and arose from my sleep. I took it, kissed it, broke the seal and read it. In accordance with what had been written in my heart were the words of my letter. I remembered that I was the son of kings and that my free-born spirit sought its like. I remembered the Pearl, for which I had been sent to Egypt, and began to charm the terrible hissing serpent. I plunged it into sleep by invoking the name of my father, the name of our next in rank and the name of my mother, queen of the East. I took the Pearl and turned to set off home to my father. I took off their base, unclean dress and left it in their land. I made my way toward the light of our homeland, the East.

I found the letter that had awakened me on the way before me; and as it had aroused me with its voice, now it led me with its light shining before me; and with its voice, it gave me heart in my fear, and with its love, it pulled me, and I went on [...] My parents [...] sent to meet me by the hand of their treasurers, to whom they had been entrusted, the raiment of glory that I had taken off and the mantle to cover it. I had forgotten its splendor, having left it in my father's house as a child. While I observed it, it suddenly seemed to become a mirror image of me. I saw all of myself in it and it saw everything in me, so that we were two and separate but one in sameness of form ... And it was covered all over with the image of the King of Kings ... And I saw the movements of gnosis vibrating all over it. I saw that it was about to speak and I heard the sound of the songs it murmured during the descent "It is I that acted in the actions of him for whom I was raised in my Father's house and I felt within myself that my stature was growing in correspondence with his labors." And with kingly movements it offered itself entirely to me and hastened from the hands of those carrying it so that I might take it. And I too was moved by love to rush forward and receive it. And I stretched out and took it and wrapped myself in the beauty of its colors. And I threw the royal mantle all around me. Thus clothed anew, I went up to the gate of salvation and adoration. I bowed my head and adored the majesty of my Father, who sent it to me, whose commands I had performed because he too kept his promise ... He welcomed me with rejoicing and I was with him in his kingdom, and all his servants praised him with the voice of an organ, singing that he had promised that I would reach the court of the King of Kings and appear together with him having brought my Pearl.[85]

The reading of this myth is actually rather surprising but not because it presents any direct and immediate similarities and correspondences with the *Kəbrä nägäśt*. On the contrary, such similarities appear either non-existent or very vague, and the very symbol of the pearl basically suggests clearly different things in the two texts. Their kinship is nevertheless discovered by taking a broader approach that does not involve correspondence in terms of individual passages (and hence quotations) or symbolism. In our view, there are instead structural correspondences regarding "figures" (or situations) and narrative sequences, as listed below.

- An initial situation of wealth and glory, a noble birth
- External circumstances beyond the protagonist's control, which lead to his departure from this initial situation in search of something
- The essential importance of this something, without which the kingdom cannot be inherited
- A journey
- A test: the need to charm the serpent or lull it to sleep in order to gain possession of the Pearl
- A condition of exile
- A loss of memory
- A letter
- The letter being brought by a bird or compared to a bird
- Renewed memory of origins and the tasks to be performed
- Possession of the Pearl
- Guidance on the journey home provided by the letter
- A raiment of glory sent by the parents

---

[85] Hans Jonas, *Lo Gnosticismo*, Torino, 1991, pp. 131-33.

- Apotheosis and glorification on return to the native land

The initial sequence (1-4) is also found in the *Kǝbrä nägäśt*, albeit with different characteristics. The test (5) is the journey to King Solomon. The most important test, namely to obtain possession of the Ark, which is present in the above-mentioned Coptic Arabic source, is instead omitted in the *Kǝbrä nägäśt*, where it is the sons of the Israelite elders that steal the Ark. The feeling of exile (6) prompts Mǝnilǝk to return to his homeland but he never forgets who he is. The letter (8) is replaced by the ring that Solomon gives to the Queen of Sheba on her departure. Possession of the Pearl (11) corresponds to the theft of the Ark by the sons of the elders, to which Mǝnilǝk does not, however, object. The guidance provided by the letter (12) is provided in the *Kǝbrä nägäśt* by angels. The clothing with precious garments (13) takes place both after Mǝnilǝks meeting with Solomon and in final apotheosis (14). It therefore happens twice, on Mǝnilǝk's arrival in Israel and above all on his return to Ethiopia, his home.

The overall impression is that the structural components of the *Hymn of the Pearl* have been reassembled in new sequences but with numerous similarities. Moreover, some elements either absent from the *Kǝbrä nägäśt* or present in a different form, like the letter, the serpent, the involvement of a bird, and the tests (5), are to be found in parallel narratives, i.e. other versions of the *Kǝbrä nägäśt*, or in its sources.[86] In addition to all this, the purpose of the *Kǝbrä nägäśt* as a whole is to help Mǝnilǝk rediscover his true origins, which is also the substance of the narrative in the *Hymn of the Pearl*.

In the light of the above, it is our view that rather than being influenced by the *Hymn of the Pearl* in its composition, the *Kǝbrä nägäśt* constitutes in all respects a complex and sophisticated reworking of the

---

[86] Mǝnilǝk is tested by Solomon in the narratives addressed under the title "Modern Legends of Solomon and the Queen of Sheba" in the introduction to Ernest A. Wallis Budge, *The Queen of Sheba and her only son Menelik*, London 1932, pp. LI-LV. Moreover, the Queen of Sheba does the same thing with Solomon in order to ascertain his wisdom.

hymn, which was in any case well-known in Egypt and circulated there in a Coptic version translated by a Gnostic.[87]

We must pause here once again, however, because the above considerations do reveal a close relationship between the *Hymn of the Pearl* and the *Kəbrä nägäśt* but not as yet between the *Kəbrä nägäśt* and Gnosticism. This is because the scholars are not unanimous in attributing a Gnostic origin to the *Hymn of the Pearl*. Birger A. Pearson points out in the work referred to above[88] that the *Gospel of Thomas* and the *Acts of Thomas* (and therefore also the *Hymn of the Pearl*, which forms part of the text and is wholly coherent with the rest) contain no trace of the doctrine of emanations, the myth of Sophia or the wicked and ignorant Demiurge. The only elements these texts have in common with Gnosticism are aversion to the flesh; rejection of the human world and its conventions; emphasis on knowledge of oneself and one's true, divine nature, and therefore on a higher level of knowledge and "wisdom"; constant references to this higher wisdom as light; and the Platonic idea of the two levels of truth, the human and the divine, which present correspondences and similarities that must, however, serve solely as stimuli to attain a higher understanding of the true world of the spirit. These are not, however, themes peculiar to Gnosticism. According to Pearson. these texts reflect the model of Christianity peculiar to Mesopotamia (which then spread into Syria and Egypt), which he calls "Thomas Christianity." Themes characteristic of Gnosticism are present in Thomas Christian texts but the major focus is on the divine origin of the soul and the return to its origins, which is clearly Platonic first and

---

[87] It should be noted that while passages from the *Acts of Thomas* are present in Ethiopia in the *Gädlä hawaryat* (*Acts of the Apostles* or *Combat of the Apostles*), there is no trace of the *Hymn of the Pearl* among them. A translation of the Ethiopian text of the *Acts of Thomas* appears as an appendix to Ernest A. Wallis Budge, *Baralam and Yewasef—Being the Ethiopic Version of the Christianized Recension of the Buddist Legend of the Buddha and the Bodhisattva*, Cambridge, 1923, pp. 298-338.

[88] Birger A. Pearson, *Ancient Gnosticism*, op. cit., pp. 256 ff.

Gnostic second.⁸⁹ Moreover, the discovery of the divine nature of the soul is also a discovery of the Christ dwelling within us, thus emphasizing the close relationship Thomas is supposed to have enjoyed with Christ as his brother.⁹⁰

Logion 73 of the *Gospel of Thomas* states that whoever knows everything but not himself has nothing, which encapsulates one of the key tenets of Thomas Christianity. The *Gospel of Thomas* takes the form of a collection of Christ's sayings and—notwithstanding the customary internal contradictions, especially as regards the imminence of the kingdom of heaven—displays greater affinity with the *Gospel According to John* than the other gospels. Despite this similarity, however, the sayings of Jesus in the *Gospel of Thomas* differ in tone, focusing more on the need for self-knowledge as a way to rediscover one's true origins. Hence also the insistence on the need to rise above the apparent opposites of this world:

> Jesus said to them, "When you make the two into one, and when you make the inner like the outer and the outer like the inner, and the upper like the lower, and when you make male and female into a single one, so that the male will not be male nor the female be female, when you make eyes in place of an eye, a hand in place of a hand, a foot in place of a foot, an image in place of an image, then you will enter [the kingdom]."⁹¹

and on the fact that the kingdom is already present:

> His disciples said to him, "When will the rest for the dead take place, and when will the new world come?"

---

⁸⁹ There is also a very close similarity to the themes of the *Corpus Hermeticum*. In more or less the same period as the spread of Gnosticism and Christianity, this expressed a form of pagan philosophy that also presented similar features like the divinity of man, the yearning to rediscover one's true identity, and the mystic pursuit of the divine through esoteric rituals.

⁹⁰ The *Gospel of Thomas* is attributed to the apostle Didymos Judas Thomas, and both "Didymos" and "Thomas" mean twin, respectively in Greek and Aramaic.

⁹¹ *The Gospel of Thomas*, translated by Stephen Patterson and Marvin Meyer, logion 22, http://gnosis.org/naghamm/gosthom.html.

He said to them, "What you are looking forward to has come, but you don't know it."[92]

This idea is repeated:

His disciples said to him, "When will the kingdom come?"

"It will not come by watching for it. It will not be said, 'Look, here!' or 'Look, there!' Rather, the Father's kingdom is spread out upon the earth, and people don't see it."[93]

These sayings seek to introduce the idea that redemption is already present in the person of Christ and not something in the future. Awaiting the apocalypse thus gives way to a mystical dimension of direct dialogue with God.

6.4.5 Gnosticism or "Thomas Christianity"

The above considerations on the *Hymn of the Pearl* and the hypostases present in the *Kəbrä nägäśt* spontaneously give rise, however, to the suspicion that there may be other explanations for the apparent Gnostic characteristics of the *Kəbrä nägäśt*. The ideas of duality (Thomas himself was regarded as the counterpart, brother or twin of Christ), the return to the divine origins, the negation of opposites, and knowledge as understanding of one's divine nature are closely related to Platonism and the correspondence between the human world and the world of ideas (the earthly Ark and the heavenly Ark). Apart from a few other points that could be attributed to what the scholars call the "strongly Gnosticizing character of Alexandrian Christianity," which would, for example, explain the multiplication of hypostatic entities, there thus appear to be no particular grounds for detecting a real and telling Gnostic influence in the *Kəbrä nägäśt* rather than just traces of the influence of Thomas Christianity. This surmise must, however, be reconsidered in the light of an examination of the whole body of texts belonging to the period of translations from Arabic.

---

[92] Ibid., logion 51.
[93] Ibid., logion 113.

6.5 The Book of the Mysteries of Heaven and Earth

This is an apocalyptic work again dating from the mid-15th century, an esoteric text for initiates purporting to contain divine revelations imparted by an angel to the abbot Bäṣälotä Mika'el and passed on to a monk (Yəshaq or Zosimas, regarded by some as the same person). It claims to reveal the secrets of creation and the interpretation of inspired texts such as the *Book of Revelation* as well as the eschatological mysteries of the end time. As clearly stated at the beginning, the work "unfolds the mysteries of the first and the last tabernacle, and explains the mysteries of the whole creation."

The first books of this text were published by J. Perruchon in 1903[94] and the last three by S. Grebaut in 1911.[95]

The text also includes a pearl,[96] born here after eighty-two others of a bird fecundated by the sun. Despite the symbolic references, according to which this magnificent pearl is the one true Faith, and despite the beauty and evocative power of the myth, there appear, however, to be no particular references here other than to virginal purity (the fecundation by the sun). This is indeed a direct reference to the *Life of St Anne* and the *Kəbrä nägäśt* but certainly not to the *Hymn of the Pearl*. The other points of possible Gnostic reference to be found here are the battle in the heavens between the forces of good and evil, the power of demons (which clearly derives from the *Book of Enoch*, one of the sources of the *Book of the Mysteries of the Heavens and the Earth*), and the need to conceal these doctrines:

> Do not reveal this to all men but only to the wise and learned. If you reveal these words to all, you will have no share in the kingdom of heaven, said the angel sent to me.[97]

This too is, however, already present in the *Book of Enoch*.

---

[94] J. Perruchon, "Le Livre des Mystères du Ciel et de la Terre," in *Patrologia Orientalis*, Tome I, Fascicule 1, 1903.

[95] S. Grébaut, "Les Trois Dernièrs Traités du Livre de Mystères du Ciel et de la Terre," in *Patrologia Orientalis*, Tome 6, 1911.

[96] J. Perruchon, op. cit., pp. 13-15.

[97] Ibid., p. 35.

Finally, attention should be drawn to the general visionary and prophetic character of the text and the model of expression through myths and combinations of symbols, which are features shared by Gnosticism with other schools of thought.

6.6 The Christian Novel of Alexander the Great

6.6.1 Historical Outline

The *Zena Ǝskəndər*, referred to here as the *Christian Romance of Alexander*,[98] was translated into Ge'ez during the 14th century, when the tales of Alexander the Great had already been developed and reworked for over a thousand years. The initial version, called the *Alexander Romance* and attributed to Callisthenes of Olynthus (Pseudo-Callisthenes), was composed in Egypt in the 3rd–4th century AD and presents Alexander the Great as the liberator of Egypt from Persian rule and the founder of Alexandria. The work gave rise to countless narratives, adaptations, translations, and retranslations in areas where previous versions had already circulated. Gianfrancesco Lusini has traced a possible line of descent of the Ge'ez version of the *Alexander Romance* of Pseudo-Callisthenes starting from a lost Persian version of the 6th century translated into Syriac in the 7th.[99] This would then have been used in the 9th century by a Muslim author for the Arabic version, numerous traces of which survive in a whole range of Islamic texts. The Ethiopian *Romance of Alexander* would instead have been translated from the Arabic only in the 15th or 16th century.

The version of the *Christian Romance of Alexander* known today, the text of interest to us here, is instead regarded as a product of the 14th century. It presents Alexander as an ascetic Christian hero who launches crusades against unbelievers and peoples guilty of abominable practices. Despite these unmistakably Christian characteristics, however, the

---

[98] Gérard Colin, *Alexandre le Grand, héros chrétien en Ethiopie. Histoire d'Alexandre (Zênâ Eskender)*, Leuven, 2007. The thesis adopted here is the one put forward by Gianfrancesco Lusini, for whom the work is not an original Ethiopian text but rather a translation from Arabic, albeit with possible local additions.

[99] Gianfrancesco Lusini, "Origine e significato della presenza di Alessandro Magno nella letteratura etiopica," in *Rassegna di Studi Etiopici* 38 (1994), pp. 95–118.

narrative is just as unmistakably influenced by the Quran and the tales of the *Arabian Nights*.

Given that Alexander lived and died long before Christ (356–323 BC), it should be recalled that the Christianized reworking of the story of his life was written in the 7th century, after Jerusalem had been wrested from the Persians by Heraclius (628 AD) and before it fell definitively under Arab rule (637 AD). The work was clearly designed to glorify the feats of the Byzantine emperor, who had also regained possession of the relics of the Cross, by comparing them to those of the great Macedonian, the anachronism of Christianization being deliberately ignored to this end because the figure of Alexander actually stood for Heraclius.[100]

6.6.2 Gnostic Characteristics?

In the *Christian Romance of Alexander* the Great, the most distinctive feature revealing a possible link with Gnosticism is renunciation of the flesh and the pursuit of bodily purity. As this is unquestionably characteristic of Gnosticism but even more so of Manichaeism and in any case shared with the strict rules of monastic communities, it does not appear sufficient by itself to prove a Gnostic relationship. Nor do the occasional references to magical practices, which may have been present in Gnosticism but were certainly not distinctive characteristics of it.

An aspect of this narrative that does appear to suggest more definite Gnostic influences is one mentioned also by Enrico Cerulli in *La Letteratura Etiopica*.[101] With a view to explaining this point more fully, Cerulli's short quotation will be expanded here to make it more complete. The following text is part of a dialogue on the resurrection of the dead between Alexander the Great, whose death is now imminent, and his follower Komsat. In the course of his arguments in response to the various objections raised by Komsat, Alexander describes the Last Judgment at the moment when the trumpet sounds for the second time:

---

[100] A tradition linking the achievements of Heraclius with those of Alexander the Great, thought to date from the early 7th century, has been discovered in Edessa. See Barbara Baert, *A Heritage of Holy Wood*, Leiden-Boston, 2004, p. 139 and note 30.

[101] Enrico Cerulli, *La Letteratura Etiopica*, Florence-Milan,1968, pp. 46-48.

"The angels of light will receive the souls of the righteous that trusted to the Promise. The angels of darkness will receive the souls of the sinners. The souls will return into their bodies. There will be a perfect man without corruption in the likeness of our father Adam, whom God created. A little child or a pauper, blind or crippled, each will be alive like our father Adam with no corruption, living by the word of God. Everything that is on the earth will be forgotten and no one will remember the desires that are on earth because they are vain. All thought of down here will be forgotten, forgotten as a dream that has vanished. (Mankind will be) as Adam was at first, before he sinned by eating of the tree. They will become children of the light of intelligence and spiritual beings because the flesh will have been absorbed by the spirit of life and the folly of darkness will have been renewed by knowledge, by the light of intelligence and knowledge, not (as) men or women, righteous or sinners. All those who are perfect will be children of light, like the angels of God, children of light and spiritual beings."[102]

Clearly evident here is the typically Manichaean idea of individual souls dissolving into a single undifferentiated divine entity in which all memory of earthly life will be lost. Moreover, the expression "children of light" is commonly used in Manichaean texts.[103] This is not the only characteristic to attract our attention, however, as the earlier eternal damnation of sinners is subsequently attenuated in virtue of divine omnipotence:

If a man will not mend his ways and keep God's commandment, God will destroy him by death and bring him back to life when He so wishes.[104]

The possibility of salvation therefore exists also for sinners. Finally, Komsat makes this remark a few pages further on: "the pursuit of wisdom is worth

---

[102] Translated here from the French version by Gérard Colin, *Alexandre le Grand, héros chrétien en Ethiopie*, op.cit., pp. 145-47.

[103] Hans Jonas *Lo Gnosticismo*, op. cit., p. 238.

[104] Translated from the French version by Gérard Colin, *Alexandre le Grand, héros chrétien en Ethiopie*, op.cit., p. 147

more than all the treasures of gold and silver."[105] This is an evident reference to Wisdom, as confirmed also by Alexander's response.

In any case, despite the Manichaean or Gnosticizing themes, it appears evident to us on closer examination that the most important point of reference is not Gnosticism in the strict sense but Thomas Christianity, the presence of which is revealed also in the first quotation by the phrase "not (as) men or women," an idea typical of the *Gospel of Thomas*.

The text also contains, however, a number of hints or allusions to ideas that are never fully expressed. One example is provided by this explicit statement made in the first of the above quotations: "They will become children of the light of intelligence and spiritual beings because the flesh will have been absorbed by the spirit of life and the folly of darkness will have been renewed by knowledge, by the light of intelligence and knowledge, not (as) men or women, righteous or sinners. All those who are perfect will be children of light, like the angels of God, children of light and spiritual beings." It is true that this regards the "children of light," but in that case what sense can the reference to "sinners" possibly make? The crucial point is perhaps the idea that "[a]ll those who are perfect will be children of light," which could be taken in the light of the second quotation as suggesting the possibility of salvation for whoever has sinned but has become "perfect." And what is this perfection if not wisdom? As stated in the first quotation above, "the folly of darkness will have been renewed by knowledge, by the light of intelligence and knowledge." This is an idea deeply characteristic of the Christian Gnosticism of Valentinus, which clearly states that the matter is born out of ignorance and that salvation from darkness therefore lies in knowledge. Once again, however, this theme is characteristic not only of Christian Gnosticism but also of Thomas Christianity, albeit perhaps with slight differences in emphasis. Moreover, connections with Thomas Christianity also emerge from the above-mentioned *Acts of Thomas* translated into Ge'ez (*Gädlä hawaryat*), where we find, for example, the passage quoted below. The text begins with the words spoken by the multitude. Having heard Thomas preach and having seen his miracles, they wish to be converted but are aware that they have lived in sin and ask whether they can still be admitted to the new faith:

> "But if He will have compassion upon us, and will show mercy upon us, and redeem us, and will deliver us from our former

---
[105] Ibid., p. 153.

works, and from all the evil and from the error wherein we have erred and gone astray, and will neither keep in mind, nor remember against us our transgressions of former times, we will conform unto His Will, and we will keep His commandment wholly."

Then the Apostle answered and said unto them, "He will neither keep in mind, nor remember against you your transgressions, nor the error wherein ye have lived, and He will not keep beneath his eye the sins which ye have committed."[106]

The idea arises spontaneously that if God can forget man's sin, there is all the more reason to assume that man, an imperfect creature, will be able to forget it too, either due to his imperfection or by the will of God, and that this act of forgetting will indeed be the prerequisite for the full enjoyment of closeness to God after death.

If this is so, then the premises subsequently developed in the *Christian Romance of Alexander*—whereby the soul is attributed with the Manichaean character of an indistinct fragment of light devoid of individual identity—are evidently already present in Thomas Christianity and the Ethiopian versions in which it is expressed. The same holds as regards the deliverance of all regardless of their sin. An example is provided by the Ge'ez version of the *Acts of the Apostles* (*Gädlä hawaryat*), where Thomas intercedes to obtain forgiveness for a sinner guilty of murder.[107] It should be noted in passing that in the 14th century, when the *Gädlä hawaryat* was translated, the power to obtain forgiveness for any kind of sin through intercession was attributed to Christ and not to the Virgin Mary, as it was later. To conclude, while Gnostic elements are unquestionably present in the *Christian Romance of Alexander*, they are ambiguous and could also be attributed to other influences. Overall appraisal of the characteristics present in this work and the others belonging to the period of the translations from Arabic may make it possible to resolve this ambiguity.

---

[106] *The Acts of Saint Thomas in India* in Ernest Wallis Budge, *Baralam and Yewasef*, op. cit., p. 324.

[107] Ibid., pp. 332-38.

6.7 The *Combat of Adam*

6.7.1 The Genesis of the Work

The Combat of Adam is a work of complex genesis that took its final shape in Ethiopia in the 14th century during the great period of translations from Arabic into Ge'ez. A brief survey of the existing sources enables us to state that the work in its Ethiopian form must be regarded as the result of combining two different traditions. The first half unquestionably derives from a Christian Arab reworking of a Jewish text. This Arabic source bears the same title as the narrative in question. Summary comparison is sufficient to show that the first part is in fact, with negligible differences, a perfect translation into Ge'ez of the text of the *Combat of Adam* circulating in Christian Egypt.[108] Despite the efforts made in the Arabic version to Christianize the text, its Judaic origin is still clearly evident in the geographic references, the precise similarities to Jewish written sources, the fact that God is often referred to simply as the Creator, and the absence of all reference to Christ other than in the Christianizing interpolations.[109]

The second part of the book is instead of different origin. While it is unquestionably based on a clearly identified Arabic source, this appears to be the product of the translation of repeatedly reworked Syriac texts. The Arabic version probably dates from the 8th century and was translated into Ge'ez, as we have seen, several centuries later. Comparison of this Syriac-Arabic source, entitled the *Cave of Treasures*,[110] with the second part of the *Combat of Adam* shows such extensive reworking and expansion as to suggest that the work of a copyist was not sufficient for this part and that—taking the English edition of 1882 by Solomon Caesar Malan as our term of comparison[111]—over twenty pages of additional text were

---

[108] This Arabic version has been published in Antonio Battista and Bellarmino Bagatti, *Il Combattimento di Adamo*, Jerusalem, 1982.

[109] For specific indications on this point, see the introduction to Antonio Battista and Bellarmino Bagatti, *Il Combattimento*, op. cit.

[110] Antonio Battista and Bellarmino Bagatti, *La Caverna dei Tesori*, Jerusalem, 1980.

[111] Solomon Caesar Malan, *The Book of Adam and Eve, also called the conflict of Adam and Eve with Satan, a book of the early Eastern Church, translated from the Ethiopic, with notes from the Kufale, Talmud, Midrashim, and other Eastern works*, Edinburgh, 1882. This edition is the source of all the quotations from the Ethiopian version of the *Combat of Adam* given here.

required to link the two halves. Moreover, the presence of Christ is explicit and in harmony with all the text in this second part, which means that the original source was unquestionably Christian.

6.7.2 The Influence of Gnosticism and of Origen

The possible references to Gnosticism in the Ge'ez version of the *Combat of Adam* are minimal but unquestionably more certain and decisive, as will be shown by the quotations presented below.

These are the words spoken by Adam to Eve after the original sin:

> And Adam said to Eve, "Look at thine eyes, and at mine, which afore beheld angels in heaven, praising; and they, too, without ceasing. But now we do not see as we did: our eyes have become of flesh; they cannot see in like manner as they saw before."
>
> Adam said again to Eve, "What is our body today, [compared] to what it was in former days, when we dwelt in the garden?"[112]

Now it is God speaking to Adam:

> "But when I heard of thy transgression, I deprived thee of that bright light. Yet, of My mercy, I did not turn thee into darkness, but I made thee thy body of flesh, over which I spread this skin, in order that it may bear cold and heat.[113]

The next passage comes after a very long fast on the part of Adam and Eve, which starts with their expulsion and is prolonged by their refusal to eat earthly food because they still hope for God's forgiveness and readmittance to Eden. Finally, in desperation and starving to death, they decide to eat the fruit of the fig tree given to them by God but suffer from stomach ache the following day:

> Then Adam besought the Lord and said, "O Lord, let us not perish through the food we have eaten. Lord, smite us not; but deal with us according to Thy great mercy, and forsake us not until the day of the promise Thou hast made us."
>
> Then God looked upon them, and at once fitted them for eating food; as unto this day; so that they should not perish.

---

[112] Solomon Caesar Malan, *The Book of Adam and Eve*, op. cit. p. 6.
[113] Ibid., p. 15.

> Then Adam and Eve came back into the cave sorrowful and weeping because of the alteration in their nature. And they both knew from that hour that they were altered [beings], that their hope of returning to the garden was now cut off; and that they could not enter it.
>
> For that now their bodies had strange functions; and all flesh that requires food and drink for its existence, cannot be in the garden. Then Adam said to Eve, "Behold, our hope is now cut off; and so is our trust to enter the garden. We no longer belong to the inhabitants of the garden; but henceforth we are earthy and of the dust, and of the inhabitants of the earth. We shall not return to the garden, until the day in which God has promised to save us, and to bring us again into the garden, as He promised us."[114]

The first two quotations clearly refer to the early Christian thinker Origen (c. 185–254), who suggested that God gave Adam and Eve their bodies after the original sin, before which they were spiritual entities without a body made of flesh. Origen's teachings were condemned around the 6th century but, as pointed out by Gianfrancesco Lusini, traces of their influence, mediated by now lost Arabic sources, are evident in Ethiopia before the 15th century, especially in the region of Lake Tana.[115]

The last quotation clearly carries on from the first two and suggests that in giving Adam and Eve a body, God omitted to equip this with an anus, the necessary creation of which required additional divine intervention. While it is not known to the present author whether this tradition draws on previous sources, the three quotations and the loathing of the flesh manifest in them suggest the possible influence not only of Origen through the mediation of Arabic sources but also of Manichaeism.[116]

Finally, attention should also be drawn to a perhaps vaguer but equally significant reference. It is in fact the very idea of the "combat" of Adam against Satan and the reasons for Satan's hatred of man that appear

---

[114] Ibid., pp. 76–77.

[115] Gianfrancesco Lusini, "Tradizione Origeniana in Etiopia," in *Origeniana Octava. Papers of the 8th International Origen Congress*, vol. II, Leuven, 2003, pp. 1177-84.

[116] Manichaean influences had indeed also manifested themselves in Europe more than two centuries earlier with Catharism. Morover, Manichaeism survived in the East until around the 17th century, even though no evidence of the transits has yet been found.

to emerge from a Gnostic-Manichaean background in this passage, where Satan speaks to Adam:

> "But now, Adam, by reason of thy fall thou art under my rule, and I am king over thee; because thou hast hearkened to me, and hast transgressed against thy God. Neither will there be any deliverance from my hands until the day promised thee by thy God."
>
> Again he said, "Inasmuch as we do not know the day agreed upon with thee by thy God, nor the hour in which thou shalt be delivered, for that reason will we multiply war and murder upon thee and thy seed after thee. This is our will and our good pleasure, that we may not leave one of the sons of men to inherit our orders in heaven."[117]

Three reasons are therefore given. Man is part of Satan's kingdom, the realm of evil, because Satan was able to trick him into disobeying God's command. If man were forgiven by God, Satan would lose his kingdom or it would become less important. Satan knows that God will forgive man sooner or later, but this gives him all the more reason to delay that moment by increasing his efforts against man. Finally, Satan fears that man, once redeemed from sin, will be given the role he himself once held as an archangel. The three concepts—the existence of a lower kingdom of evil and matter; the fight to prevent man from regaining his divinity as part of the effort to prevent the reunification of the godhead and the fullness of the kingdom of light; and finally the envy of Satan, who seeks to prevent man from being endowed by God with the dignity that was once his—are all indicative of a Gnostic-Manichaean tradition. Yaldabaoth envies man because it was he himself, misunderstanding Sophia's advice, that endowed man with divinity, thereby losing part of his own. Yaldabaoth and the Archons seek to prevent man from returning to heaven after death. Finally, there is the very idea of the kingdom of darkness. All these elements are indicative of the presence behind these narratives of heterodox sources, possibly mediated again through the teachings of Origen as probably reworked by Manichaean thinkers or communities.

---

[117] Solomon Caesar Malan, *The Book of Adam and Eve*, op. cit. pp. 64-65.

6.8 Barlaam and Josaphat

6.8.1 The Genesis of the Work

A brief examination of *Barlaam and Josaphat*, a curious hybrid work constituting a Christianized life of the Buddha, may prove useful at this point and enable us to take a small step forward. Research on its genesis has traced a path leading from Indian traditions or texts to Persia, where the work was translated into Arabic after Islamization and the Buddha became a Muslim saint within the sphere of Ishmaelite mysticism. It is in this form that it entered Georgia during a period of Arab rule and was translated into Georgian with the figure of the Buddha undergoing Christianization. Through shifts in the balance of political influence, Georgia became a satellite of the Byzantine Empire and this version reached its capital, where a Georgian scholar translated it into Greek in the 10th century. Subsequent translation into Latin and inclusion in the *Golden Legend* of Jacobus da Varagine ensured the success of the now Christianized narrative and expanded its circulation throughout the Mediterranean and neighboring areas. An Arabic retranslation of the Christianized Greek version was then translated into Ge'ez in 1553 during the great period of Ethiopian translations from Arabic.

6.8.2 Gnostic Influences and Traces of the Dispute on Iconoclasm

This text includes some of the themes already found in the course of our investigation, albeit expressed here with particular effectiveness, as in the following example, where a noble convert to Christianity bluntly refuses to obey his king and abandon the faith:

> I will not submit myself unto thee, and I will not consent to do thy bidding in this matter, and I will not deny Him Who hath done good unto me and delivered me. Supposing thou dost give me to the wild beasts, or dost hack me in pieces with swords, or dost hurl me headlong from the rocks, or dost cast me into the fire over which thou hast power, I am not afraid of death. My heart doth not desire the things that pass away, the worthlessness and transient character of which I know well. What profit is there in them at this present? Is there any one of them about

which a man would care to think uninterruptedly? And their profitless character is not the only thing, for besides this there are the things that appertain to them, that is to say, much misery, great sorrow, and grief that is endless. The riches of this world are poverty (or, beggary), and the glory thereof is shame.[118]

Condemnation of the world of human customs and conventions, and an appeal to a higher, divine identity as the only true one for man are expressed in the strongest terms. Other recurrent themes are the occasional reference to "perfect wisdom" and the malignant power of the Archons, and the use of the typically Manichaean term "children of light" for the chosen. These are, however, elements already touched upon.

What does offer us a new avenue of investigation and a new link with later themes is the idea of the unknowability of God, which is recurrent in this text. We see it emerge repeatedly in different forms, including the assertion that "it is impossible to see God"[119] and that the divine mysteries cannot be understood by reason.[120] There is also a direct and repeated attack on idols and the conception of divinity presupposed by those who believe in them. In line with the Judaizing school of thought, the text appears to deny that God can be represented other than in the figure of Christ, who is representable by virtue of having taken human form. An icon can therefore bear witness to sacrality only if it takes the likeness of Christ.[121] Other witnesses to sacrality are the cross, as the symbol of Christ, and the relics of saints, which are such in virtue of being part of their bodies or having touched them (earth walked upon by a saint could also be a relic).

The development of this theme suggests on the one hand that the book summarizes the more mature conclusions formulated by the iconophiles after the debate against iconoclasm held in

---

[118] Ernest A. Wallis Budge, *Baralam and Yewasef—Being the Ethiopic Version of the Christianized Recension of the Buddist Legend of the Buddha and the Bodhisattva*, Cambridge, 1923, p. 13.

[119] Ibid., pp. 43 and 109-13.

[120] Ibid., p. 50.

[121] It was believed in medieval times that the Image of Edessa or Mandylion and other images of Christ had actually been produced or painted with Christ Himself as the model.

Seals of Solomon. This typical shape is achieved by superimposing two equilateral triangles in such a way as to obtain a star with six points. In the two above images the seal is enriched with other forms increasing their symbolic value: one of the examples above has the cross in its center, in the other, forms resembling climbing branches, probably a hint to the tree of life, intersect the symbol (Photographed by the author from Ethiopian churches).

Constantinople,[122] and on the other that the conception of the non-representability of the divine already present in the Buddhist[123] and Muslim traditions was taken up during this process of formulation and the attempt to rebut the iconoclastic argument that every icon is an idol. As we shall see, this theme was to undergo important development in the formulations expressed in certain writings that Cerulli attributes to followers of the Mikaelite heresy, which will be addressed in one of the following sections.

6.9 The *Ləfafä ṣədəq* and Other Talismanic Works

6.9.1 A "Magical" Christian Literature

The last group of works to be addressed in the period of translations from the Arabic comprises talismanic works of a markedly Christian character, of which the *Ləfafä ṣədəq*[124] is only one example. While similar in certain respects to the Arabic *Testament of Solomon* and *Seal of Solomon* discussed above, these texts leave no doubt whatsoever as regards the sphere to which they belong, being unequivocally Christian in their explicit reference to Christ, the Trinity, the Virgin Mary, angels, the evangelists, and the Cross.

Despite this, however, they are just as unequivocally magical works serving as talismans or amulets to be worn on the person or hung around the neck of the deceased so as to guarantee the bearer life, salvation, health, and the forgiveness of sins after death. They also contain instructions for the family of the deceased, who are required to make the

---

[122] Ernest A. Wallis Budge, *Baralam and Yewasef*, op. cit., pp. 124-25. Budge's translation seems inaccurate in places and does not appear to render correctly the relationship between image and prototype, which emerges with greater clarity in the translation from Greek. See for example S. Ronchey and P. Cesaretti, *Storia di Barlaam e Ioasaf. La vita bizantina del Buddha*, Turin, 2012, pp. 132-33.

[123] Footprints on a surface were used as an image of the non-representable Buddha in the iconographic traditions of India prior to Alexander's conquest.

[124] The "Bandlet of Righteousness," understood as the badge, amulet or talisman of the chosen. E.A. Wallis Budge states in the introduction to his edition and translation of 1929 that the "bandlet" is the "shroud" or cloth with inscriptions in which the body of the deceased was wrapped, as was customary also in ancient Egypt after mummification. See Ernest A. Wallis Budge, *The Ethiopian Book of the Dead* – Ləfafä ṣədəq, London, 1929, pp. 21-22.

The Second Phase of Gnostic Influences in Ethiopia 99

1. The cannibal of Kemer eating human flesh
2. He tries to buy a yoke of oxen for a bow and two arrows
3. He offers an additional arrow

(*Illustrating Miracle No. XXIX*)
From MS. A.

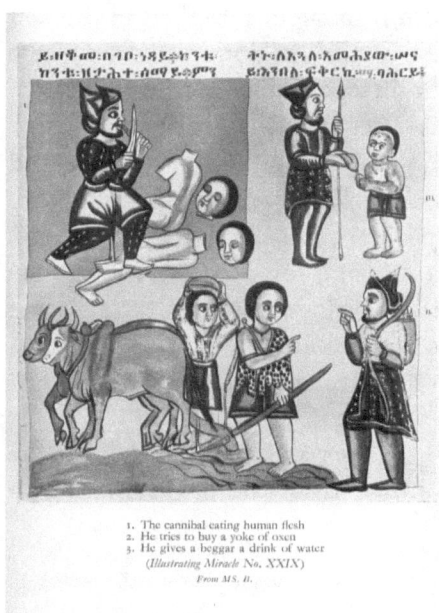

1. The cannibal eating human flesh
2. He tries to buy a yoke of oxen
3. He gives a beggar a drink of water

(*Illustrating Miracle No. XXIX*)
From MS. B.

1. The cannibal's soul is carried off to hell
2. An angel weighing the drink of water against seventy-two souls whose bodies the cannibal had eaten, and it outweighs them
3. Our Lord in glory
4. Mary protecting the cannibal's soul

(*Illustrating Miracle No. XXIX*)
From MS. B.

The above images illuminate the story of the cannibal who obtains salvation, at his death, thanks to the intercession of the Virgin (from Ernest A. Wallis Budge, *One Hundred and Ten Miracles of Our Lady Mary*, Oxford, 1933, plates LIV, LV and LVI).

sign of Solomon's seal[125] three times on the corpse in order to save his or her soul. As the text[126] must contain the name of the deceased, blanks are left for the insertion of this information whenever it is copied. Their essential character appears to be the power to ensure eternal life regardless of the nature and gravity of the sin, which are questions never considered. On the contrary, another of the prayers published by Budge in the appendix to the above-mentioned book makes it clear that the attitude of the Virgin towards the celestial powers (angels) required to assist her in helping whoever appeals to her for aid is the same as that of the magician towards the diabolic or in any case inferior powers. For this reason, all the types of problems and illnesses for which the Virgin offers protection[127] are listed in the prayer together with the following entreaty attributed to her:

> I beseech you this day, O ye whose names are hidden, and who dwell nigh unto the Veil of the Father, to come unto me wheresoever I am, and fulfil the good wish which I have, for ye have not the power to disregard my wish.[128]

This assertion is not so explicit in the *Ləfafä ṣədəq* but implicit in the fact that no inquiry is made into the nature of the sin committed and that there is no stated limitation on the Virgin's power to offer salvation to whosoever turns to her with an acceptable act of faith.

The *Ləfafä ṣədəq* is found in Ethiopia in a number of variants and with different names such as the *Book of Life*, *Prayer of Salvation* or *Prayer of Redemption*. Given the central importance attached to the Virgin, scholars attribute its production to the reign of Zär'a Ya'əqob, the sovereign responsible for the glorification of Mary, not least through the translation of *The Miracles of Mary* from the Arabic. But why is the Virgin so important in the *Ləfafä ṣədəq*? What has she to do with magical practices?

A recurrent figure in *The Miracles of Mary* is a great sinner on the point of death who manages to save himself from the devils waiting to

---

[125] Two equilateral triangles superimposed so as to form a six-pointed star (see the image on the page).

[126] The term "text" is used here rather than "book" because, as we have seen, it was written on a scroll, a piece of cloth or any support serving to wrap or accompany the corpse.

[127] Ernest A. Wallis Budge, *The Ethiopian Book of the Dead - Ləfafä ṣədəq*, op. cit., p. 104.

[128] Ibid., p. 109.

The Virgin is moved while watching the suffering of sinners in hell (Photographed by Emanuele Ragni from the church of Kura Kidanä Məhrät, Lake Tana).

Image showing the salvific role of the Virgin after the death of the sinner (Manuscript, British Library, EAP286/1/1/412, https://eap.bl.uk/archive-file/EAP286-1-1-412, copyright Institute of Ethiopian Studies, Addis Abeba. The image is from the Endangered Archives Programme of the British Library, Ethiopian Manuscript Imaging Project [DOI:https://doi.org/10.15130/EAP286]).

bear his soul away either by calling upon the Virgin or for having performed one good act in his life in her name.[129] This is an important figure and one that found mythical justification in Ethiopia in an authentic pact between the Virgin and the Son, namely the Covenant of Mercy,[130] whereby forgiveness cannot be denied if Mary intercedes with Christ on behalf of a sinner. This special power of the Virgin, one of the cornerstones of the Marian cult promoted by Zär'a Ya'əqob, found numerous opponents in the Ethiopian Church and gave rise to expressions of dissent that were then condemned as heretical, as in the case of the Stephenites, derogatively labeled "enemies of Mary."

This special ability or power of the Virgin is the logical cornerstone of the talismanic writings examined here. In the *Ləfafä ṣədəq*, after seeing the punishments inflicted on the damned in Hell, the Virgin asks Christ if there is any way out for them. Mentioning her own parents, she asks whether they too can be saved despite their sins. Christ is reluctant to answer and promises to ask God for permission to impart this revelation.

He then returns with the *Ləfafä ṣədəq*, a book written by God himself before the Virgin gave birth to Christ. The text presents the customary magical elements already seen in the Arabic *Seal of Solomon*: the injunction to keep the revelation secret; the list of the secret names of God, Christ, and the nails of the Cross; the assurance that whoever believes in God, Christ, and the Virgin will be saved as long as they follow the book's instructions, whereas whoever believes in Satan will be damned; the reference to the power of the Cross as the Tree of Life and to the *Seal of Solomon*. While the magic squares seen in the Solomonic thaumaturgical literature are absent from the *Ləfafä ṣədəq*, we do find the components of the Sator Square, the most famous and widely circulated magic square of antiquity:

SATOR

AREPO

TENET

OPERA

ROTAS

---

[129] In one case, even a man guilty of cannibalism is saved. See Ernest A. Wallis Budge, *One Hundred and Ten Miracles of Our Lady Mary*, Oxford, 1933, Miracle XXIX, p. 94.

[130] The *Kidanä məhrät*.

This is a palindrome that can be read top-to-bottom, bottom-to-top, left-to-right or right-to-left and contains a concealed cross formed by the intersecting of the word TENET in the center.[131] The reason why the Sator Square is not presented in its graphical form as a square is that the five component words are altered in the Ethiopian tradition into SADOR, ALADOR, DANAT, ADERA, RODAS, thus losing the magical effect whereby the sequence of words remains the same in whatever direction they are read. The importance of the palindrome is preserved, however, because the five component words are thought to be the names of the five nails of the cross. At the same time, while less space is devoted to the magic squares mentioned in connection with the Arabic *Seal of Solomon*, the greatest importance is instead attached to listing the secret names of God, Christ, angels, and other entities like the heavens, the heavenly bodies, the sun and the moon, which become central in the texts translated by Budge in the appendix to the *Ləfafä ṣədəq*. These are sequences, sometimes presented side by side, which take on the function of the square in all respects. One of them, in the last pages of the *Ləfafä ṣədəq*, appears to be an authentic song, comparable to the vocalic sequences of the eastern religious and hermetic traditions, with a probable hypnotic effect.[132] In this case, the magical effect no longer derives from mathematical or alphabetical mechanisms but from the obsessive repetition, as in a rosary or novena, of verbal sequences that are initially identical and then develop with ritualized variations that are repeated in turn. It is therefore unquestionably a Christian magical text but one that clearly draws on the ancient Egyptian *Book of the Dead*, which performed the same function of ensuring the survival of the deceased.

What are the most original themes, those either not found in the previous works or developed more widely in this talismanic text? There are essentially two. The first is the theme of names, already seen in the *Testament of Solomon* but emphasized here to the highest degree, thus attesting to links with the Jewish and Egyptian tradition. The second is the birth of this new and simultaneously magical and Christian approach

---

[131] Different meanings have been ascribed to this sequence of words, which is not wholly interpretable in terms of the Latin language. One constant feature of all the various interpretations is, however, the sower (*sator*, interpretable as a metaphor of the Creator or Christ) who takes care (*tenet*) of his work (*opera*). According to others, the whole can be seen as a magical formula, a seal or a protective talisman in virtue of its graphic form, in which the cross is concealed, and of its palindromic construction.

[132] Ernest A. Wallis Budge, *The Ethiopian Book of the Dead - Ləfafä ṣədəq*, op. cit., p. 85.

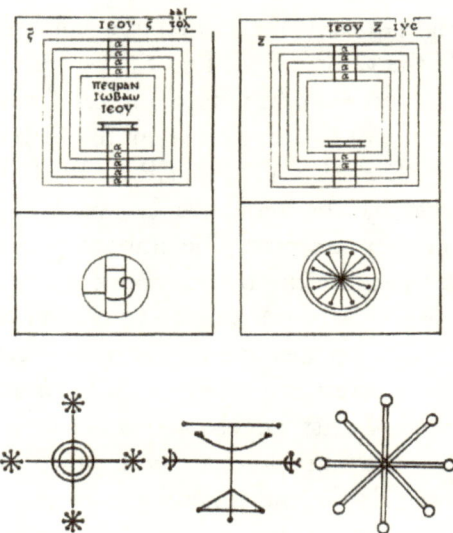

Seals from the *Books of Jeu*.

King Solomon in an Ethiopian magic scroll (Photo (C) musée du quai Branly - Jacques Chirac, Dist. RMN-Grand Palais / Claude Germain).

to the question of deliverance: the use of this sacred book, written by God, as a talisman to obtain salvation and the accompanying creation, also within the sphere of the orthodox faith, of a "loophole" for the sinner, enabling whoever possesses the book or performs the actions laid down in it to possess the wisdom it contains and obtain salvation even if he or she has committed the greatest sins. The above-mentioned names are also obviously part of this wisdom.

6.9.2 The Theme of Names and Egyptian Influences

E.A. Wallis Budge addresses the question of the elements converging in the formation of the *Ləfafä ṣədəq* at some length in the introduction to his edition of 1929. The fusion of the different influences appears to have found ideal terrain in the hybrid culture born out of the encounter between the Greek civilization and the traditions of ancient Egypt, from which Gnosticism also sprang. The primary influence in this cross-fertilization, according to Budge, is the *Book of the Dead*, the earliest formulations of which were discovered as carved inscriptions on ancient tombs and sarcophagi. According to ancient Egyptian beliefs, the transcription of parts of this on strips of cloth placed on the body guaranteed the deceased proximity to the gods or entry to the afterlife, the opening of the gates of heaven, and immunity from the attacks launched by evil spirits on souls.

At the same time, it was customary in ancient Egypt to give the gods different names constituting manifestations of their powers and attributes. These names were thought to include some of a secret, hidden nature and therefore of particular efficacy. According to Budge, the Egyptians, Gnostics, Copts, Muslims, and Ethiopians all shared the same idea of the value of names:

> All these peoples ascribed to the name of God or of a man an importance which it is impossible for us to realize fully because we do not know the exact meaning which they attached to their words for "name." It is clear, however, that they believed that the life and existence of a god or a man were bound up with the existence of his name inextricably; neither god nor man could

[THE EIGHTH SECTION]

IN THE NAME OF THE FATHER, and THE SON, AND THE HOLY GHOST, ONE GOD.

THE NAMES OF OUR LORD JESUS CHRIST, SIDRÂ-LÂWÎ—that death may not come unto me except at my appointed time.

'Awlâkît	Derdâs	Nârôs
'Elôn	Dalfôgîn	Gâdên
Yôṭâ	Bîbakuolâdîn	Sîdrâḵâ'êl
Kîraḵîṭîn	Dôlôtôlôn	Zarûbâ'êl
Sefûfâ'êl	Dôlôhôlôhîn	Tôlakîn
Kafâzîn	Gâzên	Fûlâka'êl
'Alfâ'êl	Dârâtân	Zerâ'êl
Galmâlâwî	Galawdeyân	'Iyâfên
Kalâdîn	'Abdâwî	Menâsîlâwî

The last four pages of the translation of the Ləfafä ṣədəq published by E.A. Wallis Budge. In the eighth section the salvific function attributed to the names of God and to the three persons of the Trinity is particularly evident (from Ernest A. Wallis Budge, *The Ethiopian Book of the Dead – Ləfafä ṣədəq*, London, 1929, pp. 84–87).

TRANSLATION 85

[Fol. 25a]
Selnôdes   Delâwî   Gôldâfôn
Ḳalâ'êl   Dafû'êl Sedrâḳâ'êl
Sîlî

[In these names] I take refuge, I, Thy servant STEPHEN.

IN THE NAME OF THE FATHER, AND THE SON, AND THE HOLY GHOST, ONE GOD.

'Alfâ and 'Ô (Omega)
'Alfâ 'Alfâ 'Alfâ 'Alfâ 'Alfâ 'Alfâ 'Alfâ
'Îyâ'êl 'Îyâ'êl 'Îyâ'êl 'Îyâ'êl
Îyâ'êl 'Îyâ'êl 'Îyâ'êl
Hîdâ'êl Hîdâ'êl Hîdâ'êl Hîdâ'êl
Hîdâ'êl Hîdâ'êl Hîdâ'êl
Yôdnâ'êl Yôdnâ'êl Yôdnâ'êl Yôdnâ'êl
Yôdnâ'el Yôdnâ'el Yôdnâ'êl
'Ûrnâ'êl 'Ûrnâ'êl 'Ûrnâ'êl 'Ûrnâ'êl
'Ûrnâ'êl 'Ûrnâ'êl 'Ûrnâ'êl
Hîrnâ'êl Hîrnâ'êl Hîrnâ'êl Hîrnâ'êl.

[Fol. 25b] Hîrnâ'êl Hîrnâ'el Hîrnâ'êl
'Amîs 'Amîs 'Amîs 'Amîs
'Amîs 'Amîs 'Amîs

Dâhdâ	Negdekînî	Hehdâdî
Serâyâsyâl	Suryâl	Fârdyâl
'Arâdyâl	Sadrâl	Mûdûyâl
'Adônây	Mâsyâs	'Amânû'êl
'Akoâr	Marâdyâl	'Arâdyâl
Kaf'êl	'As'al	'Afteyâl
'Armâyâl	'Aḳte'al	'Ares'al
'Akyâl	Fânû'êl	Ḳatîtyâl
Retyâl	'Alyâl	Tîtâ'ôl
Yûlyâl	Kartîyâl	Sabteyâl
Mîtâ'ôl	Mîrâ'ôl	'Aksîfâ'ôl

86   " BANDLET OF RIGHTEOUSNESS "

'Awketyâl	Bîtyâl	Fêwâl
Sarwâl	'Anwâl	Fîlala'ôl
'Akrestîyâl	'Absî'ôl	'Awnewâl
'Arne'êl	Wâtîr	Nâ'ûs
Tîrân'arnâs	Zarik'abeg	Termen
Yâ'asîkô	Mîsônkes	Mâtîr

[Fol. 26a]

Nâsâkîb	'Aksenûnîyôs	'Ûnâr
Barâkîyâs	Rûstîwôn	Dâkîyâs
'Ôrneyâs	Ṭerâs	Kînâs
'Abṣâlôn	'Ansekô	Mûd
Meṭôs	Mût	Ketonâ
Lî'aṣâ(?)	Kînâ	'Araṣâ(?)
'Anyôs	Sârdî	Kalâsîn
'Ûsûrân	Mîrâ'ak	Wârôka
Wardî'aka	'Aṣamâ'ôl	Kônâ'al
Dôrân	'Arnî	Mârîk
Lasanek	'Amîyôs	Dawra
Bared	Meyâl	Mâsidenyâl
'Armeyâl	'Aryâmî	'Anâmyâl
'Aldyâl	'Awyâl	Yâ'ab
Fû'amâ	Fûyâmâ	Sardûr
Matawâdây	'Arâdyâl	Rawer
Fârûl	Ferteka	Sûhâl
Mîkâ'êl	Gabre'êl	Sûryâl
Sadâkyâl	Sarûtyâl	'Anânyâl
Rûfâ'êl	'Akhrâṭyâl	Khârmâsyâl
'Aḵmayyâl	'Afdâmyâl	'Arenyânyâl

[Fol. 26b]

'Asrâm	Zîdâ'ôl	Sûrûk
Mensûk	'Akhabreyânôs	Kîrûbêl
'Afnânyâl	'Atlewâ	Beresteyâl
'Abreyâl	'Abrâḵ	Rāg

> TRANSLATION 87
>
> Ferteyâl   Ferfâr   Fâmâwâwâl
> Fânânyâl   Dîdyâl   Marâdkeyâl
> 'Afdekyâl
>
> O Holy Trinity, I, your servant WALDA MICHAEL, take refuge in each of your Names, and in the Names of your angels, and of your priests, so that the foul spirits and the hosts of Diabolos may not approach me on my right hand, or on my left hand, or before me, or behind me, wheresoever I may be.
>
> 'Iyâsyôn Rôdakhn Hedrâ
> 'Û'ûsûsînôyâkek 'Ayûwôs
> Salâs'êl Hêsêwôn Dênpes
>
> [I take refuge in these your Names, I your servant] STEPHEN.

exist without his name, and the "killing" or destruction of his name was equivalent to the destruction of his existence.[133]

The introduction also includes an outline of the legend of the Egyptian divinities Ra and Isis, which presents interesting similarities to the *Ləfafä ṣədəq*. Envying Ra and coveting his powers, Isis engineers a plot to discover his secret name, knowledge of which will also allow her to obtain his powers. She fashions a serpent of clay, brings it to life, and places it in his path. When Ra is bitten and the effects of the poison begin to manifest themselves, Isis claims that she can cure him only if she knows his secret name, which will enable her to attain her desires. He resists for a long time but finally yields, whereupon Isis cures him. Something similar happens in the *Ləfafä ṣədəq*, where Mary entreats Christ to have pity and reveal the true name of God in order to save her parents from hell. The *Ləfafä ṣədəq* is nothing other than this, a series of prayers and invocations, and a list of the names of God and the divine powers that draws closer and closer to the most secret and recondite truths. As in the Gnostic *Books*

---

[133] Ibid., pp. 9–10.

of Jeu, another text composed in Alexandria, the names increasingly take on the character of emanations, lesser divinities, and magical formulas endowed with power independently of their meaning.

It is hard to determine the channels through which these conceptions arrived in Ethiopia, from Egypt. The transit could date from the ancient period of trade based on the port of Adulis or be later, mediated by Alexandria and the Gnostic influences on Egyptian Christianity as seen, for example, in the *Books of Jeu*, which also display similarities with the magical scrolls studied by Jacques Mercier and discussed here below. What is certain, however, is that we have no evidence of such transits and this section is therefore to be regarded as a preview of the discussion of the undatable sources to be developed below.

6.9.3 The Names of God and Jewish Influences

An explicit reference to Jewish influences is found in *the Ləfafä ṣədəq* at the beginning of the second section. Of the forty-four names of God listed there, twenty-two correspond to the letters of the Hebrew alphabet and appear in precisely the same order as in the Jewish cultural tradition.[134] While the reason for this could of course be ignorance of the meaning of this sequence on the part of the author of the *Ləfafä ṣədəq*, it unquestionably constitutes evidence of the arrival in Ethiopia of Jewish traditions or of traditions mediating Jewish influences.

As regards the Jewish nature of this idea, it should be noted that Jewish mystics regarded the Torah, the Scriptures or the Law, as the name of God. For them, the Torah came into existence two thousand years before the creation of the world. It is a divine emanation, part of the divine essence, a hypostatic entity in a certain sense. According to some interpretations, it could be said that the Torah was to become the Word in the Christian sphere. The Torah is the wisdom of God. The name of God and the wisdom of God are one and the same, and it is the Torah that created the world.[135]

The Torah is read by man as a narrative but the true Torah is the name of God, a sequence of consonants that is nothing other than a name.

---

[134] Ernest A. Wallis Budge, *The Ethiopian Book of the Dead - Ləfafä ṣədəq*, op. cit., p. 36.

[135] Gershom Scholem, *La Kabbalah e il suo Simbolismo*, Turin, 1960, p. 54.

The name of God is, however, a supreme concentration of strength and power. If the Torah is the name of God, the instrument with which He gave life to Adam, then any man can use it to create. In order to avoid this absurdity, some rabbis claimed that the various sections of the Torah were not given in their correct order and for this reason only God can create. Man could do so too, however, by discovering this order. The following quotations will help to clarify this.

> The letters of the alphabet, and *a fortiori* those of the name of God or even of the entire Torah, which was the instrument used by God in the creation of the world, have a mysterious, magical power.[136]

> It is well known that in the Hellenistic period and later the Torah was put to magical use both by Jews and non-Jews: divine names gleaned from the Torah were used for purposes of incantation. Often the methods of combination by which such magical names were derived from the Torah are unintelligible to us.[137]

Scholem goes on to state that according to some ancient texts, Moses ascended to heaven to receive the Torah, where

> God gave him not only the text of the Torah as we know it, but also the secret combinations of letters which represent another, esoteric aspect of the Torah.[138]

All this comes, however, only in part from the orthodox Jewish tradition. The major source is instead the Kabbalah, a mystical school of Jewish thought with Gnostic characteristics that is difficult to date precisely but certainly developed after the year 1000.

Scholem expressly rules out the possibility that all this may have derived from direct Gnostic influences and speaks rather of psychological developments and structural parallels leading some elements of Judaism

---

[136] Ibid., p. 211.

[137] Ibid., p. 50.

[138] Ibid.

spontaneously to formulations of a Gnostic type.¹³⁹ At the same time, however, he notes that:

> The Kabbalah was fed initially by subterranean sources, probably of Eastern origin, and came to light for the first time in southern France in the same regions and the same period as saw the culmination of Catharism or neo-Manichaeism in the non-Jewish sphere.¹⁴⁰

This dating should be remembered, as it will prove useful in our discussion of the origins of certain Gnostic or Manichaean influences in Ethiopia.

With respect to Budge's suggestion of two sorts of influence, ancient Egyptian and Jewish, it must be pointed out that while we have no evidence of the former, there is some for the Kabbalah that certainly regards the entire area of the Mediterranean but not Ethiopia directly. We refer to the well-known historical event of the expulsion of the Jews from Spain in 1492, which led to the scattering of the Jewish community through all the areas where no such provisions were in force. It is no coincidence that major European philosophers of the time, like Pico della Mirandola and Paracelsus, knew and studied the Kabbalah. While there is obviously nothing as yet to show that these transits made their way into Ethiopia, we have already found marked imprints of the mysticism of the Kabbalah and the science of names in Egyptian manuscripts included in the *Seal of Solomon* and the above-mentioned Muslim Arabic manuscripts discovered in Ethiopia.

6.9.4 Similarities and Possible Relations: The *Picatrix*

The concepts presented above are of interest because of their marked similarities to a text produced in Spain around the 11th century, a magical work that enjoyed extraordinary success throughout the

---

[139] Ibid., p. 124.

[140] Ibid., p. 114. Other scholars have, however, pointed out that the ancient Zoroastrian religion of Persia, which already had dualistic tendencies, probably influenced Judaism in ancient times during the period of Babylonian captivity. As a result, they suggest the possibility of attributing Jewish origins to the Gnostic movements that developed as from the 1st century AD. See W. Barnstone and M. Meyer (eds.), *Essential Gnostic Scriptures*, op. cit., p. 233.

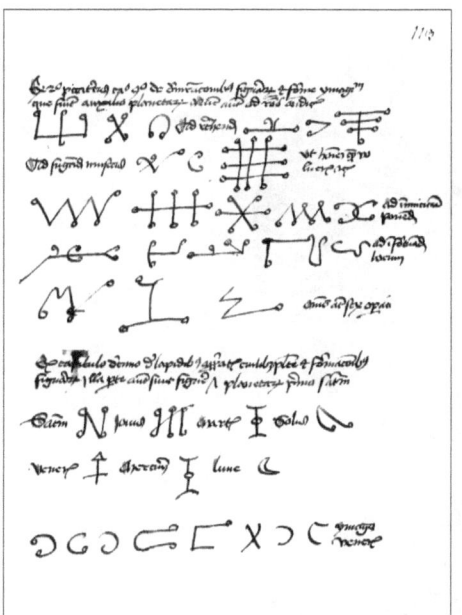
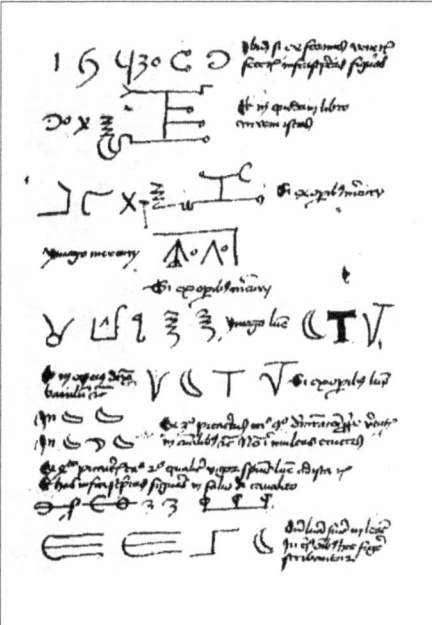

Talismanic symbols in a manuscript of the *Picatrix* (MS 3317, Fol. 113r and Fol. 113v, Osterreichische Nationalbibliothek, Wien)

Mediterranean area. We refer to the *Picatrix*, the original version of which was in Arabic and appears to have been produced between 1047 and 1051. It was translated into Spanish in 1256 and then into Latin from that language. There is some uncertainty regarding the author, Muslama al-Magritti, for whom we have no reliable information and who has been variously identified. The manuscripts have been found all over Europe.[141]

The following quotation on the subject of names will shed light on the above-mentioned similarities:

> Aristotle said this in his books on talismans: "What is best and highest in talismans comes to them from the seven planets and their effect will be longer lasting if good fortune accompanies them." It is essentially a matter of bringing the spirits and the

---
[141] Paolo A. Rossi, *Picatrix. Dalla versione latina del Ghayat al-hakim*, Milan, 2011.

The symbol of the cross takes the place of the body of Christ in the crucifixion set. Note the sun and the moon on the two sides of the cross (Ampulla from Jerusalem, 6th or 7th century - Copyright Dumbarton Oaks, Byzantine Collection, Washington, DC (BZ.1948.18)).

virtues of the heavens down to earth. He also said that there are names of powers which, if uttered with the intention of summoning those spirits, will cause them to descend, and their virtues, each in its own time, can also kill whoever is not deeply versed in the nature of the spirit and the planet suitable for that particular work on receiving them; a nature such as to conform it to the body. Thus is created what is reported by those who operate in the greatest name, who claim to be able to change

This symbol, created by superimposing two letters of the Greek alphabet, is an abbreviation of the name of Christ, but it takes also the shape of the antique Egyptian symbol of the sun. The circle around it hints to the cosmic meaning of Christ and his role of universal salvation (Part of a wall painting from a Lullingstone's Roman villa, Kent, England).

> the essence of things by means of the virtues of those names and work wonders all over the world, even though most of those who have acted in accordance with the said name disagree over its determination.[142]

While the above is just one of many possible quotations regarding the subject of names, there are also innumerable references to other subjects present in texts of the Ethiopian tradition found in the period of translations from Arabic. The following, which refers to the teachings of the ancient sages, regards astrology:

> It is also said that in the heavens there are beautiful, well-shaped forms and others less beautiful that are generated by the

---

[142] Ibid., p. 50.

Cross from the church of Makina Medhane Alem (surroundings of Lalibela). Note the sun and the moon on the two sides. (photographed by the author).

> arrangements and configurations of the fixed stars. If some are born while beautiful, well-shaped figures are ascending and while the Sun and Moon are also in beautiful figures, this means that they will be fortunate in their acts and actions. If ugly, misshapen figures are ascending in the hour of birth with the Sun and Moon in similar figures, this means that those born in these conditions will be ill-fated in their actions, their transactions, and their motivations.[143]

Slightly later we read: "A talisman is nothing other than the power of the celestial bodies that operates through them."[144] The most powerful talisman is, however, the cross, which is referred to below in the chapter that lists the elements required to perform works of magic and explains how the spirits of planets depend on simulacra and suffumigations:

> Take material appropriate to the same planet from a stone and with it construct a cross. Having done all this under the due constellation, erect the cross on two feet. Then place the figure

---

[143] Ibid., p. 76.

[144] Ibid.

Another example of cross-christogram with the same characteristics as the previous one (Circular metal plate from Vatican Museum, inv. 60587, Photo © Governatorato SCV – Direzione dei Musei).

or simulacrum of your prayer upon it in a way that is consistent with the spirit of the planet. For example, if you want to compose a simulacrum capable of provoking disputes or vanquishing and terrifying enemies, make it in the figure of a serpent or a lion. If you want to favor flight or escape, you should make the cross like a bird. If you want to increase your wealth, power, honor and position, make the cross in the form of a man sitting on a chair. Act in all your prayers in such a way that the cross is in relation to the prayer.[145]

An explanation is then given:

> The reason why this figure is to be made in the form of a cross has already been given: all things are connected with the figures that exist in relation to the quality of the thing itself and shun the opposite figures. We ask the powers of the planetary spirits for their figures to combine but do not know the figure of the

---

[145] Ibid., p. 139.

spirit and cannot attain it with experiments other than by making use of the figure of a man, an animal or another thing. It follows from this that each of the said virtues consists above all of figures. And since we clearly see that the figures and forms of trees, plants, animals, and minerals are all different from one another, so that we are not permitted to know properly the forms of the planetary spirits themselves, it is for this very reason that the ancients wise in this art chose the cross as a universal figure, because all bodies can be represented on its surface. The surface has a longitude and a latitude, and the relationship of these gives birth precisely to the image of a cross. Therefore, for the very reason that no other figure flees from it, we can call the cross the universal master of those who work magic and almost a receptacle of the powers peculiar to the planetary spirits. And this is one of the secrets of this art. And when the virtue of a planetary spirit is combined with the figure of the cross, then the work acquires virtue and power over every other figure, so that if it is made in the form of a man, its power works on men, if in animal form, then likewise on the other animals.[146]

The next step:

Therefore take the appropriate suffumigations and burn them with fire in the thurible. Place the cross just over the thurible so that the smoke rising from it passes from the lower arm of the cross to the higher. Let all this be done at the right moment in the presence of the dominant planet, as said before. If everything is done in due order, the smoke of the suffumigation will reach the sphere of the signs following straight lines and will not be torn away by the radial lines of planets opposed to the one dominant. And if your work is performed on the inferior beings of the earth, the spirit of the planets will be joined to it and its virtue will descend on what has been done on the earth through its own directions. Then will the worker's wishes be granted.[147]

---

[146] Ibid., p. 140.

[147] Ibid., p. 140–41.

Cross held up by two Roman figures of the Victory sculpted on one long side of the so called "Sarcophagus of the Prince" (Archeological Museum of Istanbul – image from Bruno Leoni, *La croce e il suo segno*, Verona, 1968, plate out of text n. 10).

The text also indicates rituals to be performed in mosques, supposedly ordered by Hermes Trismegistus himself,[148] and suggests that numbers derived from "calculations of love" be written on food or stones for people to swallow, after which "they will be seen to join together in absolutely perfect mutual friendship and love."[149]

6.9.5 Magic and the New Man

Without lingering too much over this point and in full awareness both of the differences between the Ethiopian and European contexts and of the lack of any evidence whatsoever that the *Picatrix* ever arrived in Ethiopia, our impression from the above is that Ethiopia did experience something of this shift toward magic, this glorification of a new man capable of endowing himself with powers such as to force the lesser divinities to obey him, and perhaps even God through the Virgin Mary; a being that fashions talismans, draws symbols, knows the secret names of God or the lesser divinities or devils, and knows the right perfumes to be burnt in rituals, through the Egypt of the Arabic *Seal of Solomon* and through Arab-Muslim manuscripts on the names of God. This new man is clearly hailed by the *Picatrix* in an important passage quoted here in extracts:

---

[148] Ibid., p. 170.

[149] Ibid., p. 204.

Cross on the throne from the mosaics of the Arian Baptistery in Ravenna – Italy (image from Bruno Leoni, *La croce e il suo segno*, Verona, 1968, plate out of text n. 20).

Man is similar to the animals in all natural things but separated from them by his precepts and knowledge. [...] He has fingers and palms composed in a straight line, a round head, and the ability to judge and to learn writing and the sciences, to discover precepts and to overcome all the animals, while none of them can overcome him. He laughs, weeps, and sighs. In him there is the power of God and the knowledge of justice to govern cities. He is a simulacrum that contains a light and is powerful in the spirit and uniform in its representation. [...] He has discovered subtle precepts and the subtleties thereof. He works miracles, creates wonderful representations, and is able to understand the abstraction of the sciences [...] God made him such as to discover and formulate his sciences, to explain his qualities and those of all the things of the world, capable of receiving the prophetic spirit, the treasures of his wisdom, of knowing everything that exists in the world and the relationship of one thing to the other [...] Everything is at his service while he is at the service of none [...] As a whole, the human figure is the ark of the universal spirit, the universal spirit is the ark of the

Angel holding up a cross to chase away some demons in an Ethiopian magic scroll (Asmat Prayers [late 19th-early 20th century], British Library, EAP286/1/1/44, https://eap.bl.uk/archive-file/EAP286-1-1-44, copyright Institute of Ethiopian Studies, Addis Abeba. The image is from the Endangered Archives Programme of the British Library, Ethiopian Manuscript Imaging Project [DOI:https://doi.org/10.15130/EAP286]).

universal intellect and the universal intellect is the ark of light, from which understanding proceeds. Light is therefore the matter of general understanding, which is superior to everything that is inferior [...] Man is therefore complete as regards the composition of his figure, as all the other bodies partake of it and he himself is combined with the other substance.[150]

It is possible to discern in the cult of the Virgin Mary instituted by Zär'a Ya'əqob a strongly magical and pagan element not unlike the one emerging from the power of the names of God, as seen here in the writings of Scholem and the magical practices that made indiscriminate use of Christian or Muslim symbols and references, astrology, and the wisdom of letters of the alphabet or numbers in order to fulfill the desires of whoever requested the magician's aid.

There is, however, something different in Ethiopia. It is as though the whole that manifests itself in the *Ləfafä ṣədəq* displayed not only its similarity to the models of thought found in the *Picatrix* but also its radical difference at the same time. This difference is to be seen not only in its immediate and unquestionable Christian identification but also in the model of magic put forward and employed. Our previous section on the *Testament of Solomon* has already mentioned the classification of different branches of magical practices and the distinction constantly maintained between black magic, which harnesses the powers of demons and spirits, and natural magic and theurgy, which constitute a form of cooperation with God's action in the universe through the spirituality of persons initiated into esoteric practices. This magic in conformity with God's law makes use of the divine names, the power of numbers, amulets, talismans, symbols, and plants as well as spells and enchantments, but follows paths that always draw on the powers of the Virgin Mary, saints, angels, and holy relics in what we could describe as a form of Christian gnosis.

Is it quite certain, however, that the discovery only of texts demonstrating the circulation of these models of Christian magic also proves the absence in Ethiopia of other models closer to the *Picatrix* and black magic? The answer can only be no, as there is evidence that Zär'a Ya'əqob also declared names not mentioned in the testamentary writings to be demonic and forbade their use. He also ordered the destruction of the collections of names compiled during the reign of his brother Yəshaq.

---

[150] Ibid., pp. 54–55.

In view of the fact that the "science of names" is the essential instrument of the Ethiopian magical literature, it seems to follow from all this that the lack of evidence of forms of pagan magic is probably due to the campaigns for the destruction of manuscripts repeatedly launched by the Ethiopian civil and religious authorities.

6.10 A Summary of Gnostic Influences in the Period of Translations from Arabic

Let us now seek to draw some conclusions from this examination of works that appear to present signs of Gnostic influence in the period of translations from Arabic.

With respect to those drawn above at the end of our analysis of the works translated from Greek, there appears to be substantial continuity as regards the following points:

- demonology, the natural powers of demons, the connection between demons and heavenly bodies, natural phenomena and illnesses, and, in close connection with this, the need for talismans, above all to protect souls in their journey after death;
- the corresponding existence of hierarchical formations of angels, albeit no longer connected with social injustice and the fight against the rich and mighty, essential themes of the *Book of Enoch* and the *Shepherd*.

At the same time, these themes appear to be enriched with some new characteristics:

- Talismans, seen above all in the period of translations from Greek as formulas to counteract the attempts of Archons to block the soul's path, or seals to be placed on the body of the deceased, are now endowed with the power of names, numbers, and letters of the alphabet, thus accentuating their magical and transversal character with respect to the religions. Moreover, their use is also extended to the living.
- In harmony with the previous aspect, apocryphal Christian narratives common also to the Jewish and Muslim traditions appear in some texts.

As regards the other two points identified in the period of translations from Greek:

- The appeal to wisdom, the feeling of exile, and the messianic expectation of social upheaval appear to lose importance. All that survives is the idea of esoteric revelation to be concealed from all but the chosen few. Messianic expectation instead acquires spiritual, eschatological characteristics less connected with the idea of social redemption and oriented rather toward the fulfillment of the promise of Christ's return before the Last Judgment in the kingdom of the just, which will last for a thousand years.
- The distortion of trinitary frameworks disappears and attention is focused primarily on the incarnation of Christ. In the *Kəbrä nägäśt*, as we have seen, the three instruments or intermediaries of the incarnation, the Pearl, the Ark and the Cross, become hypostatic entities, divine emanations in a certain sense, created before the birth of the cosmos. It is interesting to note that in *The Mother of Books*, composed in Fatimid Egypt (10th-12th century) and therefore a work of the Shiite Muslim faith, the same form of pre-existence, i.e. creation before the birth of the cosmos, is attributed to Mohammed, Ali, and Fatima. The question therefore arises of whether this model of hypostatic entities also reached Ethiopia through Alexandrian influences that must have been common to both Christian and Muslim beliefs at the time.

Grafted onto this framework of continuity with variations are some elements that are new for Ethiopia even though apparently deriving in some cases from very ancient thinkers and heresies:

- The unknowability of God and hence the impossibility of representing Him other than in the human figure of Christ
- The salvation of all those who does not belong to evil, irrevocable damnation thus being reserved exclusively for devils and those guilty of the worst sins (e.g. Judas Iscariot)
- The dissolution of individual human souls after death. On their way through the heavens, souls lose their earthly determinations and all memory of their identity before death to blend into spiritual wholes susceptible of complete absorption into a higher divinity that appears to have many characteristics in common with the Manichaean god of light.

As a whole, the above elements suggest a reappearance of Gnostic or Manichaean conceptions still more radical than those examined in the period of translations from Greek, even though the channel of transit may have been the Christian philosophy of Origen. The ideas of the unknowability of God, already found in Philo, and of deliverance of all certainly belong to Origen, while is unclear whether his concept of apocatastasis could also encompass the idea of individual souls dissolving into the divine. The first two could, however, also derive from the arrival of Jewish influences in Ethiopia. The unknowability and non-representability of God is certainly Jewish, while the salvation of all could be a development of the messianic expectation of God's deliverance of the chosen people from foreign domination and the collusion of rich Jews with the invaders. Subsequently, with the beginning of the Jewish diaspora and the extension of preaching to the non-Jewish Gentiles, the idea of salvation would thus have taken on spiritual overtones and become available for whoever converted. While it is true that it was Zär'a Ya'əqob who did most to promote the idea of a close relationship between Ethiopia and Israel, it is equally true, however, that he had to take some drastic choices in doing so, emphasizing the dynastic derivation from Solomon but denying other equally important Jewish characteristics. As regards the ideas examined here, the non-representability of God was not accepted by Zär'a Ya'əqob, who was instead wholly in favor of representation, and neither was the deliverance of all, even though he did, as we have seen, promote a new model of salvation for the aristocracy. Sin and individual responsibility were instead to remain paramount for all other men.

There are, however, two motifs emphasized in the texts examined above that can be seen as new in a certain sense:

- Magic and the use of talismans, which are rooted in ancient demonology and astrology but take on wholly new meaning by drawing on the Jewish and Muslim traditions regarding Solomon and his powers as a magician. The magical instruments attributed to Solomon include the letters of the alphabet and numbers, magic squares, and the secret names of God, knowledge of which was part of his wisdom. The power of these symbols and instruments is wholly independent of the faith or religion of whoever uses them.[151]

---

[151] In some Muslim and Jewish narratives about Solomon, a devil gains possession of his ring and uses it for a long time, assuming his identity and having him driven out of his palace.

Emerging from all this is a new conception of man as capable through wisdom of imposing his will on demons. This new sage is a magician but such insofar as he knows the power of the heavenly bodies, symbols, names, and minerals, and is able to control them also with the aid of demons or angels, who are spirits too.

The new Christian knowledge of magic and talismans, possibly fostered by Zär'a Ya'əqob himself. This uses ancient demonologies and the science of talismans as the basis for a new mythology of deliverance available to all regardless of the sins they may have committed. This is, however, a salvation for aristocrats, which entails possession of the book of God and compliance with the requirements laid down in it, and therefore a special kind of knowledge. The pillar of this mythology is the Virgin Mary, who employs and Christianizes all the magical instruments examined above (names of God, numbers, letters of the alphabet, seals, symbols, and books) to guarantee the spiritual salvation of all those who possess the *Ləfafä ṣədəq* and entreat her in the due form laid down in the new magical-religious liturgy. Within this framework, it is the Virgin's intercession with God that can enable even the worst sinner to obtain salvation. This is a model that in no way seeks to disrupt the spiritual or cosmic hierarchies but rather confines itself to studying and applying their rules and laws. The ritual thus becomes something like a succession of reasons and causes that must produce the effect, namely the salvation of the sinner. Here too we find the figure of a "new" man capable of interaction with the divine, the master of his own destiny, perhaps the kind of man Zär'a Ya'əqob himself hoped to be.

7

THE "MIKAELITE" OPUSCULA: A THIRD PHASE OF GNOSTIC INFLUENCES?

7.1 Background Information on the Mikaelite Heretics and the Publication of the Opuscula by Enrico Cerulli

Reference has already been made in the third section of this book to the publication of these 17th-century tracts by Enrico Cerulli in 1958, his attribution of the same to followers of the Mikaelite movement, and his identification in them of Gnostic influences that would in his view account for their peculiar characteristics. It should be recalled that Cerulli regarded these texts, which are highly complex and hard to interpret, as the clearest evidence of the supposed presence of Gnosticism in Ethiopia. The third section also outlines the debate that arose amongst scholars after their publication and points out the substantial disagreement of some as regards both their attribution to the Mikaelite heretical movement and their interpretation as Gnostic writings, albeit without going into the grounds put forward. It will therefore be advisable at this point to start from the beginning with a general outline of the Mikaelites and the associated sources.

The Mikaelite movement and its name are thought to derive from the monk Zämika'el, about whom very little is known. The confutation of his doctrines by Zär'a Ya'əqob (1434–68) is supposed to have taken place in the early years of his reign.

In the *Mäṣḥafä Bərhan*, a text attributed to Zär'a Ya'əqob and one of the sources of information on the Mikaelite heresy, the king states that he summoned Zämika'el together with 'Aṣqa, another heretic, in order to refute their doctrine. He adds that the Metropolitan Bärtälomewos had been suspected of the same heresy during the reign of Yəshaq (1414–29) and obliged to recant. It appears to follow from this both that the Mikaelite heresy was already present in Ethiopia even before Zämika'el and that it had found favor in circles that were close to the Coptic patriarchate and therefore influenced by the doctrines circulating in Alexandria. These surmises appear to be borne out by the fact that the two new metropolitans Mika'el and Gäbrə'el and the bishop Yoḥannəs were asked by Zär'a Ya'əqob on their arrival in 1438–39 to make an explicit anti-Mikaelite declaration.

According to Cerulli, further confirmation is provided by the fact that in his *Book of the Mystery*, a compendium of Christian heresies, Giyorgis of Sägla refuted the Sabellian heresy—which blurs the distinction between the three persons of the Trinity, the Father being likened to a man, the Son to his word and the Holy Spirit to his breathing—in 1424 and therefore prior to the presumed date of Zämika'el's condemnation. The Sabellian view could obviously have given rise to the idea that the three persons are indistinguishable, and it is strongly suspected that the heresy was the first to be addressed in the *Book of the Mystery* precisely in order to attach primary importance to its refutation by the author. At the same time, if Giyorgis of Sägla made no specific reference to its advocates, who were presumably present in Ethiopia, it was perhaps because they must have held influential positions in the court or patriarchate, and he preferred to avoid any direct clash with them.

It should in any case be pointed out that there is no evidence from inside the Mikaelite movement. It appears from the above-mentioned *Mäṣḥafä Bərhan* and from one of the narratives in the *Book of the Miracles of Mary*[152] that what Zämika'el and his followers were actually accused of was rejecting observance of the Sabbath and "denying Mount Zion."

As regards the first point, the Mikaelites, in line with Alexandrian practice, probably condemned observance of the Sabbath, which was instead supported by Zär'a Ya'əqob. On taking the throne, the king had taken a wholly unambiguous stance on this question in order to avert the risk of a schism within the Ethiopian church between supporters of the Alexandrian patriarchate and those espousing the views of Eustachius,[153] who had championed observance of the Sabbath for decades.

---

[152] Enrico Cerulli, *Il Libro etiopico dei Miracoli di Maria e le sue fonti nelle letterature del Medio Evo latino*, Roma, 1958.

[153] The founder of this movement was the monk Ewosṭatewos (Eustachius), who was forced to flee from Ethiopia when his teachings were condemned. They later obtained the approval of Zär'a Ya'əqob and became part of the Ethiopian creed.

The question of the denial of Mount Zion will instead require longer examination because the sources are not clear. In his commentary on the narrative on the death of the monk Giyorgis, a Mikaelite heretic,[154] Cerulli interprets this as denial of the supper on Mount Zion. Since this was a metaphor of the Eucharist, it comes to mean the denial of transubstantiation, i.e. of the eucharistic transformation of bread and wine into the body and blood of Christ. In the above-mentioned *Mäṣḥafä Bərhan*, Zär'a Ya'əqob states that his confutation of Zämika'el regarded the mystery of the Trinity. Given the obscure nature of the reference, Cerulli summarizes his interpretive thinking as follows:

> Denying both that the Creator can be likened to the image of His creatures and that the Trinity can be divided into distinct persons also meant denying that the species can be transformed into the body and blood of the Son and that this transmutation—the transubstantiation—can take place through the descent of the Holy Spirit invoked with the Father (and the Son) in the epiclesis, as was instead the general belief of the Eastern Churches. It can thus be understood why this denial is indicated as the "denial of the existence of the supper of Mount Zion," i.e. of the institution of the Eucharist.[155]

In other words, if the question of transubstantiation is placed alongside that of the Trinity and the denial that God made man after his own likeness, it appears to follow from the above arguments that it makes no sense to speak of the Eucharist as transubstantiation, i.e. the transformation of bread and wine into the body and blood of Christ. If God is unknowable to man and if human instruments cannot even serve as metaphors to know Him, then the very idea of transubstantiation is unacceptable, thus giving rise to a spiritualized, non-bodily conception of Christ. There would thus be a close relationship between the conceptions of the Trinity that we shall now see in the opuscula and the denial of the Eucharist, i.e. of Mount Zion.

Cerulli's interpretation of the denial of Mount Zion has, however, been challenged by other scholars, who see this instead as a reference to the eschatological expectation of Christ's return before the end of the world to reign on earth for a thousand years in the Kingdom of the Just.[156]

---

[154] Enrico Cerulli, *Il Libro etiopico dei Miracoli di Maria*, op. cit., p. 112.

[155] Ibid., p. 114.

[156] See Gianfrancesco Lusini, "Eschatology", in Siegbert Uhlig (ed.), *Encyclopaedia Aethiopica*, op. cit., vol. II, pp. 379-82.

The Mikaelite denial of Mount Zion would therefore actually be the denial that Christ was to return and reign on the earth. In any case, we are dealing with the doctrinal expression of a spiritualized Christianity averse to the ideas both of the incarnation and of the earthly reign of Christ. As pointed out above, however, these are interpretations purely based on evidence and indications left by those who condemned Zämika'el and his followers and did everything in their power to prevent any dissemination of their beliefs. We have no way of knowing the real substance of Mikaelite thought and its grounds.

The three texts published by Cerulli in 1958 are entitled *Exposition of the Divinity*, the *Ship of the Soul* and the *Safe Haven*.[157] He regards them as having been written within the Mikaelite movement, already declared heretical under Zär'a Ya'əqob, in the period when the Society of Jesus was active in Ethiopia, i.e. between 1557 and 1632. Cerulli therefore explicitly suggests that the condemnation of the Mikaelites by Zär'a Ya'əqob (1434–68) only curbed the manifestation of doctrines that nevertheless survived for over a century and resurfaced when representatives of the Ethiopian Orthodox Church launched their attack on the Roman Catholic presence and proselytism.

According to Cerulli, the authors of the three tracts pursued two mutually conflicting aims:

- to take part in and contribute to the debate that developed in Ethiopia in the 16th–17th century after the arrival of the Jesuit missionaries on the side of the Ethiopian Orthodox Church;
- to do so without clearly stating their ideas so as to preserve a margin of ambiguity (sometimes through obscurity) enabling them to participate without being marginalized due to the evident heretical implications of their formulations.

In his view, this was a strategy adopted by the authors of the three works and perhaps their communities as a result of the condemnation of their founder and his followers during the reign of Zär'a Ya'əqob and the subsequent survival of the movement as an outcast heretical sect. Another possible interpretation of the birth of these tracts is that while the exemplary condemnation of Zämika'el and his followers by Zär'a Ya'əqob

---

[157] In Italian: *Spiegazione della Divinità, La Nave dell'Anima* and *Il Porto Sicuro*; Enrico Cerulli, *Scritti Teologici Etiopici dei Secoli XVI-XVII, I. Tre Opuscoli dei Mikaeliti*, Vatican City, 1958.

did put an end to the most blatant manifestations of the Mikaelite heresy and curb its growth in the patriarchate, it only prevented the free expression of beliefs that instead lived on and indeed found mature manifestation in the tracts over a century later.

The dispute with the Jesuits enabled the Ethiopian church to regain its unity momentarily in an understandable attempt to close ranks against Roman Catholic penetration, and this was perhaps regarded as the best possible opportunity to regain freedom of expression by these movements, which thus sought, albeit with anomalous formulations, to fight alongside the other representatives of the Ethiopian church and stem the tide of Jesuit initiatives.

7.2 Cerulli's Gnostic Interpretation

The Gnostic interpretation of the opuscula published by Enrico Cerulli[158] and the objections raised some years later by Father Agostino Tedla[159] and Pierluigi Piovanelli[160] concentrate on a number of passages regarded as particularly relevant. Cerulli's interpretation thus focuses in particular on parts of *Exposition of the Divinity* and one passage from *The Ship of the Soul*. At the same time, for reasons that will be made clear below, the said debate focuses in particular on a passage from the first tract, which Cerulli entitles *The Mystery of the Trinity* and interprets as an authentic Gnostic cosmology. We shall quote the entire passage both because it merits particular attention and so that it can be referred to in the course of this investigation, which will also seek to put forward a different interpretation:

> Two actions (*two active principles*)[161] have entered a house through a door, whose lock has a unique sound and repeats no other *sound*; and through the arrival of this voice, its will is made known to the listener. And these *two*, for the concupiscence

---

[158] Enrico Cerulli *Scritti Teologici Etiopici dei secoli XVI-XVII – Tre opuscoli dei Mikaeliti*, op. cit.

[159] Agostino Tedla, "A proposito di alcuni passi oscuri negli Scritti teologici etiopici pubblicati da E. Cerulli," in *Proceedings of the Third International Conference of Ethiopian Studies*, Addis Ababa, 1970, vol. II, pp. 217-42.

[160] Pierluigi Piovanelli, "Connaissance de Dieu et Sagenne Humaine en Ethiopie," in *Le Museon*, 117, Leuven, 2004, pp. 193-227.

[161] The words in italics are insertions or additions by Cerulli to make the text more comprehensible.

of the warmth of the house, possess a girl—without waiting—a girl of honorable charm, desirable by all, forbidden in beauty by her parents. But while they, having entered by one door, go to their homeland the morning *after*, they will leave by twice three doors. And their daughter, born that night, the only child of her mother and unique by name and forbidden in beauty, will leave by twice two doors. Shortly after, having left, she will give birth to three sons, for wisdom of intelligence, because she *was* pregnant; and she will call them by three names: one: "Be praised among the poor"; the second: "Be blessed among the rich"; and the third: "Be glorified among the lofty in honor." And if they are united, His foundation is rapid, as He appears in a single person. And her initial denomination perishes when they are born.

Come now, tell us the meaning of the birth of that *girl*, beautiful in form and in name, in a single night, while her youth, when she leaves, instead appears adult. I present her parable and abandon the foundation of the perceptibility of the two that entered; and I repudiate the disappearance of the abyss of the root of the garden of the parents of her, who from that (*abyss*) sprang, in the Persons of the Father, the Son and the Holy Spirit, three in Persons, one in Divinity. We shall not say that, like the sons of the girl, one has less glory than the other; and the second is more blessed than the third; and the third is more glorified than *the other two* in honor. Were we to say that, far be it from us to believe this comparison true *to the letter*. They instead exist in honor, glory and magnificence in a single reign, single power, single council, single glory. And they receive a single prostration from the earthly and the celestial with no emulation, as handed down to us by the Fathers, ancient and recent. Therefore we too shall comprehend them with the intellect without approaching their commencement, which has no end; and we shall know them with our thought without feeling or reaching their foundation, which is far away from any interpretation and sublime to speak of.[162]

---

[162] Enrico Cerulli *Scritti Teologici Etiopici dei Secoli XVI-XVII – Tre Opuscoli dei Mikaeliti*, op.cit. pp. 144-46.

Cerulli's interpretation, put forward in note 1 on page 145 of the text, is as follows:

> The entire passage is of the utmost importance for an understanding of the Mikaelite doctrine. This theogony hinges on two Active Principles, which are aroused to generate by the warmth of the dwelling they have entered and have from a female Being another female Being. No sooner has this second female Being been born than it generates in turn Three Persons destined to be united. And these Three Persons are those of the Trinity of Christianity. The birth of the Trinity is thus arrived at through successive previous emanations.
>
> Within this general idea, so closely akin it appears to the Gnostic theogonies, there are several points whose symbolism is not clear to me, e.g. the departure of the two Active Principles—after the initial act of generation—"through twice three doors" and the departure of their only begotten Daughter "through twice two doors" before giving birth to the Three Persons. In the same way, I can only draw the attention of scholars to the names that the Mother gives the Three Persons, elevating each of them respectively over the "poor," the "rich" and the "lofty." Another point, which remains unspecified in our text, regards the unification of the Three Persons. The text uses the third person plural with a highly indeterminate meaning: "they are united." But who is the Unifier or who are the Unifiers of the Three Persons? Or does the unification take place through causes that are not personified?

The same interpretation is put forward in the introduction to the edition:

> If the interpretation I have put forward is correct, here the Mikaelite inserts the Trinity of Christianity into a Gnostic theogony. This starts with two Active Principles, which both couple with a female Being. She gives birth the same night to a second female Being, which is born already pregnant and gives birth to Three sons. The Mother gives these sons different names but they are united in a single Person.[163]

---

[163] Ibid., pp. XI–XII.

This passage on the mystery of the Trinity is unquestionably the part of the opuscula that lends itself most readily to an interpretation of Gnostic character. Though open to similar interpretations, the passage from *The Ship of the Soul*[164] presents fewer footholds and its ambiguity is in any case such as to make them far less secure. What are the characteristics of the passage on the Trinity that make it susceptible of a Gnostic interpretation? There are actually only two: 1) the metaphor of the two principles that possess the honorable girl (images of sexual violence and illegitimate birth are recurrent in all the Gnostic cosmologies); 2) the interpretation of the different figures taking part in the cosmology as emanations. The impression thus emerges from this interpretation that the three figures of the Trinity are in turn emanations, which fits perfectly into a Gnostic cosmological model.

7.3 The Debate on the Gnostic Interpretation of the Supposedly Mikaelite Opuscula

The above interpretation is criticized and an alternative reading is put forward by Father Agostino Tedla in the work referred to above, where we find the following:

> As stated above, the author invites to us to solve the riddle. "Just answer this little question, he says, … Come on, tell us, what is the essence of the birth of that (daughter)?"

> Here is the answer to the riddle. The two things that enter are *food* and *drink*, or more specifically *bread* and *wine*, with an obvious allusion, as a point of departure, to Psalm 103, verse 15: […] *vinum laetificat cor hominum … panis roborat fortitudinem hominum.*

> The house is the *stomach*, the door is the *mouth*, the knocker with a unique sound making known the will of the speaker is the *tongue*, the concupiscence of the warmth of the house is the *heat* of the *stomach*. Those that enter possess a daughter with no delay, meaning that the food ingested immediately produces *strength*, called a daughter of honorable charm, etc., forbidden in beauty by her parents, meaning that the strength produced out of foodstuffs is different from them because it

---

[164] Ibid., pp. 193-96.

is immaterial while its parents are material. When the foods ingested through the mouth are eliminated the following day ("go to their homeland"), they leave by twice three doors, i.e. through the *eyes*, the *nostrils* and the *lower natural orifices* respectively in the form of *tears*, *mucus*, *urine* and *excrement*. The daughter born "that night" is already fit to become a mother and leaves by twice two doors, meaning that strength is expended through the *two legs* in walking and the *two hands* in work, "by wisdom of intelligence," meaning that, directed by intelligence, it is transformed into productive energy and generates the three sons that bear the following names: "Praised among the poor," meaning *food* in gheez በአዐ ; "Blessed among the rich," meaning *wealth* in gheez በዐለ ; "Glorified among the lofty in honor," meaning *stature* in gheez ለግለ ; In short, strength produces bread, wealth and honor by means of work under the guidance of intelligence. And if they are united, etc., the three sons, meaning that they በአዐ : በዐለ : and ለግለ : are distinct but since these three words are formed by the union of three letters በ : ለ : 0 : differently combined and pronounced, in their fundamental constitution they boil down to the same elements and thus form what is practically a single "person." Their mother, i.e. strength, is exhausted as soon as she has generated them and thus loses her original name.

Now, says the author in conclusion, I am not interested in the material parents, food and drink, i.e. bread and wine, or in the water that nourished the roots of the grain and the vines in the fields, but take strength alone as a term of reference to express the *Unity of God*, and the three brothers, distinct but having the same basis, i.e. the letters በ : ለ : 0 : to indicate the *Three Divine Persons*, who are distinct from one another but have *one and the same nature*, but eliminating from the Divine Persons the differences in praise, blessedness, and glory that exist between the three brothers.[165]

This interpretation is evidently antithetical to Cerulli's and has its own unquestionable appeal, especially for those familiar with the models of

---

[165] Agostino Tedla *A proposito di alcuni passi oscuri*, op. cit., pp. 221-22.

symbolism and metaphor typical of Ethiopian poetry and literature. The impression we have on reading the whole of the paper is, however, that in his attempt to shed light on the various obscure passages in the first tract—some of which are regarded by Cerulli as affording glimpses of the author's true convictions and of Gnostic influences—Father Agostino has concentrated too much on these "riddles" and sometimes lost sight of their meaning in the argument sequentially developed in the theological treatise. In particular, on reading Cerulli's edition and Father Agostino's explanations side by side, we are unfortunately aware at times that the latter sometimes channels his unquestionable acumen too narrowly into the search for scriptural references[166] and the "keys" to metaphors constructed on the "wax and gold" model,[167] and fails to grasp at least part of the spiritual and theological meaning of the passages interpreted.[168]

This is, however, not really sufficient. It should be added that it is precisely due to the solutions put forward by Father Agostino that we now realize that the *Explanation of the Divinity* is even more complex than previously thought and requires the same degree of attention and patience in the search for different meanings and levels of interpretation as the works of Dante Alighieri.[169] In other words, his paper opens up a space of interpretation from which other avenues of investigation and levels of meaning can be glimpsed, not least because in some cases his indisputably valid and credible hypotheses do not rule out the interpretations suggested by Cerulli.[170]

---

[166] For example, in the commentary on the passage of the "Six Towers," ibid., p. 225.

[167] As happens in the interpretation of the passage identied by Cerulli as a Gnostic cosmology.

[168] An example of this is the interpretation of the "Six Towers" passage, which is quoted in the essay in the appendix devoted exclusively to Gnostic elements in the "Mikaelite" opuscula. As explained below, the author has preferred to avoid long quotations and interpretive analyses of the texts during the general exposition of the subject addressed so as to maintain its accessibility to the general reader. For this reason, the more complex investigation carried out on these tracts is published separately. Readers wishing to examine the original texts of Cerulli and Father Agostino are referred to Enrico Cerulli *Scritti Teologici Etiopici dei secoli XVI-XVII – Tre opuscoli dei Mikaeliti*, op. cit., pp. 210-11, and Agostino Tedla, "A proposito di alcuni passi oscuri negli Scritti teologici etiopici pubblicati da E. Cerulli," op. cit., pp. 225-26.

[169] In Dante, as is known, there are four meanings of the Scriptures, literal, allegorical, moral, and anagogical (see the *Convivio*). This idea of the four categories of scriptural interpretation was, however, widespread throughout the Christian world in medieval times.

[170] This is clearly evident in the interpretation of the passage on the "Six Towers," to which reference has just been made in a note.

Let us now return to the passage quoted above. When read side by side with the text published by Cerulli, Father Agostino's interpretation leaves various questions still open and does not fit in perfectly with the argument subsequently developed, especially the text's specific reference to the three persons of the Trinity. He appears to have lost sight of the overall meaning in concentrating on the riddle. If it is true that "strength" stands for unity born out plurality, i.e. out of "bread and wine," it is equally true that this interpretation appears reductive and lacking in richness, as we shall see.

At the same time, Piovanelli's interpretation rests precisely on Father Agostino's reading of the same passage:

> In truth, a wholly Ethiopian cultural sensitivity was required in order to solve this mystery, and it is solely thanks to perspicacity of Father Agostino Tedla that the wax of literal interpretation has finally melted to reveal the precious gold of the hidden meaning. Because the two "things" are nothing other than bread and wine, which go through the mouth and enter the stomach, where they give birth to strength. And when this leaves through the hands and feet in work, it produces food, wealth, and honor. Strength thus becomes the symbol of the unity of the godhead, while its three sons represent the Father, the Son, and the Holy Spirit. There is a difference in scale because, with respect to the physiological phenomenon used as a term of comparison, the human intelligence must confine itself to accepting the mystery of the Trinity with no possibility whatsoever of knowing its nature and origins. And those who claim otherwise have far too high an opinion of their capacities. If they are incapable of solving a simple riddle, how can they ever understand the essence of divinity?[171]

Piovanelli's essay also gives rise to various doubts, however, as briefly listed below.

- Father Agostino's interpretive model does not answer all the questions, as "strength" is a typical example of the metaphors that Cerulli interprets in a Gnostic-Manichaean sense. Like light and

---

[171] Pierluigi Piovanelli, "Connaissance de Dieu et Sagesse Humaine en Ethiopie," op. cit., p. 204.

honey,¹⁷² it is a metaphor of the "nebular" kind of divinity that the soul rejoins after death and thereby loses all trace of its identity, memory of earthly life, and name, swallowed up like a drop in the ocean or a ray of light in the sun.¹⁷³

- Piovanelli claims (p. 212) that the monophysite Egyptian church would not have hesitated to condemn the anthropomorphism of Zär'a Ya'əqob as heretical rather than views of the Mikaelites. Once again, this is not conclusive, as Cerulli and other scholars have repeatedly addressed the Gnosticizing elements present in the doctrines of the Egyptian Coptic church.¹⁷⁴

- At the same time, denial of the anthropomorphism of God is a constant feature of all the Gnostic texts that present a complete cosmogony in that they start with the first divinity, the origin of all the emanations, which is always described in the form of a negative theology (the "Unknown God" of Birger A. Pearson¹⁷⁵).

- In any case, as we shall see, some Gnostic characteristics do appear to be present in the opuscula, and rejection of the Gnostic interpretation of the passage on the mystery of the Trinity does not therefore necessarily mean denial of the presence of Gnostic influences, at least in the first and second tracts published in the first volume of Cerulli's *Scritti Teologici*.

- Finally, the conclusions drawn in Piovanelli's essay include two somewhat dubious assertions, namely that the literal interpretation

---

[172] Enrico Cerulli, *Spiegazione della Divinità* in *Scritti Teologici Etiopici dei secoli XVI-XVII – Tre opuscoli dei Mikaeliti*, op. cit., pp. 95-96 and note 1, p. 96.

[173] See *The Gospel of Thomas*, translated by Stephen Patterson and Marvin Meyer, logion 27, op. cit., and Gérard Colin, *Alexandre le Grand, héros chrétien en Ethiopie*, op. cit., pp. 145-47.

[174] Suffice it to point out here that in the tract *Le Dieci Questioni* (in Enrico Cerulli *Scritti Teologici Etiopici dei secoli XVI-XVII – La Storia dei Quattro Concili ed altri opuscoli monofisiti*, op. cit.), which displays connections with the Egyptian Coptic Church in various respects, we find both Christ's need to conceal his identity from the devil and an attenuated version of the idea of salvation for all. Both of these are indicative of previous Manichaean influences due to the dualism of the first and the cosmological need to rejoin the two sets of divine ranks in the second.

[175] Birger A. Pearson *Ancient Gnosticism*, op. cit., pp. 102 ff.

of writings prevails over the allegorical in Ethiopia,[176] and that Ethiopia was cut off from the "outside world" for centuries.[177] As scholars would hardly agree on these points, they do not appear to offer suitable support for the arguments put forward by Piovanelli as regards the tracts attributed by Cerulli to followers of the Mikaelite heretics.

7.4 The Limitations of the Above Interpretations

While our exposition of the critical arguments put forward by Father Agostino and Piovanelli has already indicated some limitations of their reading of the opuscula, Cerulli's own Gnostic interpretation also appears to be weakened if some of the general observations formulated by the former are taken into account and an attempt is made to examine the internal harmony of the first tract and its coherence with the other two published by Cerulli in the first volume of his *Scritti Teologici*. In other words, the acceptance of Cerulli's interpretive hypothesis means addressing the text on the following assumptions:

- The intentional obscurity of certain passages is the way devised by the author to mask his true beliefs and hide them in a textual labyrinth that therefore consists of some "sincere" parts and others serving only to feign orthodox persuasions.
- The "Mikaelite" opuscula, and the first in particular, are thus a sort of jigsaw puzzle of theories and formulations that are not always coherent, and the reader must therefore be able to distinguish the sincere or true parts from those serving to feign orthodox persuasions.
- Behind this attitude and model of reading, the present author glimpses the professional approach of those accustomed to dealing with the earliest Gnostic texts. As we know, these circulated also in

---

[176] Suffice it to mention the *Book of the Mysteries of Heaven and Earth*, discussed in the previous chapter, which dates from the second half of the 15th century and constitutes evident proof to the contrary.

[177] This assertion, based largely on the lack of any evidence of translations of works into Ge'ez in the period from the 7th century to the 13th, is open to the objection that this in itself is not sufficient to demonstrate the absence of cultural exchanges, the existence of which appears on the contrary to be established by historical studies. Translations may not have arisen from these exchanges or may indeed simply have been lost.

Christian communities and were presented as "further revelations," thus generating great doctrinal confusion. With a view to the gradual introduction of Gnostic ideas into Christian communities, these texts were often interpolated into canonical Christian writings or inserted into narrative frameworks recognized by the church. This academic approach obviously makes sense, however, in addressing texts produced in a situation of doctrinal uncertainty, when the canon of writings and the credo were still to be established.

- In the historical period and situation in which the "Mikaelite" tracts were composed, as described by Cerulli himself, the doctrinal framework was instead fully established. The Mikaelites had already been condemned as heretics and a major theological battle was under way against the Roman Catholics. In seeking to rally its forces against the common enemy, the Ethiopian church reorganized its own ranks and prepared its weapons for the impending fray. In this case, the preparation of weapons means that various components of the Ethiopian church produced texts for use in the debate against Catholic propaganda. In such a situation, one wonders what sense it could possibly make to produce ambiguous texts at variance with established doctrine and open to reiterated charges of heresy. If such doubts are legitimate in abstract terms, they become all the more so on examining the texts themselves and seeing that they profess not only perfect allegiance to the Fathers of the Church but also, in some passages, to doctrines that flatly contradict Cerulli's interpretation, e.g. the repeated references to the Virgin Mary, Mother of God, in the first tract.[178] If Cerulli's interpretation were correct, such references could have been simply avoided.

- Moreover, as regards the logic of its theological arguments, the text appears to be perfectly consistent except—paradoxically enough—for the need to solve the "riddles" put forward.

- Given the above, it appears to us that Cerulli's arguments are less consistent than those developed, despite their limitations, by Father Agostino, which are exemplified below in two short quotations:

---

[178] Enrico Cerulli, *Scritti Teologici Etiopici dei secoli XVI-XVII – Tre opuscoli dei Mikaeliti*, op. cit., pp. 82, 104 and 116.

Moreover, our author's style seems to be intentionally obscure, not through any fear of being discovered by his adversaries or in order to join their ranks more easily "in the discussion under way with the Catholic missionaries [...] and take advantage of the opportunity to present the essential points of his doctrine" [...] as Cerulli suggests. The author is in fact decidedly clear and explicit in his assertions from the very outset and does nothing to mask them in any part of the work. It is rather out of personal taste that he delights in the constant accumulation of never-ending figures of speech, images, symbols, comparisons, metaphors, parables, and allegories of an original and unusual nature. He does so above all, as we shall see, in order to demonstrate one of his primary assertions, namely the weakness of the human mind with respect to the infinite Being. He therefore sets his adversaries authentic riddles in order to confound them and induce them to recognize the limitations of their intellect as regards the knowledge of God.[179]

My conclusions can already be stated. There are no "Active Principles," "emanationist theogonies" or "Gnosticism" in these writings, There are simply riddles presented in the customary form of "gold" beneath a thick coat of "wax." In any case, the Gnostic interpretation of these texts is evidently at variance and incompatible with the completely orthodox doctrine—apart from the known differences between the Ethiopian and Roman churches over Christology and the procession of the Holy Spirit—clearly presented in the tracts in question.[180]

While Father Agostino's arguments have their own unquestionable logical coherence and succeed in offering elements to cast doubt on Cerulli's interpretation, they fail to do full justice to the opuscula, which present numerous new and original characteristics in the sphere of Ethiopian literature in general and the Ethiopian literature of their time in particular.

---

[179] Agostino Tedla, "A proposito di alcuni passi oscuri negli Scritti teologici etiopici pubblicati da E. Cerulli," op. cit., pp. 218-19.

[180] Ibid.

7.5 The Need for a New Interpretation

In view of the productive disorientation generated by the reflections outlined above, the present writer has attempted to develop a new interpretation of the passage on the mystery of the Trinity. This hypothesis has, however, no place in the exposition presented here, which has been primarily aimed at the general reader so far. Any attempt to explain its process of development would involve comparing and contrasting long quotations in search of textual correspondences and similarities within the first tract and between all three as well as precise recurrent symbols. As all this is incompatible with the purposes of the present work, we shall confine ourselves to presenting a brief summary of the results of the investigation undertaken and the proposed interpretation. More knowledgeable readers interested in pursuing the literary and philosophical analysis of the opuscula in greater depth will instead find in the appendix an essay making it possible to follow the author's research on the "Mikaelite" tracts almost step by step.[181]

This investigation is based in particular on analysis of the following: the passage on the mystery of the Trinity quoted above and the pages that follow it until the end of the first tract,[182] the parable on the allegorical interpretation of the Scriptures,[183] and the "pantheist cosmology" of the earth found in the opening pages of the tract.[184] Consideration of the different passages, the symbologies they present, and the logical processes to which these different symbologies are subjected appears to reveal a complex metaphor regarding the relationship established between the Scriptures and their interpreter. In other words, the passage regarded by Cerulli as a "Gnostic cosmology" would actually be an allegorical description of how the process of interpreting the Scriptures develops. On this view, the "two principles" that enter the house are the senses and the intellect, the faculties that man uses in order to know, which are examined in the tract in the pages before the passage on the mystery of the Trinity. The "house" they enter is the Scriptures. The possession of the girl "without

---

[181] See *The "Mikaelite" Opuscula Published by Cerulli and the Hypothesized Gnostic Influences* in the appendix below.

[182] Enrico Cerulli, *Scritti Teologici Etiopici dei secoli XVI-XVII – Tre opuscoli dei Mikaeliti*, op. cit., pp. 146-52.

[183] Ibid., pp. 112-13.

[184] Ibid., pp. 67-73.

waiting" is a metaphor of rash and hasty endeavor, possibly of the literal interpretation of the Scriptures, but in any case of an effort incapable of distinguishing "the months of the seasons of the divine Scripture,"[185] i.e. one that does not allow time for ripening and a gradual approach to the divine truths. Everything that comes after this in the subsequent development of the metaphor is a symbolic description of the sterility of this process, which can only lead to a bogus "appropriation" of truth grounded on the attribution of names. The "Mikaelite" author denies, however, the cognitive value of these denominations because "we will know them with our thought without feeling or reaching their foundation, which is far away from any interpretation and sublime to speak of. Because prior to their being perceptible is their not being *such* …"[186]

Shortly after the passage on the mystery of the Trinity quoted above, we find some of the passages that prompted Cerulli to see a relationship between the opuscula and the Sabellian views referred to by Giyorgis of Sägla, and to develop his interpretation in a Gnostic light:

> **If we know it now, we call it with many names, because they were born for us on the foundation after the form of the body of the creatures was born**. And if we say "three persons," *we do not mean* that it is like Abraham, who *precedes* Isaac by a hundred years, and Isaac, who precedes Jacob by a certain amount of time. This is not what we mean to say. Like Adam, who *alone* existed at one time, these *persons of the Trinity* instead exist in parity and in union. **Their names did not come after them but exist like them *ab initio*. And their persons are called names and their names are called persons. As St Gregory Thaumaturgus said in his first homily on the Trinity**:

> "Know that every thing is of the three things that are names, i.e. substance, name and genus. We speak, *for example*, of (man) servant and steward: man by nature, servant by condition and steward by name. We also speak of the Father, Son, and Holy Spirit, and these, however, are not names subsequently adopted by them but themselves the persons. **"Man" is not a name but signifies *human* nature, because each man *then* has *his own individual* name**, differing from one to another, for example

---

[185] Ibid., p. 210.

[186] Ibid., p. 146.

Adam, Abraham, Isaac, and Jacob; these are their names. **But the hypostases of God are *themselves* the names, and the names are *themselves* the hypostases,** because the interpretation of hypostases is persons that are certain, existing in their own right, perfect in appearance and image. And these certain names are called the Trinity, being one essence and three persons and one divinity."[187]

These few short lines encapsulate the thinking of the author of the tract, the formulations that caused Cerulli to think that he was a Mikaelite, and that Mikaelite was akin to Sabellian. As we continue in the reading, however, we realize immediately that the above is not the exposition of a new metaphysics but rather the basis for the umpteenth and perhaps the most forthright assertion of the unknowability of God:

What shall we say from now on? Does the seed perhaps grow from the sea to produce crops for the fool who sowed it *there in the sea*? Or does the plant grow that was planted on the rock and burned by torrid fire at the roots while it was *also* far from the passing of water? Does hunger perhaps come in the midst of satiety or thirst in the midst of drinkers? Are there not perhaps those who do not know the distinction of the month of harvests; *and* for their laziness, proud people in misery for the plague of famine, kept to their beds by *famine* and unable to move just as the ulcerated are kept to their *beds* by *plague*? Just so, if we have sown seeds of thought in the deep sea of Divinity, going beyond the soil of humility, going beyond the fields of *our* boundaries, we too will remain not only with no fruits but without any sprouting of leaves. Brothers, let us from now on place limits on our discourse so as not to ruin ourselves, and let us measure the limits of our discourse so as not to perish. Let us say with St Paul: "O the depth of the riches both of the wisdom and the knowledge of God," the love of the Lord. And Isaiah said: "Who hath measured the waters in the hollow of his hand, and meted out heaven with the span?" There is none equal to the Lord. And who is like Him? And we the orthodox, without falsehood or deceit, believe in these testimonies.[188]

---

[187] Ibid., pp. 146–47.

[188] Ibid., pp. 147–48.

These two quotations could appear to clash with one another but do not in actual fact as long as the first is interpreted not as a metaphysical proposition but rather as the exposition of the birth of the concept in man—the idea of the Trinity—and therefore in a gnoseological perspective. The first quotation begins in fact with these words: "If we know it now, we call it with many names, because they were born for us on the foundation after the form of the body of the creatures was born." This is equivalent to saying that man can only know God in this way, through metaphors and imprecise words drawn from his own human experience. Moreover, with respect to the next phrase, for this reason we say "persons," but this name of "persons" was coined by man and in this sense, in the human understanding, in the idea of God that man has formed for himself: "Their names did not come after them but exist like them *ab initio*. And their persons are called names and their names are called persons." On close rereading, the entire passage always proves to refer to *interpretation*, i.e. to the idea of God that man has formed for himself, and not to the divine truths; to the names that we give to the divine truths and not to the divinity itself. The few pages that follow the above passages and conclude the tract contain nothing to suggest that this analysis is in any way inconsistent or flawed.

In our opinion, the above interpretation restores solid logical coherence to the sequential exposition of the first tract and also makes it possible to glimpse its connection with the other two identified by Cerulli as Mikaelite.

To conclude, we can say that the authors of the three "Mikaelite" opuscula wrote texts that, in addition to urging an allegorical interpretation of the Scriptures, in turn produce and offer the reader precise examples of texts to be interpreted allegorically, almost as a preliminary exercise before embarking on the Scriptures, or perhaps as a kind of challenge, a way of putting adversaries to the test.

7.6 The Originality of the Investigation Carried Out in the "Mikaelite" Opuscula

In summarizing and presenting the conclusions of his analysis and refutation of the Gnostic interpretation of the opuscula, Father Agostino points out that something about the tracts remains unresolved in the sense that their reading reveals characteristics alien to the Ethiopian cultural context of the time. He observes that the "Mikaelite" opuscula actually display the influence of the Catholic missionaries in various respects[189] and adds: "The broad use of psychological arguments, something truly unusual in the traditional schools, also suggests if not direct dependency, at least a certain influence of the missionaries."[190] By "psychological arguments" Father Agostino may have meant all the passages examined in the first tract that, if understood in the literal sense, oblige us to attribute God with wholly human feelings like jealousy, envy, desire for vengeance, and repentance (interpretations which are indeed abundantly present in the Midrash). Alternatively, he may have referred to the precise examination of the limitations of the human cognitive faculties, mentioned also in the monophysite tracts published by Cerulli in the second volume of his *Scritti Teologici Etiopici dei Secoli XVI-XVII* but developed in far greater depth in the opuscula. In short, Father Agostino thought that the opuscula had been at least partially influenced in their composition by the presence of Jesuit missionaries in Ethiopia, something strongly and clearly opposed in the second and third tracts, as mentioned above. It therefore appears that the influence referred to by Father Agostino derived from a combination of circumstances that forced some members of the Ethiopian Church to take the following steps:

- to formulate their doctrinal views in full and explicit terms for use in debate;
- to enter into contact with different schools of thought during the debates and also through a reading of the theological works that the Jesuit missionaries unquestionably took with them to Ethiopia;
- to enter into contact with different schools of thought when events in Ethiopia forced many orthodox members of the church to take refuge in Alexandria, where they probably continued their polemics in writings addressed to the Ethiopian rulers.

Attention should be drawn to another feature of the opuscula that also appears to be new, namely a "linguistic" approach to the Trinity, whereby the metaphysical aspect of the question is deliberately distinguished from the gnoseological. The real nature of the Trinity is an unknowable and unattainable truth. Any human attempt to approach some knowledge of the divine must be undertaken in full awareness that it can never expect to attain this truth. The endeavor therefore becomes a

---

[189] Agostino Tedla, "A proposito di alcuni passi oscuri negli Scritti teologici etiopici pubblicati da E. Cerulli," op. cit., p. 241.

[190] Ibid.

reflection on the human instruments of language and on the limitations of the human faculties of perception and imagination in order to try to speak of that transcendent reality (or perhaps rather "that we might not be altogether silent," as St Augustine put it). The "Mikaelite" opuscula display perfect awareness that the problem is linguistic, as in the following passage already quoted above:

> "Know that every thing is of the three things that are names, i.e. substance, name and genus. We speak, *for example*, of (man) servant and steward: man by nature, servant by condition and steward by name. We also speak of the Father, Son, and Holy Spirit, and these, however, are not names subsequently adopted by them but themselves the persons. **"Man" is not a name but signifies** human **nature, because each man** then **has** his own individual **name**, differing from one to another, for example Adam, Abraham, Isaac, and Jacob; these are their names. **But the hypostases of God are** themselves **the names, and the names are** themselves **the hypostases,** because the interpretation of hypostases is persons that are certain, existing in their own right, perfect in appearance and image. And these certain names are called the Trinity, being one essence and three persons and one divinity."[191]

It is clear that the author is fully aware of the difference between species, individual, and name, between category, substance, and attribute, as expressed in the following passage from Abelard:

> For example, this man is a substance, a body, an animate and sensitive being, i.e. a "rational, mortal animal," that is to say a man, and he can be white and curly haired, can be a subject and receive other accidents. And while the substance, body, and animate being are identical in him according to number and essence, they are nevertheless different from one another according to their properties and must be determined on the basis of these with different definitions. One is proper to substance, another to the body or the other things, and one is called state of substance, another of the body or the other things.
>
> In this way it is possible to attribute to individual things innumerable characteristics differing from one another in terms

---

[191] Enrico Cerulli *Scritti Teologici Etiopici dei Secoli XVI-XVII – I – Tre Opuscoli dei Mikaeliti*, op. cit., pp. 146-47.

of properties while the essence remains identical. Why is it therefore any wonder that different properties should be found in God in terms of which the three persons can be distinguished while the divine essence remains one? In a man. who is substance and body at the same time, or the other individual things stated previously [...] one is the property of the substance, another the property of the body and the other things, and another the property of the father and the son. In God, in the same way, even though the same essence is Father, Son and Holy Spirit, one is the property of the Father, whereby it generates, another the property of the Son, whereby it is generated, and another the property of the Holy Spirit, whereby it proceeds.[192]

The difference in the formulations is just as strong as the similarity between their content. Every essence, while remaining one and the same, has different properties and states. God can therefore be one in essence and trine in the relational identity between the different figures. The names are the persons and the persons are the names. While the use of the concepts is obviously not identical, there are deep similarities in the understanding of the problem. The investigation carried out appears to reveal definite similarities between the "Mikaelite" opuscula and the studies of European theologians, from St Augustine of Hippo to Thomas Aquinas, who recast the whole of previous theological speculation in his *Summa Theologiae*.

7.7 Doubts as to the Gnostic Interpretation of Opuscula

On the basis of the foregoing discussion, it appears possible to state that Cerulli's interpretation has lost much of its importance because the critical observations of Father Agostino and his alternative solution of the "riddles" as well as the hypothesis outlined here are capable of accounting for all the characteristics present in these writings that leave the reader surprised or incredulous on first reading.

At the same time, it is true that despite this analysis, some Gnosticizing elements still appear to be present in the tracts. We refer in particular to the figures of speech or comparisons that recall the concept

---

[192] M. Parodi, M. Rossini (eds.), *Fra le due rupi, La logica della trinità nella discussione tra Roscellino, Anselmo e Abelardo*, Milan, 2000, pp. 220-21.

of a "nebular" divinity, i.e. one that will absorb the individual souls into itself, as part of itself, at the end of time to create a whole no longer susceptible of division or differentiation. The individual souls will lose all memory of earthly life, all specific determination of gender, human history, and so on, and any other characteristic making them different and unique. Among the various allusions of this kind present in the opuscula, attention can be drawn to the particularly effective comparison drawn in the first between the persons of the Trinity and honey in a quotation from Athanasius of Alexandria:

> They (*the persons of the Trinity*) are neither comprehensible nor knowable as creatures are, neither comparable nor visible, just as honey is not visible while it is *still* with the things from which it is born, *i.e.* in the wide open countryside, on the trees and in the grass, distributed in the individual flowers, in the bitter and the sweet. But now come the tricksters to show us with their wisdom the corporeal form of the *floral species* in which the taste of the goodness of the Creator was mixed. But the wise *bee instead*, when it gathers the *essences of the flowers* through patient toil, from far and near, makes a body *of those essences* (*that is, the honey*) so that it might be visible. On the contrary, *once the honey has been made*, it is no longer possible for *the bee* to turn it *once again* into its *different* essences. Such is divinity. While it is diffused everywhere, it cannot be seen, just as it is impossible to return the honey of which we have spoken to the individual flowers.[193]

The reference that comes immediately to mind is the Manichaean fragments of light dispersed in matter, which must be distilled in order to join together once again, travelling in the vessels of the sun and the moon with the king of light. Closer reflection suggests, however, that these metaphors too could fall within the conception of divinity as "ineffable mystery," which moreover informs the long "journey in search of the knowledge of God" found in the first of the opuscula and published by Cerulli also in his *Letteratura Etiopica*.[194] This is an idea of divinity that is

---

[193] Enrico Cerulli, *Scritti Teologici Etiopici dei secoli XVI-XVII – Tre opuscoli dei Mikaeliti*, op. cit., p. 95.

[194] Enrico Cerulli, *La Letteratura Etiopica*, Florence-Milan, 1968, pp. 147-49; also in *Scritti Teologici Etiopici dei secoli XVI-XVII – Tre opuscoli dei Mikaeliti*, op. cit., pp. 125-28. The passage is also quoted here in the appendix.

always expressed through metaphors of indiscernibility (like the nectar of the different flowers in honey), infinity, and incalculability. While these are unquestionably characteristics also of the primal Gnostic divinity, the conception had also become an integral part of the thinking of some schools of Christian mysticism.

Other apparently Gnosticizing characteristics, albeit of lesser importance, include the figure of the serpent in the symbolic narrative on erroneous interpretation of the Scriptures in the *Ship of the Soul*,[195] which immediately recalls the identification of the serpent in Genesis with Christ by some Gnostic sects.[196] Anyone wishing to challenge this reference would do well to consider the ambiguous role of this serpent, which appears to act in full accordance with the will of God (something that is moreover also suggested for "Evil" in the *Pseudo-Clementine Homilies*).

Another is found in the *Safe Haven*, which again presents the "figure" of Christ intent on concealing Himself and His work from Satan.[197] This figure, which we have already found in the *Ascension of Isaiah*, also appears in the opuscula contained in the second volume of Cerulli's *Scritti Teologici*. While it obviously suggests a dualistic conception of the world, such beliefs were in any case widely held by Egyptian Coptic Christians and may be no more than surviving remnants of ancient narratives of Manichaean origin.

On the whole, however, these are aspects of lesser importance. On the one hand, they prompt reflection on the Gnosticizing characteristics present, according to Cerulli, in Egyptian Coptic Christianity. On the other, they remind us that the *Exposition of the Divinity* is in any case an intentionally provocative text, as attested for example by the above-

---

[195] Enrico Cerulli, *Scritti Teologici Etiopici dei secoli XVI-XVII – Tre opuscoli dei Mikaeliti*, op. cit., p. 210. See also the appendix below for the entire passage on the erroneous interpretation of the Scriptures.

[196] Birger A. Pearson, *Ancient Gnosticism*, op. cit. p. 119.

[197] "Il Porto Sicuro," in Enrico Cerulli, *Scritti Teologici Etiopici dei secoli XVI-XVII – Tre opuscoli dei Mikaeliti*, op. cit., p. 286.

mentioned figure of the serpent and the marked ambiguities also with apparent sexual references.[198]

7.8 A Summary of the Gnostic Elements in the "Mikaelite" Opuscula Published by Cerulli

In concluding our examination of the supposedly Gnostic elements in the "Mikaelite" opuscula published by Cerulli in 1958, we shall start by referring readers to the analysis developed in the appendix, which is far more complex but also far more precise and detailed.

As regards the Gnostic elements identified by Cerulli on the basis of his interpretation of some passages as symbolic formulations presupposing a doctrine of emanations, this is regarded as questionable by various scholars, as we have seen, and the present author has also found it evidently wanting as an explanation of the overall meaning of the opuscula. Cerulli probably saw the fact that Zär'a Ya'əqob required various metropolitans to condemn the Mikaelite doctrines explicitly as evidence of a link between these doctrines and Alexandria. His awareness of the major role played by Alexandria in the production and dissemination of Gnostic doctrines then probably led him to discern a link with Gnosticism in the Mikaelite doctrines. His reading of the opuscula, with their numerous ambiguities, gave him an opportunity to bring all these elements together and attribute the tracts to late followers of the Mikaelite movement. This attribution in 1958 was also facilitated by the scarcity of reliable sources on Gnostic thought. The recent publications of original Gnostic texts have instead shown that the characteristics present in the opuscula examined here do not appear to correspond to those either of Gnosticism or of Christian Gnosticism. On the contrary, some of them indeed demonstrate the opposite, such as the importance attached in the opuscula to the observation of nature,

---

[198] While mention has already been made of the metaphor of the rape of the girl in the passage examined above, ambiguous metaphors with possible sexual references are found in various parts of the three tracts. It may be worth recalling here that the Gnostics interpreted the words "And the Spirit of God moved upon the face of the waters" at the beginning of Genesis as a reference to Sophia wandering over the waters in shame and repentance of her actions (see Birger A. Pearson, *Ancient Gnosticism*, op. cit., pp. 111–12).

regarded instead by Gnostics as the realm of darkness and evil, and in any case as incapable of offering the observer any possibility of approaching the divine or an understanding thereof.

While some Gnostic elements can be discerned in the opuscula, they are in any case characteristics that we have already discovered in other works from the period of translations from the Arabic:

- A few allusions that bring to mind what is referred to above as "nebular divinity," which souls rejoin and thereby lose their individual identities;
- The "figure" of a Christ seeking to conceal Himself and His work from Satan, which suggests the possibility of Manichaean influences;
- The strange figure of a serpent in a parable, which recalls the Christ-serpent of some Gnostic sects.[199]

As these are, however, evidently no more than faint, ambiguous traces that can also be interpreted as related to other kinds of influence, the opuscula must be denied any original and important value as evidence of the presence of Gnosticism in Ethiopia. It further follows that we must deny the validity of any attempt to "work backward" on the basis of Cerulli's analysis and argue as follows: if it is certain that strong and unquestionable traces of Gnosticism emerge in Ethiopian literature during the presence of the Jesuits in Ethiopia, and if it is certain that these traces date back to the period of the Mikaelites in the 15th century, i.e. more than a hundred years earlier, then it is reasonable to suggest on the grounds of continuity that such influences may stretch back even further in time.

Our investigation has instead ruled out the presence of Gnosticism and cast doubt on the existence of Gnostic influences on the Mikaelites of the 15th century. We are therefore forced to narrow our horizons and state that the traces of Gnosticism discovered in Ethiopia are confined to those identified in the periods of translations from Greek and from Arabic. There are also some undatable traces, as discussed in the following chapter.

---

[199] The serpent-Christ that incited Adam and Eve to eat the forbidden fruit so as to make them aware of their divine nature.

8

SOME UNDATABLE SOURCES—TALISMANIC AND THAUMATURGICAL PRACTICES

The study as developed so far has focused on writings and traditions emerging in the history of Ethiopian literature and religion that appear to suggest Gnostic influences. If it is to be regarded as complete, however, it must also address some evidence of another kind that is much hazier in character and in any case undatable. This is why, even though the materials in question are closely related to the literary sources examined above, it has been decided to consider them in a separate section. We refer here to the studies carried out by Jacques Mercier[200] on some forms of popular religiosity and talismanic or thaumaturgical practices. Attention has already been drawn to the relationship between demonology and illness, which is present also in Gnosticism, during our examination of the *Book of Enoch* and the *Book of Mysteries of Heaven and Earth*. One evident logical consequence of this relationship is that any practice concerned with health therefore also involves exorcism. As seen above, this logical connection can also be found in the period of translations from Arabic.

While Jacques Mercier's studies cannot be summarized here, the following outline will help to understand the approach adopted by this scholar.

According to Mercier. the cult of *zars*, minor divinities or spirits through which it is possible to alter a person's health or circumstances of life, spread in Ethiopia during the 16th and 17th century. A *zar* is, however, also the shaman or the figure regarded in Ethiopia as the "horse" of the *zar*, i.e. the one through which the spirit speaks. The practices

---

[200] Jacques Mercier, *Le Roi Salomon et les maîtres du regard: art et médecine en Ethiopie*, Paris, 1994.

Talismanic symbol from an Ethiopian magic scroll. The eyes have the function of watching over and protecting against evil or even of attacking demons (Asmat Prayers [19th century], British Library, EAP286/1/1/38, https://eap.bl.uk/archive-file/EAP286-1-1-38, copyright Institute of Ethiopian Studies, Addis Abeba. The image is from the Endangered Archives Programme of the British Library, Ethiopian Manuscript Imaging Project [DOI:https://doi.org/10.15130/EAP286]). See also other images in the following pages

Some Undatable Sources—Talismanic and Thaumaturgical Practices

Talismanic symbol from an Ethiopian magic scroll (Asmat Prayers [19th century], British Library, EAP286/1/1/38, https://eap.bl.uk/archive-file/EAP286-1-1-38 copyright Institute of Ethiopian Studies, Addis Abeba. The image is from the Endangered Archives Programme of the British Library, Ethiopian Manuscript Imaging Project [DOI:https://doi.org/10.15130/EAP286]).

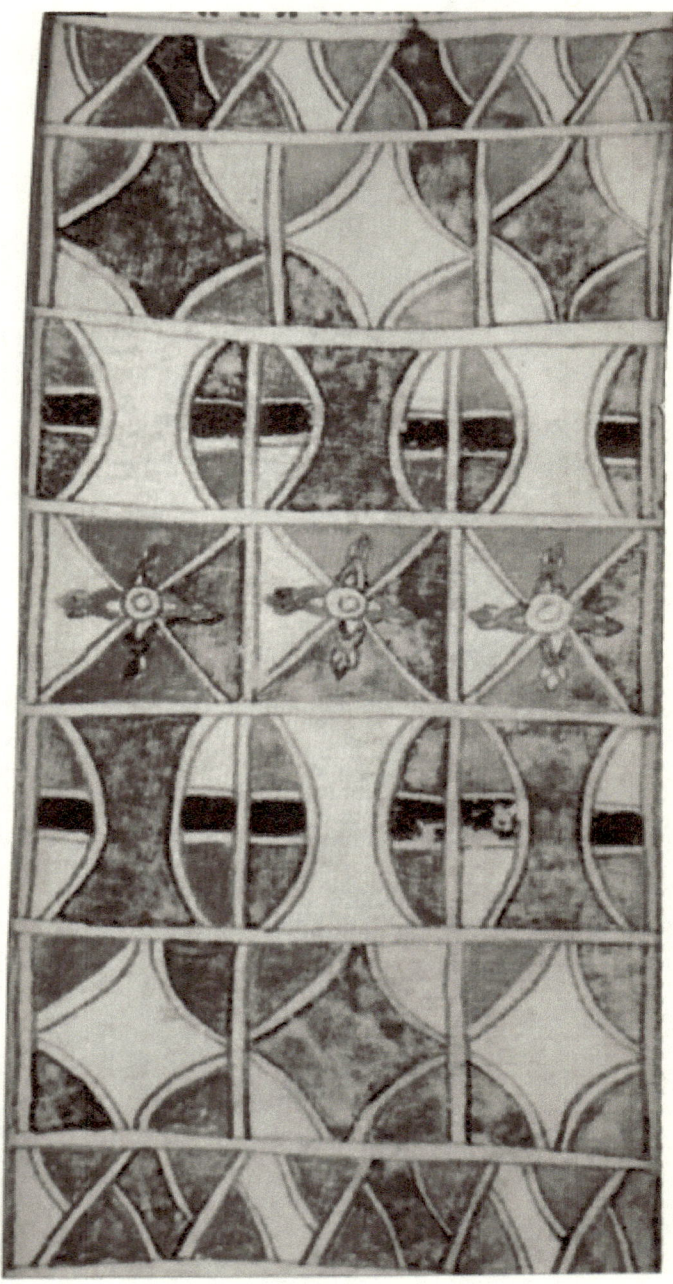

Talismanic symbol from an Ethiopian magic scroll (Asmat Prayers [19th century], British Library, EAP286/1/1/42, https://eap.bl.uk/archive-file/EAP286-1-1-42, copyright Institute of Ethiopian Studies, Addis Abeba. The image is from the Endangered Archives Programme of the British Library, Ethiopian Manuscript Imaging Project [DOI:https://doi.org/10.15130/EAP286]).

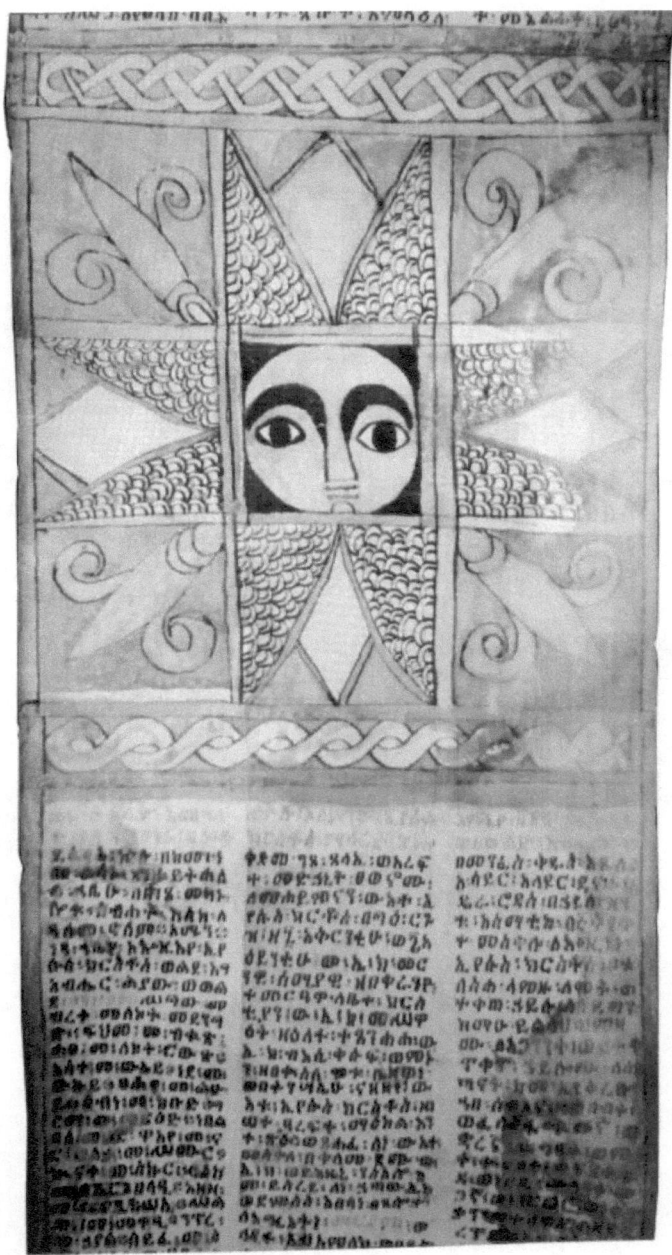

Talismanic symbol from an Ethiopian magic scroll (Asmat Prayers [19th century], British Library, EAP286/1/1/74, https://eap.bl.uk/archive-file/EAP286-1-1-74, copyright Institute of Ethiopian Studies, Addis Abeba. The image is from the Endangered Archives Programme of the British Library, Ethiopian Manuscript Imaging Project [DOI:https://doi.org/10.15130/EAP286]).

Talismanic symbol from an Ethiopian magic scroll (Asmat Prayers [19th century], British Library, EAP286/1/1/89, https://eap.bl.uk/archive-file/EAP286-1-1-89, copyright Institute of Ethiopian Studies, Addis Abeba. The image is from the Endangered Archives Programme of the British Library, Ethiopian Manuscript Imaging Project [DOI:https://doi.org/10.15130/EAP286]).

Talismanic symbol from an Ethiopian magic scroll (Asmat Prayers [19th century], British Library, EAP286/1/1/93, https://eap.bl.uk/archive-file/EAP286-1-1-93, copyright Institute of Ethiopian Studies, Addis Abeba. The image is from the Endangered Archives Programme of the British Library, Ethiopian Manuscript Imaging Project [DOI:https://doi.org/10.15130/EAP286]).

Talismanic symbol from an Ethiopian magic scroll (Asmat Prayers [19th century], British Library, EAP286/1/1/93, https://eap.bl.uk/archive-file/EAP286-1-1-93, copyright Institute of Ethiopian Studies, Addis Abeba. The image is from the Endangered Archives Programme of the British Library, Ethiopian Manuscript Imaging Project [DOI:https://doi.org/10.15130/EAP286]).

involving *zars* make no distinctions with regard to the religious identity of the person seeking aid. They are transversal and remain substantially the same for Christians, Muslims, and animists. The cult is thought to have spread through transits and exchanges with the Arabian peninsula, Sudan, Egypt, and Persia along the routes of the slave trade. It is, however, a cult of the type that absorbs the cultural beliefs and products of a region on penetrating it. As a result, on entering Ethiopia, its practices came to incorporate local beliefs and symbolic figures such as King Solomon, whose image often appears in the talismans produced.

This is clearly a marginal form of religiosity with respect to the official traditions and one that Christian priests were obviously not permitted to practice in Ethiopia. According to Mercier, however, esoteric practices closely resembling those of the *zars* and manifesting themselves in particular in the preparation of talismans were in fact developed and tolerated also within the sphere of Ethiopian Christianity. It should be pointed out that it is not clear whether the practices Mercier describes involve *zars* or *däbtärà*, figures of the Ethiopian Church performing these rites, or indeed whether he actually refers to both, given the great similarities between them. It is in any case not easy to verify Mercier's investigations, as these are practices of an esoteric character and perhaps dying out. In the Christian sphere, as noted above, the practices were forbidden to priests but performed by *däbtärà*, who were generally cantors or other figures of lesser rank in the Church. At the same time, however, the very word *däbtärà*, being derived from the Greek *diphtéra* meaning *skin, parchment* or *book*, alludes to knowledge, to a kind of revealed wisdom drawn from a book.

There are books of limited circulation providing information on the rules and rites involved. One of the practices involves mathematical calculations on a person's name in order to arrive at a number from 1 to 12 determining what would correspond in Europe to an astrological sign, i.e. the person's ruling planet. The *däbtärà* takes this as the starting point for investigations carried out with the aid of the book and also of a medium, generally a boy, through whom the spirits speak as he gazes into a mirror.[201] The *däbtärà* then interprets the medium's words and uses these "revelations" to create a talisman, generally a strip of leather marked with magical

---

[201] Esoteric practices involving the use of a mirror were also found in the Dionysian cults of ancient Greece.

symbols, letters of the alphabet and texts, and corresponding in length to the height of the person seeking help. Referred to by Mercier as *rouleaux magiques* or magical scrolls, these talismans developed over the years into an authentic form of art with its own recurrent symbols and iconographic language, as examined in his work. It may be useful to recall here that astrology is the basis of all the other rites involved in the magical practices examined above in the previous sections.

Even though the cult of the *zars* is fairly late, Mercier believes that the use of talismans in Ethiopia stretches back further (before the 14th century) and originally involved other divinities rather than *zars*. It should also be noted that similar talismans were already used in the Jewish sphere.[202]

As regards the origin of the books containing the wisdom of the magical scrolls, Mercier puts forward some hypotheses that cannot, however, be verified at present. He thus speaks of evident contacts with Jewish traditions and with some Egyptian and Greek schools of philosophy that subsequently developed into alchemy and other esoteric sciences born in the Mediterranean area in the 15th and 16th century. There is, however, no documentary evidence to support these claims, which are indeed developed by arguing backwards from the existence of such beliefs in the contemporary era that they therefore penetrated Ethiopia in some indeterminate period in the past and taking "affinity" or similarity as a criterion to identify the precedents. This is evidently a procedure susceptible of no verification whatsoever and we are therefore left to conclude once again in the case of these beliefs, as with our previous examination for other types of Gnostic influence, that it is impossible to ascertain the channels of penetration. At the same time, the existence of such channels is probable, as some of these beliefs—including the use of talismans and belief in intermediary divinities and the demonic causes of illness—are indications of possible, albeit not exclusive, links with Gnosticism.

It is in any case probable that practices similar to those described above did exist during the reign of Zär'a Ya'əqob and perhaps earlier, as the ruler proclaimed that names not mentioned in the Scriptures were demonic and forbade their use. Moreover, he also ordered the destruction of the collections of names compiled during the reign of his brother

---

[202] See the illustration of a Jewish talisman in James B. Pritchard (ed.), *Solomon & Sheba*, London, 1974, facing p. 72.

Yəshaq. Mercier argues that these facts are of importance because, in accordance with what is written above on the power of the name of God, the Ethiopian magical literature is essentially a science of names. The name, the true name of a thing, like the name of God, is a crucial instrument because knowledge of the same gives power over the thing itself. It was fairly common in Ethiopia not so long ago for people to conceal their Christian name so as to protect themselves against the possibility of being subjected to malevolent influence, because this is the name known to and recognized by God, and therefore the true name of the person, the uppercase Name of Gnosticism. The lists destroyed were probably thought to contain the names of intermediate divinities, spirits or demons, knowledge of which would confer the power to obtain anything from them.

This brief excursus on the studies of Jacques Mercier provides us with some additional information and above all reveals that many of the beliefs and practices of popular Ethiopian religiosity examined by him present characteristics similar to the magical or talismanic books discussed above, such as the *Testament of Solomon*, the *Seal of Solomon* in Arabic, the Arab-Muslim manuscript *The most brilliant light on the explanation of the most beautiful Names of God* and the *Ləfafä ṣədəq*. As already pointed out, these sources are undatable, meaning that they could belong to any of the historical periods examined here, and it is therefore impossible to determine any contacts or derivations of use for the purposes of historical research. At the same time, however, it should be noted that there are great similarities, e.g. between the uses to which the *Ləfafä ṣədə* and the magical scrolls were put, and that the scrolls could be regarded as more elementary forms of the same type of cult or ritual.

9

ANALYSIS OF THE SOURCES OF A POSSIBLE ETHIOPIAN GNOSTICISM

9.1 Components, Transits, and Intermediaries

The above chapter concludes our brief overview of the three historical periods during which Ethiopian culture produced texts apparently displaying Gnostic influences. The results of this excursus are in any case not to be regarded as definitive. If it is possible to use the formula introduced above suggesting the influence of Alexandrian Christianity, which presents marked Gnostic tendencies, and if it is even possible to speak of Gnostic influences *tout court*, the intermediary of these influences, which also constitutes their substance, remains wholly undetermined. If it is true that Gnostic influences are present in Ethiopia, they appear to manifest themselves at a distance of too many centuries with respect to the documented historical presence of Gnostic thought and the possibility of its direct transmission. There must therefore have been intermediaries of these transits that had probably—apart from a generic derivation from one component or another of Gnostic thought—already established their own autonomous status, a rationale historically grounded in the period in which they manifested themselves independently of the historical positioning of the Gnostic schools.

In other words, if Gnostic or Manichaean influences resurfaced repeatedly also in Europe,[203] they drew their meaning, credibility, and

---

[203] During the 20th century some scholars sought to identify in the romances of the Holy Grail and Parsifal the traces of a sequence of ancient symbols starting in pagan fertility rites

power of dissemination every time from the historical circumstances in which they developed, and these circumstances in turn found in ancient Gnostic texts (as in the case of the Cathars) or in new theories and writings based on earlier formulations, the reasons for this new exigency or the need to give expression to new expectations. For this reason it appears more correct to abandon generic reference to Gnostic influences present in Christianity and in the Ethiopian cultural fabric, and instead continue the investigation conducted above and extract the specific components defined above from the writings of the periods examined, breaking down the characteristics of Ethiopian Gnosticism in order to describe it better. This work, with its construction of logical and chronological aggregations, is already in fact a map of the sources of influence, which we shall endeavor to define below.

9.2 Judeo-Christian Influences in the Period of Translations from the Greek

Consideration of the sources of influence and the texts analyzed reveals a particular characteristic in the period of translations from Greek, namely the fact that all the works cited here as translated from Greek, as well as others translated in Ethiopia from the same language during the Aksumite period, have been identified by some scholars as Judeo-Christian. At the beginning of this study, in discussing the *Book of Enoch* and some Gnosticizing features identified therein, we suggested that the reason for their presence lies in the fact that Gnosticism was actually born as a Jewish heresy and that it finds one of its sources in the rebel movements that produced the Jewish apocalypses. As pointed out, however, by Maxime Rodinson, a scholar already mentioned above, the books of the Jewish apocalyptica[204] that entered Ethiopia, albeit in Christianized form,

---

and their contacts with Mithraism, and supposedly coming through Gnostic rituals and philosophy to influence Neoplatonism and then flow into British Christianity, out of which the narratives in question were born. These do in fact present highly ambiguous forms of Christian symbolism that sometimes appear to allude to pagan symbols. See Jessie L. Weston, *From Ritual to Romance*, New York, 1957.

[204] Or works deeply influenced by the apocalyptica.

are numerous and include not only the *Book of Enoch* but also the *Book of Jubilees*, *2 Esdras*, the *Ascension of Isaiah* and the *Shepherd of Hermas* as well as others not mentioned in our study. These works, which share a number of distinctive features, have been grouped together under the heading "Judeo-Christian." Their most important characteristics are outlined below.

- They are visionary works that speak of journeys to heaven and revelations received directly from God or angels. In this sense, they fall immediately within the tradition of Jewish apocalypses.

- They are works in which Christ is often identified in an anomalous way through allusions or locutions, and from which unorthodox conceptions of the Trinity emerge including Adoptionism, i.e. the belief that Christ was born a man but adopted by God as His son at the baptism. The figure of Christ can also be either completely absent or present but devoid of any bodily qualities.

- Angels are assigned a particularly important role. In some cases they become the actual creators of the world and Satan's rebellion leads to the birth of what are sometimes referred to as the "two kingdoms."[205]

- There is a radical rejection of sex, the flesh, and sometimes also of meat as food.

- They present a rich demonology and demons play an important part in the functioning of the cosmos below the heaven of the fixed stars.

The objection has been raised that during the period when these works were written—or Christianized in the case of those produced in the Jewish sphere and then subjected to interpolation by Christian copyists—the canon of the Christian creed (the dogmas defined by the early councils) had still to be established, and disagreement and divergence were somewhat frequent over matters on which Christians of the different faiths appear to have no doubts today. In any case, drawing upon the analysis of Judeo-Christianity formulated by Jean

---

[205] See the *Pseudo-Clementine Homilies*, another Judeo-Christian text, albeit not actually an apocalypse.

Daniélou,[206] we realize that while this concept, regarded as too imprecise by some scholars, cannot be used for the precise identification of a set of works or the precise definition of the social group thought to have produced them, it can serve as a historical category of research for application to the period of the first centuries immediately after the birth of Christianity: a time when no boundaries had yet been drawn between Christianity and Judaism; when heresy and orthodoxy coexisted without excluding one another; when writings later to be condemned were still regarded as "other revelations"; and when—most importantly of all for our purposes—Gnosticism had not yet been condemned or the condemnation had not yet produced its effects.

The usefulness of this historical category of research lies in the fact that a marked presence in Ethiopia of texts classified by Daniélou as Judeo-Christian could effectively account for the existence of Gnostic influences that can otherwise prove difficult to understand and explain. In this case, they would evidently not stem from Gnosticism in the strict sense but from Christian texts—some of which very ancient and therefore regarded as highly authoritative—that were subsequently not always accepted into the canon (e.g. the *Book of Jubilees* and the *Book of Enoch*, which are canonical in Ethiopia but not in Roman Catholicism) and that possess characteristics regarded as heterodox by the Church, probably because they attest to beliefs held in periods before the dogmas were established. Examples include the alteration of roles in the Trinity; a conception of Christ as spirit rather than flesh; Adoptionism; the connection between demonology and astrology, with demons seen as divinities or guardians of the different heavens and attributed with powers over natural phenomena and human illnesses; the role of Wisdom; and the messianic expectation of social revolution. Further consequences of all this are accentuated dualism and the attribution of special roles to angels too.

The other characteristic peculiar to Judeo-Christianity as defined by Daniélou is an attempt to establish solid continuity between the Old and the New Testament, and hence a tendency to interpret the former in allegorical terms as foreshadowing or heralding what was to be told in the Gospels. This does not appear to be a dominant feature in Ethiopia during the period of translations from Greek, however, and will therefore be examined in the context of the later phase of Jewish influences.

---

[206] Jean Daniélou, *Théologie du Judéo-Christianisme*, Histoire des doctrines chrétiennes avant Nicée, vol 1, Tournai, Desclée, 1958. English translation: *The Theology of Jewish Christianity*, trans. and ed. by John A Baker, London, Darton, Longman and Todd, 1964.

9.3 Gnostic Influences on Egyptian Coptic Christianity

This source of influence comes directly from Egypt and is unquestionably characterized by the Gnostic influences on Egyptian Christianity. In the work mentioned above, Pearson examines two texts[207] in which he detects elements of the Valentinian Gnosticism and Manichaeism thought to have influenced the Alexandrian church. The primary characteristics are as follows: a revisionist approach to Genesis; the soul's struggle to reach heaven; the lesser divinities and their power over the heavens; and the idea of "safe conducts" to overcome the obstruction of these malignant beings. Connections also become evident here with Gnostic cosmology and with the doctrine of emanations and hypostases. As we know, the latter include Sophia (Wisdom) in one or another of the countless roles and hierarchical positions attributed to her by the different Gnostic sects.

As pointed out in the section on the *Kəbrä nägäśt*, the gulf between the divine world and the human is bridged in Christian Gnosticism by a multitude of hypostatic entities, some of which are abstract (like Truth and the Ineffable) while others are authentic personifications of institutions or symbols, like the Church and the Cross. Some figures are instead multiplied, like Christ and Adam, who reappear repeatedly in the sequence of divine emanations. The rule of demons over the heavens and their efforts to impede the soul on its way toward God form part of this succession of entities, thus causing ever-increasing distance from the divine and contamination with matter, which is ignorance. The possibility of dualist leanings, potentially influenced by Manichaeism, is also included in this nucleus of influences.

In order to document this source of influence, reference will be made here to the *Storia dei Quattro Concili* (Treasure of Faith) published by Enrico Cerulli. This monophysite work, which should therefore be in line with orthodox doctrines, asserts that there was no evacuation of the bowels and urine in Christ or in Adam before his expulsion from Eden.[208] The short text *Le Dieci Questioni* ("The Ten Questions") also included in the same volume describes the stratagems used by Christ to disguise himself from Satan. Here we find an almost immediate reference to the *Ascension*

---

[207] Birger A. Pearson, *Ancient Gnosticism*, op. cit. The two texts are *On the Origin of the World* (2nd century) and *Hypostasis of the Arcons* (3rd century).

[208] Enrico Cerulli, *Scritti Teologici Etiopici dei secoli XVI-XVII – La Storia dei Quattro Concili ed altri opuscoli monofisiti*, op. cit. pp. 100-01.

of Isaiah: "Being omnipotent, He could have incarnated Himself and been born instantaneously but did not. He instead waited patiently for nine months so that His action might remain hidden from the Enemy [...] He could also have grown and become adult instantaneously but did not."[209] Though translated into Ge'ez and circulated in Ethiopia, this work is—according to Cerulli—an expression of the Gnosticizing Christianity practiced in Egypt and in any case originated in the sphere of the Ethiopian patriarchy.

9.4 Thomas Christianity

As we have seen, the hallmarks of this belief include hatred of the flesh, the sense of not belonging in the world, and the need to recognize one's true divine identity and be reunited with it in the place of origin. The model of "Wisdom" that derives from Thomas Christianity indicates the path of a spiritual quest exemplified by the myth of the Pearl. This was, however, substantially limited to the *Kəbrä nägäśt* and the *Life of St Anne* in Ethiopia,[210] where it in any case served the less abstract (or perhaps less universal) purpose of inserting the Virgin into a sequence of causes originated before the creation of the cosmos.[211] In Thomas it was instead a message of liberation addressed to all human beings, the creation of a "figure" of the true world and the true identity to be sought after, the dwelling place of Wisdom as well as Salvation and Light.

While the evident Platonic inspiration of these formulations might suggest the possibility of arriving from Thomas Christianity at the hypostatic entitles, this theme does not actually appear to emerge in the Thomasite model. While reference is made to a world in which human contradictions will be eliminated, this world is not described and the associated quest for God belongs to the mystical dimension. The origin of this source is undoubtedly Alexandria, the place from which the myth of the Pearl reached Ethiopia. Given the Platonic influences present in this source, it should be noted that some studies on the various components of the Christian community in Alexandria have indicated the existence also

---

[209] Ibid., p. 232.

[210] Enrico Cerulli, *La Letteratura Etiopica,* op. cit, pp. 45-46.

[211] We refer to the path of the Pearl, from the belly of Adam to St Anne and then its phenomenal manifestation in the Virgin.

of one or more communities of Platonizing Christians.[212] Moreover, the part of the *Gädlä hawaryat* devoted to Judas Thomas appears to look forward to the ideas of the dissolution of individual souls in the undifferentiated divine entity and the possibility of salvation for all regardless of the sins committed.

9.5 The Influence of Origen

As stated above, it is impossible to document the influence of Origen because his works were not translated in Ethiopia. While unmistakable traces can be found, these are late, belonging to the 14th century, and thus confront us with the paradox of an early Christian thinker apparently influencing Ethiopian literature about a thousand years after his death. This is evidently not a case of linear transit, of one or more manuscripts arriving in Ethiopia and prompting the circulation of new theological ideas. Origenism probably reached Ethiopia through news of the uprisings that had shaken the Church in Europe after the 11th century with the birth of violent neo-Manichaean movements. The Ethiopian Church also found itself in a period of internal and external conflict during the 14th century with a clash between secular and regular clergy, and the hostility of the latter toward monarchs that claimed the right to control not only the life of the Church but also theological truths while indulging in morally reprehensible conduct.

Movements of opposition probably formed within the monastic communities and found fitting forms of expression for their dissent in the writings of Origen and perhaps in other now lost texts as well as works eliminated from the canon in that century, like the *Ascension of Isaiah*. Among the themes taken up and radicalized, we find in particular the denigration of the flesh and matter in the process of salvation. According to Origen, as seen above, bodies of flesh were bestowed on Adam and Eve after the original sin and the birth of Christ was not a corporeal event. In his view, the course of salvation would end with the annihilation of matter (thus negating bodily resurrection) and the deliverance of all. This idea of the salvation of all human beings—or at least (according to the formulation in the *Qälemǝntos*) all of those not entirely given over to evil—is typical of one school of Valentinian

---

[212] David T. Runia, *Filone di Alessandria nella prima letteratura cristiana*, Milano, 1999.

Christian Gnosticism. It is also formulated in terms similar to those of the *Qälemǝntos* in the *Tripartite Tractate*, a Gnostic text probably produced in Alexandria in the 3rd century. Another element included in this nucleus of influence is the divinity of man, a theme also present in Thomas Christianity, albeit with differences in accent.

These views also involve a revision of Genesis, which in the *Qälemǝntos* even includes the part played by Satan in the original sin, as well as the idea of secret revelations that must not be disclosed to all and sundry. It should be pointed out that Origen drew some of these elements from the writings of Philo of Alexandria, the intermediary for Platonism in the Jewish religious tradition. The revision of Genesis and the unknowability of God are certainly to be found in Philo, who stated moreover that only the parts of the Bible written by Moses were inspired by God, whereas the others, written by his followers, were open to question. Finally, attention should also be drawn to the possibility of discerning within this speculative model—the path leading from the annihilation of matter to the divinity of man and the salvation of all—what we have described above as a "nebular" conception of divinity, i.e. a divinity in which individual characteristics are swallowed up and lost, an undifferentiated container of the particles of light previously dispersed in matter. A conception of this nature is expressed in the *Christian Romance of Alexander*, albeit with certain reservations. It is, however, not clear whether this is a development deriving from Manichaean influences during the complex genesis of the work or whether it has an effective basis in Origen's writings. Similar doubts arise with respect to the idea of the "kingdom of Satan" and Satan's envy of man in the *Combat of Adam*.

A neo-Manichean inspiration deriving from the influence of Origen may be identifiable in the following aspects:

- the denigration of the flesh and matter, where we find a possible link with the Catharist belief that the world was created by Satan;
- the deliverance of all human beings, which is equivalent to the negation of sin and hence evidently offers liberation from the endless obligations imposed by institutional religions and the ruling class;
- the divinity of man, which again offers liberation and urges believers to listen to other authorities superior to those that dominate civil and political life;

- the revision of Genesis, which serves the same purposes and also reinterprets the role of Satan and the serpent;
- the unknowability of God, which negates any divine seal of approval on the power exercised by rulers.

9.6 Late Jewish Influences

Consideration of the probable Jewish influences emerging in the period of translations from Arabic obliges us to state that we are faced with discordant and indeed contradictory elements that were actually used to strengthen both the "regime of truth" constructed with great care and resolution by Zär'a Ya'əqob and the case of those who opposed him and may indeed have been convicted by him of heresy.

As pointed out at the end of the section on the period of translations from Arabic, use was made of the Jewish tradition in the *Kəbrä nägäśt* to justify the power of the Solomonic dynasty through a reworking of traditions regarding Solomon and knowledge as wisdom, the wealth of Judeo-Christian sources reinterpreting the entire Old Testament as a jigsaw puzzle of typologies, symbologies, and foreshadowings of the New Testament, and stories about the Ark of the Covenant. These traditions were bent to serve Ethiopian dynastic requirements. The story of the Queen of Sheba being the daughter of a demon thus disappeared, references were made to the powers of angels rather than those of demons, and the narratives were distorted to justify the theft of the Ark on the grounds that the people of Israel were no longer worthy of their role as the chosen. Within all this, a tendency can also already be discerned to favor the miraculous or magical characteristics attributed to the Christian religion, personifying the Ark, the Cross, and the Pearl, and illustrating their peculiar powers or the special protection afforded them by angels in the course of the narrative. These themes find their rationale and their ideal synthesis in the evident aim to endow the Solomonic dynasty with the status of a monarchy by divine right, as demonstrated by the "desire" of the Ark to be transported into Ethiopia, the story of the Holy Family passing through Ethiopia on their return from the flight into Egypt and the Pact of Mercy (which guarantee the special relationship between the Virgin and the land of Ethiopia), and finally the presence in Ethiopia of the relics of the True Cross, supposedly obtained by Zär'a Ya'əqob through political initiatives and traditionally held to be preserved on Gechen Amba.[213]

The texts probably produced during the same period in the largely monastic sphere of opposition to the Solomonic dynasty instead focus on different themes—again probably of Jewish origin and in any case known to have been present in the Jewish sphere—with completely different characteristics. It is no coincidence that the *Combat of Adam* should contain the unequivocal statement that Solomon had only one son, namely Rohoboam, thereby denying any dynastic link between Israel and Ethiopia.[214] Equally indicative is the fact the first two books of the *Qälemǝntos* contain a new interpretation of Genesis with potentially subversive characteristics. If the sin of Adam and Eve, i.e. their desire to become like God, is not so serious, if it was only a sin of immaturity or failure to wait until the fruit was ripe, then it is *a fortiori* hardly sinful to disobey the ruler's wishes, given that God created man for happiness and pleasure, and that deliverance awaits all human beings. As stated above, even Satan is not such a devil on this view, as he did not lie to Adam and Eve but only talked them into not waiting for the period laid down by God.

It follows from all this that if Zär'a Ya'ǝqob fostered the introduction into Ethiopia through Arabic intermediaries[215] of Jewish traditions,[216] he did so on the basis of rigorous selection, encouraging the circulation of some and restricting that of others, which were instead taken up by opponents of the Solomonic dynasty. The latter category unquestionably includes the theme of the salvation of all and the idea of God as unknowable and non-representable, neither of which would obviously have been acceptable to Zär'a Ya'ǝqob. The idea of the deliverance of all was certainly not in line with his way of exercising power and marshaling consensus, which was indeed based on bringing charges of heresy and inflicting punishments supposedly all reflecting the will of God, who might accept the salvation of a sinner in exceptional cases but only

---

[213] A. Caquot, "Aperçu préliminaire sur le *Mashafa Tefut* de Gechen Amba," in *Annales d'Ethiopie*, 1955, vol. 1, no. 1, pp. 89-108.

[214] Solomon Caesar Malan, *The Book of Adam and Eve, also called the conflict of Adam and Eve with Satan*, op. cit., p. 187.

[215] The Jewish works translated into Arabic were very numerous indeed, especially during the early centuries of Islam.

[216] It should be recalled that according to Robert Beylot, the *Kǝbrä nägäśt* as we know it today is a reworking of an earlier text produced during the reign of Zär'a Ya'ǝqob.

through special intercession on the part of the Virgin, as shown in the *Book of Mary's Miracles* and the *Ləfafä ṣədəq*.[217]

At the same time, a divinity that cannot be known or represented was hardly in line with the model of religion promoted by Zär'a Ya'əqob in his effort to marshal consensus with epic narratives and images capable of conferring a mythic aura on his chosen figures (the Virgin, Solomon, the Queen of Sheba and Mənilək). This is why he encouraged painting during his reign as well as the representation of divine figures and indeed the worship of icons as earthly manifestations of the divine. His theology even made Christ more of a fleshly figure through the legend of the True Cross. While this does assert that the Cross was made of wood from the Tree of Life in paradise, it also states that Christ (or His humanity) suffered and died on the Cross. This unquestionably produced a figure far more capable than an abstract and unknowable or entirely spiritual divinity of arousing emotions and feelings of identification and consensus on the part of believers[218] seeking to understand the persecution of paganism under way in Ethiopia, the campaigns against the various heresies, and the efforts of monks to reconvert converts to the Muslim faith. The aim was to make Christ the image of the "mystical body" of an Ethiopian Christianity lacerated by these manifestations of dissent.

It clearly emerges from the foregoing considerations that while the Jewish themes used to endow the Solomonic dynasty with a mythic aura originated in earlier narratives, this late period saw a new synthesis of various narratives from different contexts to develop the new version of the *Kəbrä nägäśt*, a compendium offering a new and successful "regime of truth" that nevertheless coexisted with the other narratives on which it was based, which continued to circulate in Ethiopia. In this sense, these themes and narratives form an organic whole, albeit with internal contradictions, as is the case in all such regimes.[219] All this makes up an original and functional system that is the product of new and sophisticated engineering.

---

[217] Other dissenters, such as the Stephanites, instead ruled out any possibility of salvation for a sinner even in the case of intercession on the part of the Virgin to obtain salvation for grievous sins such as cannibalism, as mentioned above.

[218] Here too, the present author shares Beylot's view that the version of the *Kəbrä nägäśt* known today is the result of a reworking of earlier texts carried out during the reign of Zär'a Ya'əqob. The work contains references, albeit vague, to the legend of the True Cross, as mentioned above, including its apparition to Constantine and its discovery by St Helena, as well as numerous typological references to the rods of Moses and Aron.

[219] In this specific case, for example, the tradition that the Queen of Sheba had a foot like a goat's hoof.

As regards the salvation of all and the unknowability of God, which are not part of the *Kəbrä nägäśt* regime of truth and were probably taken up by opponents of Zär'a Ya'əqob, these themes must be recognized as closely connected to Origen, already referred to here as one of the sources of influence passing through Ethiopia. The question arises, however, of whether the doctrinal foundation of the expressions of dissent, which reached their peak in the reign of Zär'a Ya'əqob, are to be found in Origen or in other Jewish sources that entered Ethiopia through Egypt and were rejected by Zär'a Ya'əqob as out of line with his regime of truth. Finally, as already suggested, it is also possible that Origenism arrived in Ethiopia through late intermediaries connected with heretical medieval movements of a neo-Manichaean character.

Given that *Barlaam and Josaphat* is primarily concerned precisely with the unknowability and non-representability of God, particular importance attaches to the question of how it fits into this overall picture. The genesis of the work can be traced back to Buddhist sources followed by Muslim and then Byzantine, but with a particular focus for the latter on the question of the "forms" of representation of the divine, in that the work reached Constantinople after the end of the battle against iconoclasm and is in any case informed by awareness of the deep and recent reflection on the subject of icons. It follows that this work, perhaps the most theologically lucid in its approach to the questions of the knowability and representability of the divine, appears in reality to have other than Jewish sources, and that the similarity in subject matter derives solely from the fact that those mentioned above were questions considered by all the different religious traditions (even if the Islamic approach to the unknowability of God was of course deeply influenced by the speculation on the question in the Jewish sphere).

Finally, particular mention should be made of the question of the names of God and of the various lesser divinities (or demons), and of the belief that the knowledge of the name of an entity endowed the knower with power, a special ability to control that entity or obtain favors from it. This is unquestionably an element originating in the Egyptian and Jewish spheres, albeit with peculiar characteristics that are accentuated in the context of the Kabbalah, which had expressed a doctrine in which special importance was attached to demonic emanations and entities, and also for the later developments of the Kabbalah subsequent to the use of its doctrines in magic and alchemy. No particular importance is, however, given to the subject in this section on late Jewish influences because, even though its origin is unquestionably Jewish, it was to find its maximum expression in the source of influence that we are about to examine, namely late Gnosticism and magic, both of which are closely connected with Jewish influences.

9.7 Late Gnosticism and Magic

As already seen above, a tendency to emphasize the miraculous or astonishing and in certain respects "magical" characteristics of the epic narratives regarding the origins of Ethiopia is already present in the *Kəbrä nägäśt*. Similar characteristics are, however, also found in the *Christian Romance of Alexander*, a work influenced by the tales of the *Arabian Nights*, which includes various narrative components of a fantastic nature.[220] The same tendency is also present in the *Testament of Solomon* and the other works about this king, which often focus on the powers he was enabled to wield by his magical ring. The latter models are also the source of a rich demonology and a host of references to the powers exercised by these spirits. These became an authentic cosmology in the Gnostic writings because, in the map of the universe of the time, countless roles were performed by demons in controlling and governing natural realities, thus revealing that the ancient divinities, far from disappearing with the advent of Christianity, had often become "minor" figures, subordinate to the new rule but nevertheless endowed with specific powers.

This model of religiosity appears to predominate in the writings ideally close to the regime of truth put forward in the *Kəbrä nägäśt* but to be wholly absent in those indicated above as works of opposition to the same, such as the two first books of the *Qälemәntos* and the *Combat of Adam*.

It draws in particular on sources mentioned above, namely the Gnostic elements in Coptic Christianity and late Jewish influences. The former are the source of the demonology, the doctrine of "safe-conducts" and talismans, the connections between demonology and astrology, the tendency to multiply the hypostatic entities (and hence, obviously, the risk

---

[220] Suffice it to mention the automata encountered by Alexander during his travels, the journey to the Land of the Living on imaginary steeds, half-horse and half-bird, the meetings with monsters and countless other extraordinary creatures, all of which make this work a sort of compendium of the fantastic figures present in the literature of antiquity and the coeval period.

of dualistic or Manichaean leanings), and the numerous traditions about Solomon, most of which reached Ethiopia from Alexandria. The latter are instead the source in particular of the doctrine of the name of God and the power of names, as examined above, but also of a cosmological vision with markedly Gnostic characteristics that is present in the Kabbalah.[221] Even though we do not know whether it ever reached Ethiopia in direct form, i.e. with its peculiar Jewish connotations, this unquestionably left its imprint on what we regard as the new and more modern source of influence containing Gnostic features, which as such gathers the previous thematic flows together in a new synthesis. As suggested above, this is a late form of Gnosticism that was incorporated into the magical doctrines widespread throughout the Mediterranean area and Egypt, and that appears to have left traces of its presence also in Ethiopia. Priority is given within this to the elements of astrology and demonology, talismans, and the powers of a "new" man able to control nature, human will, and spirits through knowledge,[222] a man who seeks wisdom in ancient books and oracles, and endeavors to transform it into a ritual of supposedly scientific character. All this, as a whole, constitutes a form of neo-paganism that also draws broadly on Christian symbolism and cosmology, however, and makes express reference in some areas, such as Europe, to the philosophy contained in the above-mentioned writings attributed to Hermes Trismegistus. The pagan characteristics of this philosophy are also indicated above.[223]

The best expressions of this synthesis and reformulation, to which we have given the label of late Gnosticism and magic, were perhaps attained in the Muslim areas, as shown by the above-mentioned *Picatrix* and by the fact that the great model of astral influences on the history of mankind through the conjunctions of planets was compiled by the Arab astronomer Abu Maa'shir and then reworked by Al Kindi.[224] Within this overall framework, even the birth of Christ was regarded as the result of the

---

[221] See the section on the Kabbalah and myth in Gershom Scholem, *La Kabbalah e il suo Simbolismo*, op. cit.

[222] Eugenio Garin *Lo Zodiaco della Vita. La Polemica sull'Astrologia dal Trecento al Cinquecento*, Rome-Bari, 1976, pp. 55-56, which also contains a splendid quotation from the *Picatrix*.

[223] Ibid., pp. 74-75. The author takes this opportunity to state that the work by Eugenio Garin is a crystal-clear description of the system of magical-astrological thought discussed here as well as its sources of influence.

[224] Ibid. See chapters 1 and 2, pp. 1-60.

influence of forces generated by the comet, and the appearance of the star in the form of the Virgin in the Ethiopian *Combat of Adam* found its own meaning.[225] Jewish influences also played a key part in this new magical-Gnostic doctrine, however, and the doctrine of names was widely developed. While the *Picatrix* devotes numerous pages to the names of demons, which are also the names of heavenly bodies, we have already found other names of demons in the *Testament of Solomon*, where they sometimes coincide with those of the Muslim traditions. This "neo-pagan" model left few traces of its presence in Ethiopia, however, probably because of the wholesale destruction of manuscripts by order of Zär'a Ya'əqob or because its penetration was successfully limited by the civil and religious authorities. The strongest presence to be found is instead of works like the *Ləfafä ṣədəq*, where the secret names of the holy powers (Christ, God, the Virgin, and the archangels) are instead listed. Following paths already traced, symbols like the Cross, numbers, and letters of the alphabet then became signs or components of wholes through which the powers of heavenly bodies and of the human being able to harness their influence became authentic tools for the shaping and determination of destiny.

This is a path already indicated by other texts circulating in Egypt, such as the Arabic *Seal of Solomon*, which is unquestionably a late work but nevertheless presents marked similarities with the Arab-Muslim manuscript MS IES 272 discovered in Ethiopia. All this marks out the route of a hypothetical path leading to Christianized works that extracted all the possible tools, pathways, and conclusions from the pagan premises listed above so as to design a model of "Christian magic" serving to ensure the salvation of sinners after death and perhaps also well-being during life. The instruments are not too different in these Christianized works: names once again but also symbols like the Cross,[226] magical books, signs to be made over corpses, invocations, and talismans. This is why we believe that if the paganistic model described above is not present today in Ethiopia, it may have been in the past, or that, more simply, its presence in Egypt influenced the characteristics of the "Christian magic" we find in Ethiopia. The *Ləfafä ṣədəq* is the talismanic book that places the entire armory of wizardry—divine names, magic squares, crosses, the seal of

---

[225] Solomon Caesar Malan, *The Book of Adam and Eve*, op. cit., p. 204.

[226] As we have seen, however, the cross also appears in the *Picatrix*.

Solomon, symbols, numbers, letters of the alphabet, and the injunction to keep the revelation secret—at the service of salvation in the afterlife.[227]

All this was to undergo subsequent, vulgarized development with the production of magical scrolls, which encapsulate the whole of the above philosophical apparatus, simplifying the practice of reference and reducing it to the creation of a single scroll with talismanic functions instead of the copying of numerous pages required in order to obtain the guarantees offered by the *Ləfafä ṣədəq*. The only part of the above magical apparatus that appears to be missing in Ethiopia regards the complex alchemistic practices, the suffumigations, and the baking of strange elements, sometimes taken from corpses. These may well have been overly demonic in character for a people possessing the Ark of the Covenant as its talisman of election and salvation, and a book written personally by God before the birth of Christ from the Virgin as a talisman to save the few fortunate sinners from the flames of hell.

Despite these probable obstacles to the penetration of magical and paganistic doctrines in Ethiopia, however, some non-negligible traces do appear to be found in certain works. In the *Christian Romance of Alexander*, for example, it is written that the hero's father determined the position of the heavenly bodies by means of an astrolabe and bound his wife's legs together so as to prevent her from giving birth to Alexander until the hour considered inauspicious in terms of astral influences on the child had passed. In the *Combat*, when Adam and Eve are struck with terror on seeing the sun go down, God speaks to reassure them and describes its natural cycles. He also considers it necessary, however, to add that the sun is not God,[228] an assertion that is hard to understand in a text evidently circulating in restricted contexts of a clearly defined religious character, but one that could refer to paganistic theories present in Ethiopia. The sun was in any case one of the most important figures of reference in the Gnostic-magical astrology described above.

---

[227] This model of salvation granted also to sinners was of course intended to remain a prerogative of the aristocracy.

[228] Solomon Caesar Malan, *The Book of Adam and Eve*, op. cit., p. 18.

10

CONCLUSIONS

The time has perhaps come to draw the conclusions of our investigation into the presence of Gnosticism or Manichaean influences in Ethiopia. In the light of the same, any reference to Gnosticism or Manichaeism would appear improper if these are to be understood as the philosophical-religious movements developed respectively in the 2nd-3rd century (with probable survivals until the 4th for Christian Gnosticism) and the 3rd-6th century (then surviving in the Far East until the 17th). As things now stand, there is no evidence of any such contact.

These expressions of thought did, however, produce influences and generate interpretive models during the course of history that continued to reverberate for centuries and can even be detected over a thousand years after the end of Gnosticism. As stated above, we refer to the peculiar forms of Alexandrian Christianity, the teachings of Origen, the moral rigor of some monastic movements, the neo-Manichaean movements that swept across Europe in the 11th century, the anomalous symbolism to be found in the legends of the Holy Grail, and the Gnostic strands present in European Neoplatonism and Neopythagoreanism in the period of humanism and the Renaissance, not to mention the Gnostic sects still existing today and easy to find on the Internet.

We must therefore start by saying that the references examined here are probably not directly related to Gnosticism and Manichaeism but rather to these other civil, philosophical and religious movements, which drew on them centuries later to find a theoretical foundation for their present-day requirements or an answer to historically grounded questions.

On embarking on analysis of the texts that, in our opinion, present evident traces of these influences and attempting to map the sources of the same, it soon became clear, however, that further hypotheses would be needed to support our original ones, thus multiplying the levels of uncertainty. A telling example is provided by the fact that while there are evident "traces" of Origen's teaching in Ethiopian literature, his writings appear to have never been translated in the country (even though he is referred to in the work of Giyorgis of Sägla mentioned above).

In seeking to solve some of these dilemmas, we can of course refer to Egypt and to Alexandria in particular. It is indeed easy when faced with such riddles to attribute the transits to written and verbal mediators from Alexandria, and still easier, if no evidence of such mediators is found, to attribute this to the above-mentioned campaigns for the destruction of manuscripts. There is indeed historical evidence both for transits from Alexandria and for the wholesale destruction of manuscripts. The problem is that this provides a sort of skeleton key, capable of opening every door, but offers no certainty. Nevertheless, it can be used with all due caution and within limits, recognizing that in any case the presence of certain sources in Alexandria may offer no certainties but certainly does open up some possibilities. Even in the cases where there is no evidence at all of transits of these sources, transit was not only possible but also possible in forms other than the written one on which scholars usually base their research. This type of investigation hinges primarily on establishing the presence of certain sources in Alexandria and thus dispensing also with the idea of Ethiopia as a sort of impenetrable monad. The evidence to the contrary is indeed substantial and the absence of translations of literary sources is not sufficient reason to believe that Ethiopia remained untouched. Moreover, given the complexity of the past and indeed present history of the Horn of Africa, it would be legitimate to ask precisely what is meant by the word *Ethiopia* every time it is written. The above-mentioned Arab-Muslim manuscript MS IES 272 presents marked similarities with Christian texts circulating in Egypt and mentioned here in the section on the *Testament of Solomon*. At the same time, exegesis has amply demonstrated transits of Jewish and Christian sources in Islam and vice versa. In the light of this, another avenue to be explored appears to be the transit of sources between different religious traditions, not least in view both of the fact that theologians of different faiths in Alexandria were in the habit of exchanging polemics in Arabic and of the presence of Ethiopian monks in Egyptian monasteries.

While it has emerged repeatedly during our investigation that scholars have been prompted by similarities and affinities to suggest relations and derivations that find no exegetic confirmation, Ethiopia displays a particular propensity for absorbing external sources, appropriating them, and losing all memory of their origin. This makes the reconstruction of influences still more complex and can only multiply the levels of uncertainty in the case of obscure texts like the supposedly Mikaelite tracts published by Cerulli in 1958. It appears to us, however, that scholars like Father Agostino Tedla have demonstrated the ability to discern the traces of external influences in the cultural fabric of Ethiopia and its literature with no sacrifice of rigor. It is for this reason that we were led to deny the existence of Gnostic influences in the writings published by Cerulli and detect instead the influence of European missionaries. We further believe that our investigation has made an important contribution to this analysis as a whole by also demonstrating the basis of "linguistic" reflection on which the thinking of the author of the tracts is developed and thus dispelling any last lingering doubts of Gnostic influence.

The exclusion of the supposedly Mikaelite tracts from our map unquestionably simplifies the framework of reference and prompts us to look to other spheres in order to explain the highly original characteristics they present. All this enables us to confine our examination of Gnostic-Manichaean influences to the period from the 4th to the 15th century (or at most the 16th) with the sole exception of the research on talismanic and thaumaturgical practices. These are attested still later but are in any case practices and not literary sources despite their possession of a textual component.

Thanks to this simplification of the field of research, it appears clear that the six sources of influence examined above, namely

- Jewish-Christian influences in the period of translations from Greek
- Gnostic influences on Coptic Christianity
- Thomas Christianity
- the influence of Origen
- late Jewish influences
- late Gnosticism and magic

can account for all the traces of Gnostic or Manichaean thought to be found in the texts in the periods mentioned above. Moreover, identification of the last of the sources listed above has made it possible to suggest the possible inclusion of Jacques Mercier's studies on talismanic and thaumaturgical practices in our overall vision.

As already stated, all this is obviously nothing other than an overview with all the attendant shortcomings. It is a sort of map and therefore simplified, as any map proves to be on comparison with the actual topography of a coastline. Moreover, despite the best of intentions, the chronologies presented are imprecise or make assumptions that would probably not be accepted by all scholars. It is, however, our opinion that the paths of research inevitably take this course and that, after a long period during which the question of Gnostic influences in Ethiopia has been either ignored or addressed only through the exegetic analysis of a few texts, the time has now come to try and draw a new chart that, though inaccurate, will hopefully prove useful to anyone seeking to navigate the countless reefs of the seas explored here.

APPENDIX

The "Mikaelite" Opuscula Published by Cerulli and the Suggested Gnostic Influences

Background Information on the Mikaelite Heretics and Cerulli's Interpretation of the Opuscula

The Mikaelite movement and its name are thought to derive from the monk Zämika'el, about whom very little is known. The confutation of his doctrines by Zär'a Ya'əqob (1434–68) is supposed to have taken place in the early years of the sovereign's reign.

In the *Mäṣḥafä Bərhan*, a text attributed to Zär'a Ya'əqob and one of the sources of information on the Mikaelite heresy, the king states that he summoned Zämika'el together with 'Aṣqa, another heretic, in order to refute their doctrine. He adds that the metropolitan Bärtälomewos had been suspected of the same heresy during the reign of Yəshaq (1414–29) and obliged to recant. It would follow from this both that the Mikaelite heresy was already present in Ethiopia even before Zämika'el and that it had found favor in circles that were close to the Coptic patriarchate and therefore influenced by the doctrines circulating in Alexandria. These surmises appear to be borne out by the fact that two new metropolitans, Mika'el and Gäbrə'el, and the bishop Yoḥannəs were asked by Zär'a Ya'əqob on their arrival in 1438–39 to make an explicit anti-Mikaelite declaration.

According to Cerulli, further confirmation is provided by the fact that in his *Book of the Mystery*, a compendium of Christian heresies, Giyorgis of Sägla refuted the Sabellian heresy—which blurs the distinction between the three persons of the Trinity, the Father being likened to a man, the Son to his word and the Holy Spirit to his breathing—in 1424 and therefore prior to the presumed date of Zämika'el's condemnation. The Sabellian view could obviously have given rise to the idea that the three persons are indistinguishable, and it is strongly suspected that the heresy was the first to be addressed in the *Book of Mystery* precisely in order to attach primary importance to its refutation by the author. At the same time, if Giyorgis of Sägla made no specific reference to its advocates, who were presumably present in Ethiopia, it was perhaps because they must have held influential positions in the court or patriarchate, and he preferred to avoid any direct clash with them.

It should in any case be pointed out that there is no evidence from inside the Mikaelite movement itself for the first period of the Mikaelite heresy. It appears from the above-mentioned *Mäṣḥafä Bərhan* and from one of the narratives in the *Book of Mary's Miracles*[1] that what Zämika'el and his followers were actually accused of was rejecting observance of the Sabbath and "denying Mount Zion".

As regards the first point, the Mikaelites, in line with Alexandrinian practice, probably condemned observance of the Sabbath, which was instead supported by Zär'a Ya'əqob. On taking the throne, the king had taken a wholly unambiguous stance on this question in order to avert the risk of a schism within the Ethiopian church between supporters of the Alexandrinian patriarchate and those espousing the views of Eustachius,[2] who had championed observance of the Sabbath for decades.

The question of the denial of Mount Zion will instead require examination in some depth, as the sources are not clear. In his commentary on the narrative on the death of the monk Giyorgis, a Mikaelite heretic,[3] Cerulli interprets this as denial of the supper on Mount Zion. As this was a metaphor of the Eucharist, it comes to mean the denial of transubstantiation, i.e. of the eucharistic transformation of bread and wine into the body and blood of Christ. In the above-mentioned *Mäṣḥafä Bərhan*, Zär'a Ya'əqob states that his confutation of Zämika'el regarded the mystery of the Trinity. Given the obscure nature of the reference, to put forward a hypothesis, if the question of transubstantiation is taken together with that of the Trinity and the denial that God made man after his own likeness, it appears to follow from the above arguments that it

---

[1] Enrico Cerulli, *Il Libro etiopico dei Miracoli di Maria e le sue fonti nelle letterature del Medio Evo latino*, Roma, 1958.

[2] The founder of this movement was the monk Ewosṭatewos (Eustachius), who was forced to flee from Ethiopia when his teachings were condemned. They later obtained the approval of Zär'a Ya'əqob and became part of the Ethiopian credo. See G. Lusini, *Studi sul monachesimo eustaziano (secoli XIV-XV)*, Naples, 1993.

[3] Enrico Cerulli, *Il Libro etiopico dei Miracoli di Maria*, op. cit., p. 112.

makes no sense to speak of the Eucharist as transubstantiation, i.e. the transformation of bread and wine into the body and blood of Christ, because if God is unknowable to man and if human instruments cannot even serve as metaphors to know Him, then the very idea of transubstantiation is untenable, thus giving rise to a spiritualized, non-bodily conception of Christ. Cerulli puts it as follows:

> Denying both that the Creator can be likened to the image of His creatures and that the Trinity can be divided into distinct persons also meant denying that the species can be transformed into the body and blood of the Son and that this transmutation—the transubstantiation—can take place through the descent of the Holy Spirit invoked with the Father (and the Son) in the epiclesis, as was instead the general belief of the Eastern Churches. It can thus be understood why this denial is indicated as the "denial of the existence of the supper of Mount Zion", i.e. of the institution of the Eucharist.[4]

There would thus be a close relationship between the conceptions of the Trinity that we shall now see in the opuscula and the denial of the Eucharist, i.e. of Mount Zion.

Cerulli's interpretation of the denial of Mount Zion has, however, been challenged by other scholars, who see this instead as a reference to the eschatological expectation of Christ's return before the end of the world to reign on earth for a thousand years in the Kingdom of the Just.[5] The Mikaelite denial of Mount Zion would therefore actually be the denial that Christ was to return and reign on the earth. In any case, we are dealing with the doctrinal expression of a spiritualized Christianity averse to the ideas both of the incarnation and of the earthly reign of Christ. We shall return to this point below.

In 1958 Enrico Cerulli published three texts that he regarded as the first internal expression of Mikaelite doctrines to be discovered so far and attributed the movement with markedly Gnostic characteristics on the basis of the same. As shown by documentary evidence and content alike, however, the tracts are actually to be regarded as much more recent than

---

[4] Ibid., p. 114.

[5] See G. Lusini, "Eschatology", in Siegbert Uhlig (ed.), *Encyclopaedia Aethiopica*, vol. II, Wiesbaden 2005, pp. 379-82, and Agostino Tedla, "A proposito di alcuni passi oscuri negli Scritti teologici etiopici pubblicati da E. Cerulli," in *Proceedings of the Third International Conference of Ethiopian Studies*, Addis Abeba, 1970, vol. II, p. 241.

the period in which the monk Zämika'el and his followers were condemned as heretical and as belonging the period 1557-1632, when the Society of Jesus was active in Ethiopia. They appear to bear no resemblance to any other writings in the Ethiopian sphere and therefore call for examination in depth.

The three texts, which are entitled *Exposition of the Divinity*, the *Ship of the Soul* and the *Safe Haven*,[6] present high levels of philosophical reasoning that is sometimes expressed in terms of myth, albeit with strong and effective aesthetic characteristics and rhetorical effects. According to Cerulli, however, they pursue two partially contradictory aims:

- to take part in and contribute to the debate that developed in Ethiopia in the 16th–17th century after the arrival of the Jesuit missionaries on the side of the Ethiopian Orthodox Church;

- to do so without clearly stating their ideas so as to preserve a margin of ambiguity (sometimes through obscurity) enabling them to participate without being marginalized due to the evident heretical implications of their formulations.

In his view, this was a strategy adopted by the authors of the three works and perhaps their communities as a result of the condemnation of their founder and his followers during the reign of Zär'a Ya'əqob and the subsequent survival of the movement as an outcast heretical sect. Another possible interpretation of the birth of these tracts is that while the exemplary condemnation of Zämika'el and his followers by Zär'a Ya'əqob did put an end to the most blatant manifestations of the Mikaelite heresy and curb its growth in the patriarchate, it only prevented the free expression of beliefs that instead lived on and indeed found mature manifestation in the tracts over a century later.

The dispute with the Jesuits enabled the Ethiopian church to regain its unity momentarily in an understandable attempt to close ranks against Catholic penetration, and this was perhaps regarded as the best possible opportunity to regain freedom of expression by these movements, which thus sought, albeit with anomalous formulations, to fight alongside the other representatives of the Ethiopian church and stem the tide of Jesuit initiatives.

---

[6] In Italian: *Spiegazione della Divinità*, *La Nave dell'Anima* and *Il Porto Sicuro*; Enrico Cerulli, *Scritti Teologici Etiopici dei Secoli XVI-XVII, I. Tre Opuscoli dei Mikaeliti*, Vatican City, 1958.

Some Quotations

While the complexity of the tracts and the occasional beauty of some mythicized syntheses of the arguments unquestionably merit a broad, analytical discussion that is incompatible with the scope of this work, some quotations will help to give an idea of the importance and value that Cerulli attributed to them.

The following, which illustrates the grounds on which the author of the first denies that man was made in the likeness of God, takes up a celebration of the Virgin by Cyriacus of Behnesā:

> The fire of the Divinity, which is susceptible neither of examination nor of measurement and cannot therefore be compared to earthly fire, dwelt in your womb. *Earthly* fire has measurement and form, whereas it cannot be said of the Divinity that it is so much *in measurement* or like this *or that form*.
>
> The Divinity has neither a disk like the sun and moon nor stature like man but is miraculous and dwells in the highest, where it is reached neither by the thought of men nor the intelligence of angels. Neither length nor thickness has the Divinity, neither high nor low, neither right nor left, but plenitude everywhere and in everything. The Divinity has neither expanded space nor contracted space but is the divine everywhere. The Divinity has neither a roof above nor foundations below but is Himself roof and foundations. The Divinity neither looks down nor bends to lift anything from the earth but holds everything in His hand, as shown to Peter. The Divinity has no breast in front and back behind between which He is visible and between which He is contained, as man is in his body, but is instead wrapped in fiery flame, and the fiery flame is God Himself and His Divinity is pure, limpid and luminous.[7]

The subject is, however, gradually transformed during the exposition into the unknowability of God, which is given extraordinary poetic expression in the *Exposition of the Divinity* in the following myth:

---

[7] Enrico Cerulli, *Scritti Teologici Etiopici dei Secoli XVI–XVII, I. Tre Opuscoli dei Mikaeliti*, op. cit., p. 117. The words in italics are additions by Cerulli to make the passage more comprehensible.

And then I rose and ascended the mount of angels so that they might tell me what I wanted to know. On reaching them, I said straight away, "You Angels, wiser than all the creatures before and after, you bright ones, you for whom there is no problem of any creature whatsoever that cannot be explained, and none of all the secret things that were concealed is hidden from your light, now I ask you, by the law that binds you, to be masters and teachers of our ignorance and explain to me the problem of the Holy Trinity, their essence, their Persons and the breadth of their dimensions."

When the Angels heard this from my mouth, they were stricken with fear and bound by dread because heard what was not fitting for them. And if they had not overcome their terrible fear through their mercy, my soul would have melted like wax on beholding them. They answered me with a parable: "When a merciful man, out of his great charity, gives a blind man an abundance of gold, precious garments and lustrous pearls that he might have them as his possessions, and adds to these gifts delicious foods, will the blind man distinguish them in their individual form so as to rejoice in the beauty of their glow? Or will those splendid things not rather be for him like a stone? The blind man will, however, truly thank and praise the merciful one for two reasons alone: when the cold pierces, he will give thanks for the warmth of the clothing; and when hunger bites, he will give thanks for the taste of the food. Just so do we Angels thank the Lord when we fill our mouths at the table of His sweet love, which never cloys. And if we are clothed in the raiment of His grace, raiment woven with knowledge to instruct the ignorant, we praise the Lord. But if the light of our minds sought the hidden knowledge of the Divinity, this knowledge would be for it as gold and pearls cast before a blind man, who cannot rejoice in the beauty of their luster even though near. For us, our blindness would indeed be so much greater, as the ash is greater than the wood that generates it with its destruction. O earthly being, do not continue this search if you do not wish to perish!"

The narrator continues:

I went then to the Sun and said: "Explain to me the mystery of your Creator and what He is like." The Sun answered me calmly, with no anger, lest I should fear his majesty: "Go to Darkness and ask her to explain the beauty of the essence of me, the Sun, and the luster of my substance of splendor. If she answers this demand, hasten back and I too will satisfy you with falsehood like her."

And so I quickly went to seek darkness, that which is not visible to the eye, on the mountains and in the cities, but she did not meet my cry with an answer. And then I said in wonder as I was about to speak: "Is not darkness perhaps in her realm during the night, when the eyes of all are closed?"

When the Sun, who had sent me to her, returned through his windows, darkness came soon afterward, as is her habit, and stopped before me. And so I asked her with praises and thanks, saying: "I have come to you, O Darkness, over an argument with the Sun so that you might explain to me the mystery of the Sun and his essence. There is no one that sees you and no one that hears you, as you are the hiding place of everything." And she answered with wonderful and unexpected words, swearing by the Living God: "Just as you man, now, at night, cannot see the Sun, which is hidden from your eye, I too have been like you. Since I came out of my mother's womb, I have never seen the Sun and the beams of his splendor have never touched to me. On the contrary, I flee from my place, far from his voice, when the trumpet of his brightness resounds."

And so I did not return to the Sun but, on descending, I found the Wind passing by and beseeched him humbly, like the others, "Explain to me the mystery of the Divinity!" His answer was wonderful and unsurpassable for me. The Wind said: "First tie my foot with your rope and seize my hand with yours! Then your question will be answered." And I tried, running when he ran, to grasp something of the intangibility of what the Wind had told me, but could not and was left behind. The wind mocked me for my shameful weakness, as the ostrich mocks hyenas or the birds of the sky mock dogs when they chase them.

I then descended in weariness into the Abyss and the Ocean and asked them what I had first asked the highest of creation. I said to them: "Since you are my neighbors and my trusty protectors, I have come to ask you to explain the question of the mystery of God," The Ocean answered me: "Take finely ground salt and milled grain and scatter them vigorously in me. And then, shortly afterwards, take them back, sweeping with the broom of your wisdom, if you can. Take back the flour without it getting wet and the salt without it dissolving, then will I grant your wish in what you have asked me to explain." In my weakness, I said nothing to this reply.

And the Abyss, imitating the Ocean in his clemency towards me, said: "Take fire and a lamp. Leap into me holding them and turn around with them in your clenched hand so as to illuminate. Count in this way the number of grains of sand and their measure one by one, grain by grain, seeking out their secrets with that lamp. Then rise up and emerge without getting wet and without either the fire or the lamp being extinguished. When you have done that of your own power, I will explain to you the measure of those who are beyond measurement." And so I was astonished and dumbfounded, because the Abyss had placed a weight of discourse heavier than lead in my mouth with his answer.

And so I went to the earth, my mother, and I said to her in tenderness and love: "As you are my mother and my parent, so have I come to you that you might explain a question I have been unable to understand, and that is the essence of the divinity, which is hidden from thought. As you know, no mother wishes her child to appear in the clothes of poverty but rather in pride of appearance. Enrich me therefore with wisdom and let them be confounded who confounded me when I questioned them." And she replied sweetly, seeming to answer my question: "My child, do what I tell you and do it at once, then will my words help you to learn. Take a rope and measure the height of the firmament and calculate the size of the earth. Count the trees, the blades of grass, and the stones that are on it. Then dig down into it to the foundation. Pierce it vigorously and observe those beneath it, those deprived of name. When you have done that of your own power, I in turn will be able to reach the foundations of God, and on my return I will tell you the measure of the number of Him that centuries cannot number, of Him that boundaries do not circumscribe and the steps of thought cannot reach.[8]

The above quotations clearly show the original characteristics that prompted Cerulli to attach importance to the three opuscula and some of the reasons why he thought that they were influenced by Gnosticism, an interpretation that is not, however, accepted by other scholars. We shall seek in the following pages to summarize the debate under way since 1958 on these works.

The Debate on the Gnostic Interpretation of Opuscula Published by Cerulli: The Interpretations Put Forward by Cerulli, Father Agostino Tedla and Piovanelli

The Gnostic interpretation of the Mikaelite opuscula published by Enrico Cerulli[9] and the objections raised some years later by Father Agostino Tedla[10] and Pierluigi Piovanelli[11] concentrate on a number of passages regarded as particularly relevant. Cerulli's interpretation thus focuses in particular on parts of the *Exposition of the Divinity* and one passage from the *Ship of the Soul*. At the same time, for reasons that will be made clear below, the said debate focuses in particular on a passage from the first tract, which Cerulli entitles *The Mystery of the Trinity* and interprets as an authentic Gnostic cosmology. We shall quote the entire passage both because it merits particular attention and so that it can be referred to in the course of this investigation, which will also seek to put forward a different interpretation:

> Two actions (*two active principles*)[12] have entered a house through a door, whose lock has a unique sound and repeats no other *sound*; and through the arrival of this voice, its will is

---

[8] Enrico Cerulli, *La Letteratura Etiopica*, Florence-Milan 1968, pp. 147–49.

[9] Enrico Cerulli, *Scritti Teologici Etiopici dei secoli XVI-XVII – Tre opuscoli dei Mikaeliti*, op. cit., pp. XI-XIII

[10] Agostino Tedla, "A proposito di alcuni passi oscuri negli Scritti teologici etiopici pubblicati da E. Cerulli," in *Proceedings of the Third International Conference of Ethiopian Studies*, Addis Ababa, 1970, vol. II, pp. 217–42.

[11] Pierluigi Piovanelli, "Connaissance de Dieu et Sagesse Humaine en Ethiopie," in *Le Muséon*, 117, Leuven, 2004, pp. 193-227.

[12] The words in italics are insertions or additions by Cerulli to make the text more comprehensible.

made known to the listener. And these *two*, for the concupiscence of the warmth of the house, possess a girl—without waiting—a girl of honorable charm, desirable by all, forbidden in beauty by her parents. But while they, having entered by one door, go to their homeland the morning *after*, they will leave by twice three doors. And their daughter, born that night, the only child of her mother and unique by name and forbidden in beauty, will leave by twice two doors. Shortly after, having left, she will give birth to three sons, for wisdom of intelligence, because she *was* pregnant; and she will call them by three names: one: "Be praised among the poor"; the second: "Be blessed among the rich"; and the third: "Be glorified among the lofty in honor." And if they are united, His foundation is rapid, as He appears in a single person. And her initial denomination perishes when they are born.

Come now, tell us the meaning of the birth of that *girl*, beautiful in form and in name, in a single night, while her youth, when she leaves, instead appears adult. I present her parable and abandon the foundation of the perceptibility of the two that entered; and I repudiate the disappearance of the abyss of the root of the garden of the parents of her, who from that (*abyss*) sprang, in the Persons of the Father, the Son and the Holy Spirit, three in Persons, one in Divinity. We shall not say that, like the sons of the girl, one has less glory than the other; and the second is more blessed than the third; and the third is more glorified than *the other two* in honor. Were we to say that, far be it from us to believe this comparison true *to the letter*. They instead exist in honor, glory and magnificence in a single reign, single power, single council, single glory. And they receive a single prostration from the earthly and the celestial with no emulation, as handed down to us by the Fathers, ancient and recent. Therefore we too shall comprehend them with the intellect without approaching their commencement, which has no end; and we shall know them with our thought without feeling or reaching their foundation, which is far away from any interpretation and sublime to speak of.[13]

---

[13] Enrico Cerulli, *Scritti Teologici Etiopici dei Secoli XVI-XVII – Tre Opuscoli dei Mikaeliti*, op. cit., pp. 144-46.

Cerulli's interpretation, put forward in note 1 on page 145 of the text, is as follows:

> The entire passage is of the utmost importance for an understanding of the Mikaelite doctrine. This theogony hinges on two Active Principles, which are excited to generate by the warmth of the dwelling they have entered and have from a female Being another female Being. No sooner has this second female Being been born than it generates in turn Three Persons destined to be united. And these Three Persons are those of the Trinity of Christianity. The birth of the Trinity is thus arrived at through successive previous emanations.
>
> Within this general idea, so closely akin it appears to the Gnostic theogonies, there are several points whose symbolism is not clear to me, e.g. the departure of the two Active Principles—after the initial act of generation—"through twice three doors" and the departure of their only begotten Daughter "through twice two doors" before giving birth to the Three Persons. In the same way, I can only draw the attention of scholars to the names that the Mother gives the Three Persons, elevating each of them respectively over the "poor", the "rich" and the "lofty". Another point, which remains unspecified in our text, regards the unification of the Three Persons. The text uses the third person plural with a highly indeterminate meaning: "if they are united ". But who is the Unifier or who are the Unifiers of the Three Persons? Or does the unification take place through causes that are not personified?[14]

The same interpretation is put forward in the introduction to the edition:

> If the interpretation I have put forward is correct, here the Mikaelite inserts the Trinity of Christianity into a Gnostic theogony. This starts with two Active Principles, which both couple with a female Being. This gives birth the same night to a second female Being, which is born already pregnant and gives birth to Three sons. The Mother gives these sons different names but they are united in a single Person.[15]

---

[14] Ibid., p. 145, note 1.

[15] Ibid., pp. XI-XII.

The above interpretation is criticized and an alternative reading is put forward by Father Agostino Tedla in the work referred to above, where we find the following:

> As stated above, the author invites to us to solve the riddle. "Just answer this little question, he says, ... Come on, tell us, what is the essence of the birth of that (daughter)?"
>
> Here is the answer to the riddle. The two things that enter are *food* and *drink*, or more specifically *bread* and *wine*, with an obvious allusion, as a point of departure, to Psalm 103, verse 15: [...] *vinum laetificat cor hominum ... panis roborat fortitudinem hominum.*
>
> The house is the *stomach*, the door is the *mouth*, the knocker with a unique sound making known the will of the speaker is the *tongue*, the concupiscence of the warmth of the house is the *heat* of the *stomach*. Those that enter possess a daughter with no delay, meaning that the food ingested immediately produces *strength*, called a daughter of honorable charm, etc., forbidden in beauty by her parents, meaning that the strength produced out of foodstuffs is different from them because it is immaterial while its parents are material. When the foods ingested through the mouth are eliminated the following day ("go to their homeland"), they leave by twice three doors, i.e. through the *eyes*, the *nostrils* and the *lower natural orifices* respectively in the form of *tears*, *mucus*, *urine* and *excrement*. The daughter born "that night" is already fit to become a mother and leaves by twice two doors, meaning that strength is expended through the *two legs* in walking and the *two hands* in work, "by wisdom of intelligence," meaning that, directed by intelligence, it is transformed into productive energy and generates the three sons that bear the following names: "Praised among the poor," meaning *food* in gheez ብላዕ ; "Blessed among the rich," meaning *wealth* in gheez ብዕል ; "Glorified among the lofty in honor," meaning *stature* in gheez ቁግል ; In short, strength produces bread, wealth and honor by means of work under the guidance of intelligence. And if they are united, etc., the three sons, meaning that they ብላዕ : ብዕል : and ቁግል : are distinct but since these three words are formed by the union of three letters ብ : ል

: 0 : differently combined and pronounced, in their fundamental constitution they boil down to the same elements and thus form what is practically a single "person." Their mother, i.e. strength, is exhausted as soon as she has generated them and thus loses her original name.

Now, says the author in conclusion, I am not interested in the material parents, food and drink, i.e. bread and wine, or in the water that nourished the roots of the grain and the vines in the fields, but take strength alone as a term of reference to express the *Unity of God*, and the three brothers, distinct but having the same basis, i.e. the letters ስ : ሐ : 0 : to indicate the *Three Divine Persons*, who are distinct from one another but have *one and the same nature*, but eliminating from the Divine Persons the differences in praise, blessedness, and glory that exist between the three brothers.[16]

This interpretation is evidently antithetical to Cerulli's and has its own unquestionable appeal, especially for those familiar with the models of symbolism and metaphor typical of Ethiopian poetry and literature. The impression we have on reading the whole of the paper is, however, that in his attempt to shed light on the various obscure passages in the first tract—some of which regarded by Cerulli as affording glimpses of the author's true convictions and of Gnostic influences—Father Agostino has concentrated too much on these "riddles" and sometimes lost sight of their meaning in the argument sequentially developed in the theological treatise. In particular, on reading Cerulli's edition and Father Agostino's explanations side by side, we are unfortunately aware at times that the latter sometimes channels his unquestionable acumen too narrowly into the search for scriptural references[17] and the "keys" to metaphors constructed on the "wax and gold" model,[18] and fails to grasp at least part of the spiritual and theological meaning of the passages interpreted.[19]

---

[16] Agostino Tedla, "A proposito di alcuni passi oscuri," op. cit., pp. 221-22.
[17] For example, in the commentary on the passage of the "Six Towers", ibid., p. 225.
[18] As happens in the interpretation of the passage identified by Cerulli as a Gnostic cosmology.
[19] An example of this is the interpretation of the "Six Towers" passage, quoted here below, where the author confines himself to identifying the scriptural references.

This is, however, not really sufficient. It should be added that it is precisely due to the solutions put forward by Father Agostino that we now realize that the *Exposition of the Divinity* is even more complex than previously thought and requires the same degree of attention and patience in the search for different meanings and levels of interpretation as the works of Dante Alighieri.[20] In other words, his essay opens up a space of interpretation from which other avenues of investigation and levels of meaning can be glimpsed; for example, the scriptural references for the passage on the "Six Towers"[21] are unquestionably valid but this explanation does not rule out the interpretation offered here below and already outlined by Cerulli.

Let us now return to the passage quoted above. When read side by side with the text published by Cerulli, Father Agostino's interpretation leaves various questions still open and does not fit in perfectly with the argument subsequently developed, especially the text's specific reference to the three persons of the Trinity. He appears to have lost sight of the overall meaning in concentrating on the "riddle". If it is true that "strength" stands for unity born out plurality, i.e. out of "bread and wine", it is equally true that this interpretation appears reductive and lacking in richness, as we shall see.

At the same time, Piovanelli's interpretation rests precisely on Father Agostino's reading of the same passage:

> In truth, a wholly Ethiopian cultural sensitivity was required in order to solve this mystery, and it is solely thanks to perspicacity of Father Agostino Tedla that the wax of literal interpretation has finally melted to reveal the precious gold of the hidden meaning. Because the two "things" are nothing other than bread and wine, which go through the mouth and enter the stomach, where they give birth to strength. And when this leaves through the hands and feet in work, it produces food, wealth, and honor. Strength thus becomes the symbol of the unity of the godhead, while its three sons represent the Father, the Son, and the Holy Spirit. There is a difference in scale because, with respect to the

---

[20] In Dante, as is known, there are four meanings of the Scriptures, literal, allegorical, moral and anagogical (see the *Convivio*). This idea of the four categories of scriptural interpretation was, however, widespread throughout the Christian world in medieval times.

[21] We apologize for referring in advance to a text that has yet to be quoted. Readers can either simply bear the reference in mind during this initial part of the study or read the passage straight away in the section entitled *A new interpretive hypothesis*.

physiological phenomenon used as a term of comparison, the human intelligence must confine itself to accepting the mystery of the Trinity with no possibility whatsoever of knowing its nature and origins. And those who claim otherwise have far too high an opinion of their capacities. If they are incapable of solving a simple riddle, how can they ever understand the essence of divinity?[22]

This passage on the mystery of the Trinity is unquestionably the part of the opuscula that lends itself most readily to an interpretation of Gnostic character. Though open to similar interpretations, the passage from *The Ship of the Soul*[23] presents fewer footholds and its ambiguity is in any case such as to make them far less secure. What are the characteristics of the passage on the Trinity that make it susceptible of a Gnostic interpretation? There are actually only two: 1) the metaphor of the two principles that possess the honorable girl (images of sexual violence and illegitimate birth are recurrent in all the Gnostic cosmologies); 2) the interpretation of the different figures taking part in the cosmology as emanations. The impression thus emerges from this interpretation that the three figures of the Trinity are in turn emanations and, if all this has some meaning, it fits perfectly into a Gnostic cosmological model.

Cerulli's own Gnostic interpretation also appears to be weakened, however, if some of the general observations formulated by Father Agostino are taken into account and an attempt is made to examine the internal harmony of the first tract and its coherence with the other two published by Cerulli in the first volume of his *Scritti Teologici*. In other words, the acceptance of Cerulli's interpretive hypothesis means addressing the text on the following assumptions:

- The intentional obscurity of certain passages is the way devised by the author to mask his true beliefs and hide them in a textual labyrinth that therefore consists of some "sincere" parts and others serving only to feign orthodox persuasions.
- The "Mikaelite" opuscula, and the first in particular, are thus a sort of jigsaw puzzle of theories and formulations that are not always

---

[22] Pierluigi Piovanelli, "Connaissance de Dieu et Sagesse Humaine en Ethiopie", op. cit., p. 204.
[23] Enrico Cerulli, *Scritti Teologici Etiopici dei Secoli XVI-XVII – Tre Opuscoli dei Mikaeliti*, op. cit., pp. 193-96.

coherent, and the reader must therefore be able to distinguish the sincere or true parts from those serving to feign orthodox persuasions.
- Beneath this attitude and model of reading, the present author glimpses the professional approach of those accustomed to dealing with the earliest Gnostic texts. As we know, these circulated also in Christian communities and were presented as "further revelations", thus generating great doctrinal confusion. With a view to the gradual introduction of Gnostic ideas into Christian communities, these texts were often interpolated into canonical Christian writings or inserted into narrative frameworks recognized by the church. This academic approach obviously makes sense, however, in addressing texts produced in a situation of doctrinal uncertainty, when the canon of writings and the credo were still to be established.
- In the historical period and situation in which the "Mikaelite" tracts were composed, as described by Cerulli himself, the doctrinal framework was instead fully established. The Mikaelites had already been condemned as heretics and a major theological battle was under way against the Roman Catholics. In seeking to rally its forces against the common enemy, the Ethiopian church reorganized its own ranks and prepared its weapons for the impending fray. In this case, the preparation of weapons means that various components of the Ethiopian church produced texts for use in the debate against Catholic propaganda. In such a situation, one wonders what sense it could possibly make to produce ambiguous texts at variance with established doctrine and open to reiterated charges of heresy. If such doubts are legitimate in abstract terms, they become all the more so on examining the texts themselves and seeing that they profess not only perfect allegiance to the Fathers of the Church but also, in some passages, to doctrines that flatly contradict Cerulli's interpretation, e.g. the repeated references to the Virgin Mary, Mother of God, in the first tract.[24] If Cerulli's interpretation were correct, such references could have been simply avoided.
- Moreover, as regards the logic of its theological arguments, the text appears to be perfectly consistent except—paradoxically enough—for the need to solve the "riddles" put forward.

---

[24] Ibid., op. cit., pp. 82, 104 and 116.

- Given the above, it appears to us that Cerulli's arguments are less consistent than those developed, despite their limitations, by Father Agostino, which are exemplified below in two short quotations:

> Moreover, our author's style seems to be intentionally obscure, not through any fear of being discovered by his adversaries or in order to join their ranks more easily "in the discussion under way with the Catholic missionaries [...] and take advantage of the opportunity to present the essential points of his doctrine" [...] as Cerulli suggests. The author is in fact decidedly clear and explicit in his assertions from the very outset and does nothing to mask them in any part of the work. It is rather out of personal taste that he delights in the constant accumulation of never-ending figures of speech, images, symbols, comparisons, metaphors, parables, and allegories of an original and unusual nature. He does so above all, as we shall see, in order to demonstrate one of his primary assertions, namely the weakness of the human mind with respect to the infinite Being. He therefore sets his adversaries authentic riddles in order to confound them and induce them to recognize the limitations of their intellect as regards the knowledge of God.[25]

> My conclusions can already be stated. There are no "Active Principles", "emanationist theogonies" or "Gnosticism" in these writings, There are simply riddles presented in the customary form of "gold" beneath a thick coat of "wax." In any case, the Gnostic interpretation of these texts is evidently at variance and incompatible with the completely orthodox doctrine—apart from the known differences between the Ethiopian and Roman churches over Christology and the procession of the Holy Spirit—clearly presented in the tracts in question.[26]

The general considerations listed below will serve as a starting point for the new interpretation of the passage on the mystery of the Trinity to be put forward here.

---

[25] Agostino Tedla, "A proposito di alcuni passi oscuri negli Scritti teologici etiopici pubblicati da E. Cerulli", op. cit., pp. 218-19.

[26] Ibid., p. 219.

1. As clearly shown by Father Agostino in the conclusions of his study,[27] the three opuscula form a complex whole with various aims. The first, *Exposition of the Divinity*, is evidently addressed to figures within the Ethiopian Church, whereas the second and the third are avowedly intended as polemics against the Roman Catholics and their party. There is, however, a precise link between them, as the first seeks in formulating its polemical assertions with respect to the Ethiopian orthodox creed to prepare the tools required for the attacks on the Catholics to be launched in the second and third. The polemical assertions made in the first pamphlet are as follows:

- Denial of any likeness between God and man and between God and creatures in general. In particular, the author rejects any literal interpretation of all the anthropomorphic expressions used in the Scriptures, e.g. references to the "hands" or "eyes" of God.
- A broader rejection of the literal interpretation of the Scriptures.

In support of these two points, the author asserts the limitations of the human tools of knowledge, i.e. the senses and the intellect, and the unknowability of God and in particular of the two divine mysteries of the Trinity and the incarnation of Christ. This argument has its own coherence because, as Father Agostino points out, "those in the Ethiopian Church who claim that God has a *face, form* and *limbs* like those of man are by no means few ... If asked how an immaterial God can have a face and features in the somatic sense, they answer that He knows and that it is impossible to explain, being a mystery."[28] In this overall framework, what Father Agostino calls "riddles" perform the precise function of forcing adversaries to take cognizance of the limitations of their intelligence by means of the model of riddle construction of the Qəne, which was and still is widely used in Ethiopia. The author of the *Exposition of the Divinity* addresses these challenges, however, with an accentuatedly polemical and sometimes provocative attitude. This can be seen, for example, a) at the beginning of the first tract,[29] which really appears to describe a natural cosmology of the pantheistic kind that has little to do with a theological

---

[27] Ibid., pp. 239–42.

[28] Ibid., pp. 240–41.

[29] Enrico Cerulli, *Scritti Teologici Etiopici dei secoli XVI-XVII – Tre opuscoli dei Mikaeliti*, op. cit., pp. 67–73.

pamphlet explicitly claiming to put forward theories in line with Ethiopian orthodoxy, and b) in the fact that this text appears to include metaphors of a sexual nature. An example is provided by the figure of "wind", which appears to describe an erotic approach. This "wind seeks enter through the door, a door barred, prohibited, distorted and sealed, which it [the wind] cannot take by surprise."[30] "Its [the wind's] journey is not fruitless, however, as it is not left abandoned on the threshold of mockery, nor does the effort of its haste fail at the doorway of derision." Not to mention, c) the reference to the girl raped in the *Mystery of the Trinity*. This marked polemical intent evidently raises the question of whether the opuscula were really written as contributions to a debate or with other aims.

2. This polemical vein is indeed accentuated in the second tract[31] with explicit references first to similarities between Roman Catholicism and Islam, and then to unclean rituals resembling magical rites attributed to Catholics. These are accusations that appear to offer no terrain for real theological debate but simply brand the Catholic adversary as despicable. A polemical vein of such violence would hardly be fitting for a heretical movement seeking to regain support in official and fully orthodox ecclesiastical circles, as suggested by Cerulli, not even in the situation he describes, characterized by the need to restore the unity of the Ethiopian Church against Jesuit penetration and therefore to develop arguments against the common Catholic enemy. The impression is that the opuscula represent the views of those most opposed and hostile to the foreign presence, expressed in such provocative terms precisely in order to heighten the confrontation with the Jesuits and make any dialogue impossible. Another possibility is that the opuscula were not intended to contribute to any debate but simply to express the reasons for rejecting any dialogue and were therefore not aimed at the Jesuits or the pro-Jesuit party but rather at those endowed at the political level with power to grant or deny the Jesuits and pro-Jesuits the freedom to proselytize. This is made still more evident by Father Agostino's interpretation of the passage in the *Ship of the Soul* where the "Roman faith" and therefore the credo trumpeted by the Jesuits are compared—albeit in somewhat obscure terms—to the Whore

---

[30] Ibid., p. 69.
[31] Ibid., pp. 229-31.

of Babylon in the Book of Revelation.[32] The comparisons must have been far more obvious at the time, however, as the metaphors alluded to the meaning of the names of figures well-known for their political and religious views and hence easily identified by those at whom the opuscula were addressed.

3. The reader of the opuscula is surprised by the alternation to be found in them. On the one hand, we have parts that are wholly exegetic and didactic, designed to illustrate the Scriptures and their interpretation, sometimes in traditional terms and sometimes with greater freedom. On the other, we have original parts that sometimes develop complex, elaborate metaphors in the traditional style of the Ethiopian Qəne, sometimes address subjects that certainly belong to Christian speculation but are equally certainly not traditional in Ethiopia, like the limitations of the human sensory and cognitive faculties, sometimes linger over precise descriptions of natural phenomena or animal behavior, and sometimes indulge in highly emotional reflections on the incomprehensibility of God and the need to prepare the mind for the mystical abandonment of any attempt to understand. What is in any case evident, however, is the originality of the whole, which makes the opuscula almost unique in Ethiopian literature. Moreover, among the most original features, attention should be drawn to the investigation of the senses and the other tools of knowledge with which mankind is endowed as well as the precise description of some natural phenomena and forms of animal behavior. All this makes to think that in addition to his unquestionable grounding in theology, the author also possessed other kinds of knowledge.

4. The whole of the first tract is in actual fact constructed like a sort of labyrinth, which starts from a metaphor of nature, used in order to assert the difference between the characteristics of nature (of which man is part[33]) and the divine. In nature everything is lost on death and nothing preserves its identity or name, whereas the identity of the divine and its elements endures and cannot be lost. Eventually, however, at the

---

[32] Agostino Tedla "A proposito di alcuni passi oscuri negli Scritti teologici etiopici pubblicati da E. Cerulli," op. cit., pp. 231-35.

[33] Enrico Cerulli, *Spiegazione della Divinità* in *Scritti Teologici Etiopici dei secoli XVI-XVII – Tre opuscoli dei Mikaeliti*, op. cit., p. 67: "l'uomo ragionevole, congenere degli animali [rational man, akin to the animals]" The author knows of no other assertion in the Ethiopian literature of such a forthright and explicit nature, perhaps once again expressed in deliberately provocative terms.

end of a long discussion rich in quotations, symbology and parables, the author states that the three constituent entities of the Trinity are pure names, that none of the human instruments believed capable of leading to knowledge of the divine can help man to attain this end, and that, in the closing words of the text: "The Divinity knows Itself. Amen."[34] We are thus taken along a misleading path where, paradoxically enough, the initial assertion is strongly qualified by the conclusion that this truth is inaccessible to man and the fact of unknowability alone remains valid. What is the meaning of this argument? Which are its true aims? What does it seek to show? Something still appears to elude us, perhaps even the real purpose and content of this first tract.

5. Help is provided, however, by the *Mirror of the Intellect*,[35] where we read as follows at the beginning: "many have risen to speak and have turned the doctrine of the faith and religion in another direction. Some have said that the Three Persons stem from One Divinity, some that 'Divinity' comes to mean power and command, and some that the Holy Trinity exists not in persons but in names alone."[36] This passage is important because it presents a cross-section of the debate generated in Ethiopia with the arrival of the Jesuits and the adherence at the highest level to their initiatives of proselytism. It also makes us realize, however, that the debate and the attacks on the Jesuits were in actual fact anything but a united front. The writer thus explicitly attacks those who claim that "the Holy Trinity exists not in Persons but in names alone," and hence the supporters of ideas that Cerulli attributes to the Mikaelites. The above considerations appear to show that the polemic against the Jesuits in Ethiopia during that period became a sort of sounding board or forum, forcing the various elements of the Ethiopian Church to come out into the open and present their conflicting views; that the honing of weapons for use against the Jesuits was accompanied by bitter internal strife in which all the members of the Ethiopian Church took part, presenting their views and arguments in defense of what each group identified as orthodoxy. We thus have a sort of virtual forum in which these different

---

[34] Enrico Cerulli, *Scritti Teologici Etiopici dei secoli XVI-XVII – Tre opuscoli dei Mikaeliti*, op. cit. p. 152.

[35] Enrico Cerulli, *Scritti Teologici Etiopici dei secoli XVI-XVII – La Storia dei Quattro Concili ed altri opuscoli monofisiti*, Vatican City, 1960.

[36] Ibid., pp. 163-64.

elements sought to assert themselves by presenting arguments and material for debate. In doing so, however, endless opportunities for infighting were opened up. To give just one example, the author of the *Mirror of the Intellect* explicitly takes issue with the authors of the opuscula identified by Cerulli as Mikaelite tracts, attacking not only the assertion that the persons of the Trinity are no more than names but also the denial of the anthropomorphism of God, and supporting literal interpretation of the anthropomorphic passages in the Scriptures.[37] This reveals, however, that the ideas expressed by the author of the first "Mikaelite" tract were perceived in the Ethiopian context as "out of line" and unorthodox. The nature of this heterodoxy will be addressed below.

6. The foregoing prompts reflection and raises the question of identifying the internal components of the Ethiopian Church that faced one another in the dispute. Cerulli's response is to attribute the paternity of the tracts published in the first volume of his *Scritti Teologici* to followers of the heretical Mikaelite movement. Piovanelli rejects this interpretation in the study cited above on the grounds that no evidence has been discovered of the existence of a "Mikaelite movement" but only of the condemnation of its presumed founder and some other figures. In his view, the supposedly Mikaelite opuscula are instead expressions of the Monophysite orthodoxy closest to the Egyptian Coptic faith. As regards the attribution of the writings published in the first volume to followers of the Mikaelites, the present author agrees that there is no evidence to support this claim. At the same time, however, given all the evidence of the prolonged survival in Ethiopia of movements already declared heretical and condemned (as in the earlier cases of the Eustacians and the Stephanites), it is hard to imagine that the complex forces involved in the theological debate of previous centuries simply disappeared. It appears probable instead that they found different positions in the new panorama characterized by the Jesuit presence and the birth of new theological disputes. As a result, the views of Cerulli and Piovanelli do not appear irreconcilable, as it is quite possible both that the heirs of the Mikaelite heretics took their place in the new doctrinal formations, and that these were close to the circles of the Coptic patriarchy, as Piovanelli suggests.

---

[37] Ibid., pp. 174–75.

7. In certain respects, the above considerations therefore bear out Piovanelli's interpretation, which casts doubt on the existence of any connection not only between the opuscula published in the first volume of Cerulli's *Scritti Teologici* and the Mikaelites but also between the Mikaelites and Gnosticism. Piovanelli's essay itself also gives rise to various reservations, however, as briefly listed below.

- Piovanelli criticizes certain parts of Cerulli's translation of the *Exposition of the Divinity*.[38] While the points in question are certainly open to doubt they are by no means conclusive and in any case not such as to invalidate Cerulli's interpretation as a whole.
- His acceptance of Father Agostino's interpretation does not answer all the questions, as "strength" is a typical example of the metaphors that Cerulli interprets in a Gnostic-Manichaean sense. Like light and honey,[39] it is a metaphor of the "nebular" kind of divinity that the soul rejoins after death, thereby losing all trace of its identity, memory of earthly life, and name, swallowed up like a drop in the ocean or a flicker of light in the sun.[40]
- Piovanelli claims that the monophysite Egyptian church would not have hesitated to condemn the anthropomorphism of Zär'a Ya'əqob as heretical rather than views of the Mikaelites.[41] Once again, this is not conclusive, as Cerulli and other scholars have repeatedly addressed the Gnosticizing elements present in the doctrines of the Egyptian Coptic church.[42]

---

[38] Pierluigi Piovanelli, "Connaissance de Dieu et Sagesse Humaine en Ethiopie," op. cit., p. 203.

[39] Enrico Cerulli, *Spiegazione della Divinità* in *Scritti Teologici Etiopici dei secoli XVI-XVII – Tre opuscoli dei Mikaeliti*, op. cit., pp. 95-96 and note 1, p. 96.

[40] See *The Gospel of Thomas*, translated by Stephen Patterson and Marvin Meyer, logion 27, op. cit., and Gérard Colin, *Alexandre le Grand, héros chrétien en Ethiopie*, op. cit., pp. 145-47.

[41] Pierluigi Piovanelli, "Connaissance de Dieu et Sagesse Humaine en Ethiopie," op. cit., p. 212.

[42] Suffice it to point out here that in the tract *Le Dieci Questioni* (in Enrico Cerulli, *Scritti Teologici Etiopici dei secoli XVI-XVII – La Storia dei Quattro Concili ed altri opuscoli monofisiti*, op. cit.), which displays connections with the Egyptian Coptic Church in various respects, we find both Christ's need to conceal his identity from the devil and an attenuated version of the idea of salvation for all. Both of these are indicative of previous Manichaean influences due to the dualism of the first and the expression of the cosmological need to reunite the two divine ranks in the second.

- At the same time, denial of the anthropomorphism of God is a constant feature of all the Gnostic texts that present a complete cosmogony in that they start with the first divinity, the origin of all the emanations, which is always described in the form of a negative theology, what Birger A. Pearson refers to as the "Unknown God."[43]
- In any case, as we shall see, some Gnostic characteristics do appear to be present in the Mikaelite opuscula, and rejection of the Gnostic interpretation of the passage on the mystery of the Trinity does not therefore necessarily mean denial of the presence of Gnostic influences, at least in the first and second tracts published in the first volume of Cerulli's *Scritti Teologici*.
- Finally, the conclusions drawn in Piovanelli's essay include two somewhat dubious assertions, namely that the literal interpretation of writings prevails over the allegorical in Ethiopia,[44] and that Ethiopia was cut off from the "outside world" for centuries.[45] As the scholars are by no means in agreement on these points, they do not appear to offer suitable support for the arguments put forward by Piovanelli as regards the tracts attributed by Cerulli to followers of the Mikaelite heretics.

A New Interpretive Hypothesis

At this point, it becomes increasingly urgent to put forward the new interpretation of the passage quoted at the beginning. This hypothesis is based on examination of the textual correspondences and metaphors present in the first of the "Mikaelite" tracts and to a very small degree in the second. We shall begin by presenting the following passages from the *Exposition of the Divinity* side by side:

---

[43] Birger A. Pearson, *Ancient Gnosticism*, op. cit., pp. 102 ff.

[44] Suffice it to mention the *Book of the Mysteries of Heaven and Earth*, which dates from the second half of the 15th century and constitutes evident proof to the contrary.

[45] This assertion, based largely on the lack of any evidence of translations of works into Ge'ez in the period from the 7th century to the 13th, is open to the objection that this is not sufficient in itself to demonstrate the absence of cultural exchanges, the existence of which appears on the contrary to be established by historical studies. Translations may not have arisen from these exchanges or may indeed simply have been lost.

From page 72	From page 144
(passage regarding the children of the Earth, devoured by their mother in the logic of the natural cycles of life, death and rebirth)	(extract from the passage on the mystery of the Trinity interpreted by Cerulli as a "Gnostic cosmogony")
Their body was in a single body *with the Earth* and foreshadows no other kind of word to the listener. And their form, already distinct in essence and wondrous in appearance, will show—to the beholder—as ornament a single form with that of the *Earth*. **And their names, which were all distinct from one another, will be on a single heel. They entered through a single door and are closed with a single lock of names, that lends no key to open and no crack to introduce the arm of the word and distinguish their forms,** *giving them a different name from that of the Earth*. The Shepherd of the Living, who is not the Guardian of the Dead or the Feeder of the Given, cannot recognize their form, which he knew before, nor can he call them by their individual **names**, by which he called them before …	**Two actions (*two active principles*) have entered a house through a door, whose lock has a unique sound and repeats no other *sound*;** and through the arrival of this voice, its will is made known to the listener. **And these *two*, for the concupiscence of the warmth of the house, possess a girl—without waiting—a girl of honorable charm, desirable by all, forbidden in beauty by her parents. But while they, having entered by one door, go to their homeland the morning *after*, they will leave by twice three doors.** And their daughter, born that night, the only child of her mother and **unique by name** and forbidden in beauty, will leave by twice two doors. Shortly after, having left, she will give birth to three sons, for wisdom of intelligence, because she *was* pregnant; and she will call them by **three names**: one: "Be praised among the poor"; the second: "Be blessed among the rich"; and the third: "Be glorified among the lofty in honor". And if they are united, His foundation is rapid, as He appears in a single person. **And her initial denomination perishes when they are born.**

The first is taken from what is referred to above as the pantheist cosmology of the Earth and the second is the previously quoted passage on the mystery of the Trinity. The boldface added by the present author indicates some correspondences to which we shall return.

It is, however, also important to present here the parable on the allegorical interpretation of the Scriptures from the *Exposition of the Divinity*:

> There was a rich man whose coffers were full of gold and silver, and his house full of grain, and the abundance of his wealth was such that there was hardly any room left for him. And he thought that thieves might rob him, so he went to the smiths and ordered them to make him hinges of steel and doors of iron. And the craftsmen together made them. Then, in his arrogance, he gave them gold to make a lock, and they did as he told them. When they had finished, he said to them, "Go home," without keeping his promise or giving them the recompense for their work. In his great arrogance, he did *not even* ask them to teach him how to slide the bolt to open it.
>
> Poor in intellect and devoid of humility, he then stood up, ordered his servants out, closed the house with those doors, and sealed it with the peerless *gold* seal without first seeing the explanation of its opening. He then departed, leaving inside all his choicest belongings and taking with him the gold key, which neither he nor his servants knew how to use.
>
> Then came the hour of habit, which is the minister of desire, and the *rich man* sat in the shade in a place of his choosing and ordered the servants of his kitchen and the masters of his cellars to bring him in haste, as usual, everything necessary *to dine*. The servants answered, "We have brought nothing from the house here. Everything has been left inside." Then he rose up in anger and beat them savagely until blood from their heads ran to the ground because he was hungry. And they said, "Lord, listen to us and cool your temper! Did you not order us to leave in haste without taking *anything*? We did not think that after we had left, the door would be closed—due to your haste—before you saw us laden with provisions for a journey."
>
> And so he cooled his temper and went and stood before the door of his house holding the *gold* key, which gave its master no power. He put it into the door to open but it did not

work, as he had not learned the secret, but rather locked it still more securely. And so he returned to his resting place sorely grieved. Was it not perhaps out of arrogance that he had not learned before? *Nor did he make any move now*, being too ashamed to face the craftsmen whose toil *he had not recompensed*. If he had instead gone to them with humility, he would not have returned dismayed without having learned *the secret*. Because of his pride, however, he would turn to no one for his dinner and so he spent the night without eating. And so he died because of his folly and was mocked by his servants and friends. The intelligent servants instead, having *afterward* learned from the craftsmen how to open that house full of riches, enjoyed them all.

Just so, if you do not take the key of interpretation, which is the guide of the word of the learned, to *open* the doors of the Scriptures, the treasure of life, you will always hunger for the bread of knowledge until you perish like the one whose story we have told, the *rich man* lacking in humility, whose belongings were inherited by his servants, deriving succor from the word of the Prophet, who said, "Better a wise servant than a mad king."[46]

The bolt is obviously a metaphor of the secrets and riddles of the Scriptures, while the key is the tool of interpretation and the closing of the house is a metaphor of the prohibition imposed by literal interpretation.

It will, however, prove useful here to consider also another passage, this time from the *Ship of the Soul*, namely the parable on erroneous interpretation of the Scriptures:

Why do the foolish plant sin and harvest death, sow pain and reap damnation? All this *happens* because they do not carefully distinguish the months of the seasons of the divine Scriptures in order to sow the seed of spiritual health in the field of their mind at the sowing time. Because they are in poverty, because they did not go out into the countryside in

---

[46] Enrico Cerulli, *Scritti Teologici Etiopici dei Secoli XVI-XVII – I – Tre Opuscoli dei Mikaeliti*, op. cit., pp. 112-13.

the autumn of the wise and take the advice of the *wise* because of their pride.

Thus they tell of a wise man who built twice three towers and filled them with riches for all the desires of the flesh. Then he handed it over to his servants that they might enjoy them and be grateful to their lord in his munificence. But *the servants*, in the pride of their foolishness, soon rebelled against their master and drove him from the house so that he went to dwell in the wilderness. He hastened to restrain the haste of its wrath against them and spent his time in silence. After some time, however, he sent another wise man to make peace between them. The man went and urged them meekly, according to the words that the meek man, *that is the master*, had sent him to speak, to repent, in which case he, *the master*, would take no revenge on them. But they, *the servants*, refused. Then *the master* sent his burning wrath and destroyed those servants with their houses. He spared none of the dark *houses* except one, which was covered by the darkness in which its foundations had been laid, and not by design. But after a certain time, the lord sent the lamp of wisdom to that *house* so that its eyes might be opened to the light. And so *the lamp* was sent that it might enter, *and that rebellious servant too*, in his mind, stumbled into error. He fell and the serpent, the angel of the abyss, derider of wayfarers, emerged and received him straight away. He turned his face and went to that house. When she saw him, she thought he was coming to swallow her, and out of her fear for him she came to the doorway in order to flee. But on looking up, she saw who is stronger than *that serpent, even* while fire was covering her and darkness surrounding her, and she could go no farther. She immediately made entreaties and wept tears and threw away her raiment and covered herself in sackcloth, tearing her breasts and ripping her cheeks, and she called for whoever of the humble might save it. And her husband, who holds her, "donned the hair shirt and lay in ashes." When they heard the doctrine of the lamp of wisdom, after the serpent had vomited on their threshold, their mind was certainly illuminated with the light of its discourse, as they descended from the mountain of pride. Therefore did they not perish like their kind. And the fire rose to its substance and the serpent went down to its lair. Because the Lord always does this for the humble, as it was said, "near and not far from whosoever truly calls him."[47]

Attention has already been drawn above to the limitations of Father Agostino's "scriptural" interpretation of this passage, which fails to attain the broader, allegorical level of meaning.[48] To proceed with our analysis and delineate a second level of interpretation, we can say that the towers and the riches consigned to the servants are the Scriptures, the ungrateful servants are the people unable to understand the Scriptures, the patient master is God, and the wise man is Noah or perhaps the Redeemer. The towers and the servants are destroyed except for one house, which remains, however, in darkness. This may be a metaphor of imperfect (perhaps literal) understanding of the Scriptures. The lord then sends the lamp of Wisdom, but the only servant not to perish in the divine punishment "stumbles" into error. The "serpent" then appears, but the most obvious and immediate interpretation, i.e. that this is Satan, does not fit in perfectly because the serpent causes "the house", i.e. its inhabitants, to look up and see "who is stronger." Moreover, the serpent "vomits on their threshold" and "the house" receives "the doctrine of the lamp of wisdom." This is a strange serpent, one that resembles the serpent Christ of certain Gnostic sects in their

---

[47] Ibid., pp. 210–11.

[48] Father Agostino's interpretation is given here so as to facilitate the reader's understanding: "A wise man, i.e. God, built twice three towers, i.e. six cities, filled them with goods of every kind and entrusted them to his servants. These are the cities of the Pentapolis and Nineveh, whose inhabitants, instead of showing gratitude to the Lord for the riches received through his generous providence, drove him away with the wickedness of their lives so that he had to dwell in the wilderness with Abraham. He could have destroyed them immediately but waited patiently for them to repent, sending Lot, a man as meek as his Lord, to call them back to the strait and narrow. As they did not listen to his warning, the Lord destroyed the Pentapolis and spared Nineveh, which did penance in accordance with Jonah's preaching. The end of the section describes the well-known episode of the prophet Jonah in the customary metaphorical terms, but this is quite clear and requires no explanation." Agostino Tedla, "A proposito di alcuni passi oscuri negli Scritti teologici etiopici pubblicati da E. Cerulli", op. cit., pp. 225–26.

interpretation of Genesis[49] or the principle of evil in the Pseudo-Clementine Homilies, whose actions are in accordance with God's will. The call for help from the "humble" on the part of the servant's wife and the "descent from the mountain of pride" are humility in interpretation and rejection of rigidly literal interpretation. And therefore, finally, "they did not perish like their kind. And the fire rose to its substance and the serpent went down to its lair." It is striking that Father Agostino's interpretation, though always valuable for the scriptural references, should prove inadequate and above all that he should make no comment on the last part of the parable, the section with the references to the "serpent," which is instead crucial.[50] Nor does he appear to grasp the overall meaning of the passage, which is quite evident in the light of the first paragraph of the quotation as presented above. This part is instead wholly omitted by Father Agostino in his essay.

Let us now return to the passage on the mystery of the Trinity. The hypothesis formulated here is that this is not a cosmology but a sophisticated symbology of the relationship established between the Scriptures and their interpreter, and an explicit criticism of those who trust to literal interpretation and "names" rather than allegorical interpretation. As stated in the first of the two quotations presented side by side above, all living beings, on dying, "entered through a single door and are closed with a single lock of **names,** that lends no key to open and no crack to introduce the arm of the **word** and distinguish their forms." Death puts an end to names and their capacity to distinguish because, with the end of the different beings and their return to the one natural entity, "now instead 'they are found under a single form and under the only name' of earth. And they will remain in this state until the end of world."[51]

The Shepherd of the Living, who appears in the next sentence, is not God, as Father Agostino thought, but another entity, perhaps the personification of the "names" (as Father Agostino himself suggests) or perhaps the human intellect, now devoid of its ability to distinguish.

---

[49] Birger A. Pearson, *Ancient Gnosticism - Traditions and Literature,* op. cit., pp. 117 ff.

[50] Agostino Tedla, "A proposito di alcuni passi oscuri negli Scritti teologici etiopici pubblicati da E. Cerulli", op. cit., pp. 225-26.

[51] Ibid., p. 231.

Let us now try to apply this model to the passage on the mystery of the Trinity:

Two actions	Perhaps the senses and the intellect, the two instruments of knowledge addressed by the author immediately before the passage on the Trinity (pp. 139–44)
enter a house	The house is the Scriptures, the Holy Scriptures.
through a door, whose lock has a unique sound and repeats no other; and through the arrival of this voice, its will is made known to the listener	The door is the approach to the Scriptures and the lock its secrets, but its sound is the will of God, the "letter" of the Scriptures, because they are His Scriptures.
And these, for the concupiscence of the warmth of the house, possess a girl—without waiting—a girl of honorable charm, desirable by all, forbidden in beauty by her parents.	This is the attempt to penetrate, to reveal the mysteries of the Scriptures, but it takes place "without waiting," and therefore without obeying the rule of understanding "by degrees" or considering "the months of the seasons of the divine Scriptures for sowing," as seen in a previous quotation. It is therefore a violation and ineffectual.
But while they, having entered by one door, go to their homeland the morning after, they will leave by twice three doors.	The above passage from the *Ship of the Soul* speaks of "a wise man who built twice three towers and filled them with riches for all the desires of the flesh." This reference to fleshly desires and the subsequent ingratitude of the servants suggests that "twice three doors" is a figure of speech for dispersion, like "twice three towers." This interpretation is in any case consistent with the phrase "without waiting" found in connection with the rape of the girl and with the interpretation of the same passage on the "Six Towers" put forward by Father Agostino..

(*Continued*)

And their daughter, born that night, the only child of her mother and unique by name and forbidden in beauty, will leave by twice two doors.	All of the passage recalls the reference made in the cosmogony of the Earth to the wind raging against the earth without being able to violate it, even though "its journey is not without effect." The suggestion in this case is that an interpretation "without waiting" is incorrect but performs the function of prompting a different model, as symbolized by the exit "through twice two doors," which appears to be a reference to the four canonical levels of scriptural interpretation (literal, allegorical, moral and anagogic).
Shortly after, having left, she will give birth to three sons, for wisdom of intelligence, because she was pregnant; and she will call them by three names: one: "Be praised among the poor"; the second: "Be blessed among the rich"; and the third: "Be glorified among the lofty in honor." And if they are united, His foundation is rapid, as He appears in a single person. And her initial denomination perishes when they are born.	The action of the two principles, like that of the "wind," does not prove ineffective but leads rather to the birth of three sons, to whom three names are given. This is the effect of fecundation "without waiting" and the three names, in their banality, have no distinguishing power. They are mere names and appear moreover to derive from the experience of human societies, poverty, wealth, and honor.[52] Their evident inadequacy or insignificance makes it necessary to combine them in a single person, which in turn causes the disappearance of "her initial denomination [...] when they [the three names] were born."
Come now, tell us the meaning of the birth of that *girl*, beautiful in form and in name, in a single night, while her youth, when she leaves, instead appears adult. I present her parable and abandon the foundation of the perceptibility of the two that entered;	The word "perceptibility" appears rather to mean "ability to perceive," and the phrase to mean that the senses and the intellect (the two principles) are not perceptive enough to interpret the mystery.

---

[52] In this reference to poverty, wealth and honor, it may also be possible to discern a criticism of those who "have said [...] that saying 'Divinity' comes to mean power and command," as seen above in the quotation from the Mirror of the Intellect. According to Cerulli, this was probably a reference to the Jesuits. See Enrico Cerulli, Scritti Teologici Etiopici *dei secoli XVI-XVII – La Storia dei Quattro Concili ed altri opuscoli monofisiti*, op. cit., p. 163, note 4.

and I repudiate the disappearance of the abyss of the root of the garden of the parents of her, who from that (*abyss*) sprang, in the Persons of the Father, the Son and the Holy Spirit, three in Persons, one in Divinity.	Though very obscure, the phrase appears to mean that the author of the tract rejects the abyss (i.e. depth, the deep, obscure sense of the Scripture, deriving from her parents) and refuses the root of the garden of her parents, i.e. the process of generation initiated by those two principles (likened to the action of a root in a garden), and hence the generative process that led to the birth from the "abyss" of the Three Persons of the Trinity, Three Persons but a single divinity.
We shall not say that, like the sons of the girl, one has less glory than the other; and the second is more blessed than the third; and the third is more glorified than *the other two* in honor. Were we to say that, far be it from us to believe this comparison true *to the letter*. They instead exist in honor, glory and magnificence in a single reign, single power, single council, single glory. And they receive a single prostration from the earthly and the celestial with no emulation, as handed down to us by the Fathers, ancient and recent.	A rejection of the classificatory approach to the Trinity through names and an attack on the anthropomorphic approach to the divine, which interprets it through recourse to the categories of human societies.
Therefore we too shall comprehend them with the intellect without approaching their commencement, which has no end; and we shall know them with our thought without feeling or reaching their foundation, which is far away from any interpretation and sublime to speak of. Because prior to their being perceptible is their not being such. As the Elder said, "I know the Lord with no name."	This is the crowning of the symbolic episode. It is impossible to understand the mystery of the Trinity, its "commencement" and its "foundation, which is far removed from any interpretation."

It is no coincidence that the author should present a clear exposition of his trinitarian "nominalism" immediately after this passage.

> **If we know it now, we call it with many names, because they were born for us on the foundation after the form of the body of the creatures was born.** And if we say "three persons", *we do not mean* that it is like Abraham, who *precedes* Isaac by a hundred years, and Isaac, who precedes Jacob by a certain amount of time. This is not what we mean to say. Like Adam, who *alone* existed at one time, these *persons of the Trinity* instead exist in parity and in union. **Their names did not come after them but exist like them *ab initio*. And their persons are called names and their names are called persons. As St Gregory Thaumaturgus said in his first homily on the Trinity**:
>
> "Know that every thing is of the three things that are names, i.e. substance, name and genus. We speak, *for example*, of (man) servant and steward: man by nature, servant by condition and steward by name. We also speak of the Father, Son, and Holy Spirit, and these, however, are not names subsequently adopted by them but themselves the persons. **"Man" is not a name but signifies *human* nature, because each man *then* has *his own individual* name**, differing from one to another, for example Adam, Abraham, Isaac, and Jacob; these are their names. **But the hypostases of God are *themselves* the names, and the names are *themselves* the hypostases**, because the interpretation of hypostases is persons that are certain, existing in their own right, perfect in appearance and image. And these certain names are called the Trinity, being one essence and three persons and one divinity."[53]

These few short lines encapsulate the thinking of the author of the tract, the formulations that caused Cerulli to think that he was a Mikaelite, and that Mikaelite was akin to Sabellian. As we continue in the reading, however, we realize immediately that the above is not the exposition of a

---

[53] Enrico Cerulli, *Scritti Teologici Etiopici dei Secoli XVI-XVII-I – Tre Opuscoli dei Mikaeliti*, op. cit., pp. 146-47. The italics are additions by Cerulli to make the text more comprehensible. The boldface has been added by the present author to emphasize certain parts.

new metaphysics but rather the basis for the umpteenth and perhaps the most forthright assertion of the unknowability of God:

> What shall we say from now on? Does the seed perhaps grow from the sea to produce crops for the fool who sowed it in the sea? Or does the plant grow that was planted on the rock and burned by torrid fire at the roots while it was far from the passing of water? Does hunger perhaps come in the midst of satiety or thirst in the midst of drinkers? Are there not perhaps those who do not know the distinction of the month of harvests; and for their laziness, proud people in misery for the plague of famine, kept to their beds by famine and unable to move just as the ulcerated are kept to their beds by plague? Just so, if we have sown seeds of thought in the deep sea of Divinity, going beyond the soil of humility, going beyond the fields of our boundaries, we too will remain not only with no fruits but without any sprouting of leaves. Brothers, let us from now on place limits on our discourse so as not to ruin ourselves, and let us measure the limits of our discourse so as not to perish. Let us say with St Paul: "O the depth of the riches both of the wisdom and knowledge of God", the love of the Lord. And Isaiah said: "Who hath measured the waters in the hollow of his hand, and meted out heaven with the span?" There is none equal to the Lord. And who is like Him? And we the orthodox, without falsehood or deceit, believe in these testimonies.[54]

These two quotations may appear to clash with one another but do not in actual fact as long as the first is interpreted not as a metaphysical proposition but rather as the exposition of the birth of the concept in man—the idea of the Trinity—and therefore in a gnoseological sense. The first quotation begins in fact with these words: "If we know it now, we call it with many names, because they were born for us on the foundation after the form of the body of the creatures was born." This is equivalent to saying that man can only know God in this way, through metaphors and imprecise words drawn from his own human experience. Moreover, with respect to the next phrase, for this reason we say "persons", but this name of "persons" was coined by man and in this sense, in the human understanding, in the idea of God that man has formed for himself: "Their names did not come after them but exist like them *ab initio*. And their persons are called names and their names are called persons." On close rereading, the entire passage

---

[54] Ibid., pp. 147-48.

always proves to refer to *interpretation*, i.e. to the idea of God that man has formed for himself, and not to the divine truths; to the names that we give to the divine truths and not to the divinity itself. The few pages that follow the above passages and conclude the tract contain nothing to suggest that this analysis is in any way inconsistent or flawed.

In our opinion, the above interpretation restores solid logical coherence to the sequential exposition of the first tract and also makes it possible to glimpse its connection with the other two identified by Cerulli as Mikaelite.

The Originality of the Investigation Carried Out in the "Mikaelite" Opuscula

But who were the adversaries of the author of the first tract, the *Exposition of the Divinity*? What was the position of the Ethiopian Church on the question of the Trinity? Why were "names" a key subject in the speculations of the author of the first tract? The second volume of Cerulli's *Scritti Teologici Etiopici dei Secoli XVI-XVII* presents a sample of other texts written in the same period of anti-Jesuit polemics. These are grouped together as "monophysite" and hence orthodox even though in actual fact, as we shall see, the four texts in question do not appear completely harmonious in terms of content and unquestionably come from different spheres of the Ethiopian Church. Let us, however, return to the questions raised above. The position of the Ethiopian Church as regards the Trinity is clearly expressed in the *Mirror of the Intellect*, which Father Agostino rightly regards as "the most sustained and the most fully developed in the second volume."[55] As regards the meaning of "one divinity" and "three persons," the author offers the following clarification:

> They are distinct in names, in persons, in appearance, in hypostasis; and they are one in divinity, that is to say in essence, in will, in consent, in word, in life.[56]

He continues further on:

> We are convinced and persuaded by their denomination that each of Them has a name of his own that he neither gives

---

[55] Agostino Tedla, "A proposito di alcuni passi oscuri negli Scritti teologici etiopici pubblicati da E. Cerulli", op. cit., p. 240.

[56] Enrico Cerulli, *Scritti Teologici Etiopici dei secoli XVI-XVII*, op. cit., p.165.

himself nor is able pass on to another, and that is not like the name of another. This (is said) of the name of the Father with respect to the names of the Son and the Holy Spirit; of the name of the Son with respect to the names of the Father and the Holy Spirit; and the name of the Holy Spirit with respect to the names of the Father and the Son. If we speak of the intellect, we do not give it the name of word; nor to the word do we give the name of intellect; nor to the soul, i.e. to our life, do we give the name of word or intellect. Just so, when we call the Father, we do not give Him the name of the Son or the Holy Spirit. And this holds for all three.[57]

Let us say therefore that we are convinced and know that God, adorable in the name, has the speaking Word that was born of Him; and has the life-giving Life that proceeded from Him. This leads us to give the divine essence the name of Father, because the Son was born of Him as the word is born of the intellect. And we give the name of Son begotten of the Father to the Person of the Word, as we have said before, insomuch as the word is clearly born of the intellect. And this name of Word leads us to call it Son; and it is manifestly clear that the word has no origin or birth other than from the intellect. Therefore do we call the Person of the Word the Son. And we give the name of Holy Spirit, proceeding from the Father, to the person of Life, as Life comes from the intellect with no division; and therefore do we call the Holy Spirit the Life of the Father. And this designation of His vitality leads us to call him Spirit, as we call our life "soul." It is indeed acknowledged that our life is our soul.[58]

For the Ethiopian Church, the "name" was therefore one of the essential attributes of the different figures of the Trinity and one of the tools needed to ensure the distinguishability of the three figures, the one that did most to guarantee the "relational" identity, i.e. the possibility of distinguishing the three persons from one other through their relations of "family" (father-son) and function ("generation-procession"). These are expressed

---

[57] Ibid., p. 172.
[58] Ibid., p. 173.

elsewhere through precise metaphors, such as the sun with its three attributes of the disc, light, and heat, here in the same tract, and the comparison of the Father to a man, the Son to his word, and the Holy Spirit to its breath in the *Treasury of the Faith*.[59] As we have seen, the author of the first "Mikaelite" tract instead fiercely attacks the idea of knowledge through "names" and any claim to derive knowledge of the divine through "metaphors" based on human experience. What he therefore rejects is precisely examples like those offered by the above quotations, which claim to use names and human experience as the basis for drawing authentic "maps," as the third appears to do in a certain sense with its correspondences between the figures of the Trinity and the various human "functions". The author of the first tract appears to tell us that the divine can only be known through the Scriptures, which must, however, be subjected to patient study and investigation, eschewing any immediate approach and literal interpretation. This stance of the Ethiopian Church in favor of the literal interpretation of the Scriptures also emerges clearly in the *Mirror of the Intellect*, where the existence of an "image" of God is asserted in the following passage:

> It is shown by the Books of the Old and the New (Testament) that he has image and appearance. If He had no image and appearance, He would not have said, "Let Us make man in Our image, according to Our likeness." This proves that He has image and likeness. It is also said in the Scriptures that "the face of the Lord is against them that do evil" and "the eyes of the Lord are upon the righteous, and His ears are open unto their cry" ... Therefore do we believe and confess that the Lord has an effective image, which is not tangible and delimited like ours but, as His nature is neither tangible nor delimitable, so also is His image.[60]

---

[59] *Tesoro della Fede*, the first tract in the second volume of Cerulli's *Scritti Teologici Etiopici dei secoli XVI-XVII*. It is surprising that this work, which presents itself as a bulwark of the true orthodox faith, should employ this comparison, thus taking up a formulation of the Sabellian heresy and hence the heresy of which the Mikaelites were also accused. The limits of the comparison are, however, explicitly stated a few lines later. E. Cerulli, *Scritti Teologici Etiopici dei secoli XVI-XVII – La Storia dei Quattro Concili ed altri opuscoli monofisiti*, op. cit., p. 70.

[60] Enrico Cerulli, *Scritti Teologici Etiopici dei secoli XVI-XVII*, op. cit., pp.174-75.

It follows from the above that the "Mikaelite" opuscula launch a substantial attack on some cornerstones of the Ethiopian faith, which are confirmed as such also by other texts published by Cerulli in the second volume of his *Scritti Teologici Etiopici dei secoli XVI-XVII* and especially in the *Treasury of the Faith*.

Those listed above are not, however, the only original features to emerge from a reading of the "Mikaelite" opuscula. Another of particular importance regards the unknowability of the divine, as addressed through analysis of the following:

- the limitations of the senses
- the limitations of the intellect
- the limitations of the human ability to interpret the Scriptures
- the probable inability of man to love and know God even if God should reveal Himself to man, as man is satisfied with what he knows and then desires it no longer
- the reasons why it is right for the divine to remain a mystery and for the paradoxes of the divine to remain such
- the need to accept the unknowability of God, of Whom nature and the Scriptures are, however, manifestations and therefore to be addressed with respect and humility by those wishing to approach Him

Not all the elements of this complex whole can be found in the Ethiopian tradition. The *Mirror of the Intellect* certainly discusses the limitations of the human tools of knowledge and on the fact, for example, that man cannot know his own soul. The following meditation on the impenetrability of the mystery of Christ's incarnation appears slightly further on in the same tract:

> As regards those who say, "We know and are certain of how this mystery of the Union came about," this is error and deceit, since Gabriel and Mary themselves could not fathom that (mystery) even though she is His mother and Gabriel the herald of His incarnation and birth and His messenger. They (Mary and Gabriel) indeed ended their discourse with the final conclusion of the faith, saying, "There is nothing that it is impossible for the Lord." And so like us, poor and

> limited in intelligence, who are even ignorant of the formula of our humanity, which is made up of the four elements and exists in one harmony even though they are opposed to one another ... and that our humanity was formed of those elements we know and confess, but how it was made and composed we know not and cannot be certain. And if we cannot know ourselves with any certainty, how can we flatter that we might know the Union of God the Word with our nature?[61]

In certain respects, with its rhetorical overtones of emotion, this passage recalls parts of the "Mikaelite" opuscula, the first in particular. It also reminds us that mystery is one of the great historical themes of Christianity. Ethiopia is not only no exception in this sense but also a place where mystery is often invoked precisely in order to offer (or refuse to offer) answers on the two most important questions, namely the Trinity and Christ's incarnation, the object of endless speculations and among the subjects most keenly debated in the dispute with the Jesuits (to whom the phrase "those who say" probably alludes). Recourse to the concept of mystery, explicitly and repeatedly formulated,[62] was a way of making these subjects of dispute matters of faith and thus curtailing potentially endless exchanges of views. In this perspective, the position expressed by the author of the first supposedly Mikaelite tract, the *Exposition of the Divinity*, constitutes a perfectly acceptable contribution to the debate on the monophysite side, as the idea of the unknowability of God and the "Trinitarian nominalism" entailed by the limitations of the human tools of knowledge were certainly sufficient to stifle any discussion of the above-mentioned mysteries in its cradle and rule out the assertion of anything other than the monophysite views.

Another aspect of the "Mikaelite" opuscula that appears detectable also in the monophysite writings published by Cerulli is the use of complex metaphors based on the wax-gold model of the Ethiopian Qəne. The *Treasury of the Faith* offers a few examples.

---

[61] Ibid., p. 180.

[62] See for example ibid., p. 179.

- In the first, reference to the various forms in which the Holy Spirit manifests Itself to man (e.g. as flame and a dove) is followed by this assertion:

> The Lord can do anything and flawed is the faith of whosoever believes that there is something He cannot. But let us leave the Lord aside. Even water, despite its liquid nature, can become solid, it can become hail that is touched with the hand without thereby losing its essence as water. We do not call hail water or water hail, but it is understood that the nature of hail is water and in fact, after a short time, the substance of hail returns to water. Likewise the Lord, wishing to appear to men, becomes man or fire or dove or many other images but does not therefore, by the fact of revealing Himself as fire or dove, depart from His divine nature, just as hail does not depart from its nature to assume other natures but rather returns to water.[63]

- The substantial difference with respect to the Qəne lies in the fact that the metaphors, as shown here, are not formulated as riddles. The wax-gold model is, however, followed perfectly, even though the meaning is revealed in the exposition,
- Further on, a similar comparison is drawn for the generation of the soul of the unborn child by the two parents. The metaphor is based on wood and its ability to burn, which remains hidden until two pieces of wood are rubbed against one another. The potential of wood (fire) is not developed until the condition of development (i.e. rubbing) is created. In the same way, if the male seed does not combine with the "menstrual blood," there is no possibility of generation and neither new flesh nor a new soul can be developed.[64]

It is clearly evident from these examples that figures of speech and analogies, like the metaphor of wax and gold, were certainly used in the Ethiopian theological debate at the time of the Jesuit presence. They reach their highest peak of complexity, however, only in "Mikaelite" opuscula, which their interpreter Father Agostino ended up, as we have seen, regarding as tests or challenges.

---

[63] Enrico Cerulli, *Scritti Teologici Etiopici dei secoli XVI-XVII – La Storia dei Quattro Concili ed altri opuscoli monofisiti*, op. cit., p. 91.

[64] Ibid., p. 97.

At the same time, however, while it is possible to trace various characteristics and the original themes of the opuscula back to the Ethiopian cultural context of their time, something unresolved still remains. Father Agostino observes in his conclusions that in various respects they actually reveal the influence of Catholic missionaries: "The broad use of psychological arguments, something truly unusual in the traditional schools, also suggests if not direct dependency, at least a certain influence of the missionaries."[65] By "psychological arguments" Father Agostino may have meant all the passages examined in the first tract that—if understood in the literal sense—oblige us to attribute God with wholly human feelings like jealousy, envy, desire for vengeance, and repentance (interpretations which are indeed abundantly present in the Midrash). Alternatively, he may have referred to the precise examination of the limitations of the human cognitive faculties, mentioned also in the monophysite tracts but developed in far greater depth in the opuscula. In short, Father Agostino thought that the opuscula had been at least partially influenced in their composition by the presence of Jesuit missionaries in Ethiopia. At the same time, attention has already been drawn to the fierce opposition to the Roman Catholic presence clearly expressed in the second and the third tracts. It therefore appears that the influence referred to by Father Agostino derived from a combination of circumstances that forced the authors of the opuscula, as well as some elements of the Ethiopian Church, to take the following steps:

- To formulate their doctrinal views in full and explicit terms for use in debate;
- To enter into contact with different schools of thought during the debates and also through a reading of the theological works that the Jesuit missionaries unquestionably took with them to Ethiopia;
- To enter into contact with different schools of thought when events in Ethiopia forced many of the orthodox clergy to take refuge in Alexandria, where some of them, as we shall see, probably continued their polemics in writings addressed to the Ethiopian rulers.

While the above observations are made on the basis of Father Agostino's suggestions, there are two other points that appear worthy of mention

---

[65] Agostino Tedla, "A proposito di alcuni passi oscuri negli Scritti teologici etiopici pubblicati da E. Cerulli," op. cit., p. 241.

because they do not appear to fit immediately into the Ethiopian cultural context of the time.

First, the assertion of a kinship between man and animals,[66] something quite unusual in Ethiopia but habitually used by St Augustine of Hippo and by all the Christian authors acquainted with Greek philosophy, appears on the first page of the first "Mikaelite" tract.

Second, the assertion that the discovery of God must start from the contemplation of creation, as typically argued by Augustine, e.g. in the *De Trinitate*,[67] and by other Augustinian authors like St Bonaventure,[68] is explicitly stated in the third of the opuscula:

> Do not seek the Lord boldly, however, but rather in the form of the creatures that are before you, *creatures* perceptible with the senses. Reach the land of their hidden Parent by these steps and fall down for fear of your audacity.[69]

In actual fact, however, this theme emerges clearly also from the passion with which animal behavior[70] is described in the opuscula as well as natural phenomena like fog[71] and the metaphor of honey.[72]

To end this brief discussion of the elements of originality to be found in the "Mikaelite" opuscula, mention must be made of the "linguistic" approach to the Trinity, whereby the metaphysical aspect of the question is deliberately distinguished from the gnoseological. The real nature of the Trinity is an unknowable and unattainable truth. Any human attempt to approach some knowledge of the divine must be undertaken in full awareness that it can never expect to attain this truth. The endeavor therefore becomes a reflection on the human instruments of language and

---

[66] Enrico Cerulli, *Scritti Teologici Etiopici dei Secoli XVI-XVII – Tre Opuscoli dei Mikaeliti*, op. cit., p. 67.

[67] St Augustine of Hippo, *On the Trinity*, XV, 1, 1.

[68] St Bonaventure, *The Mind's Road to God* (*Itinerarium mentis in Deum*), http://www.ewtn.com/library/sources/road.txt.

[69] Enrico Cerulli, *Scritti Teologici Etiopici dei Secoli XVI-XVII – Tre Opuscoli dei Mikaeliti*, op. cit., p. 314. The word in italics is an addition made by Cerulli.

[70] Ibid., p. 72 (the leopard), p. 151 (the spider), and pp. 151-52 (the chameleon).

[71] See Agostino Tedla "A proposito di alcuni passi oscuri negli Scritti teologici etiopici pubblicati da E. Cerulli," op. cit., p. 223, in connection with the passage in Enrico Cerulli, *Scritti Teologici Etiopici dei Secoli XVI-XVII – Tre Opuscoli dei Mikaeliti*, op. cit., pp. 148-50.

[72] Enrico Cerulli, *Scritti Teologici Etiopici dei Secoli XVI-XVII – I – Tre Opuscoli dei Mikaeliti*, op. cit., pp. 95-96.

on the limitations of the human faculties of perception and imagination in order to try to speak of that transcendent reality (or perhaps rather "that we might not be altogether silent", as St Augustine put it). The "Mikaelite" opuscula display perfect awareness that the problem is linguistic, as in the following passage already quoted above:

> Know that every thing is of the three things that are names, i.e. substance, name and genus. We speak, *for example*, of (man) servant and steward: man by nature, servant by condition and steward by name. We also speak of the Father, Son, and Holy Spirit, and these, however, are not names subsequently adopted by them but themselves the persons. **"Man" is not a name but signifies *human* nature, because each man *then* has *his own individual* name**, differing from one to another, for example Adam, Abraham, Isaac, and Jacob; these are their names. **But the hypostases of God are *themselves* the names, and the names are** themselves **the hypostases**, because the interpretation of hypostases is persons that are certain, existing in their own right, perfect in appearance and image. And these certain names are called the Trinity, being one essence and three persons and one divinity.[73]

It is clear that the author is fully aware of the difference between species, individual, and name, between category, substance, and attribute, as expressed in the following passage from Abelard:

> For example, this man is a substance, a body, an animate and sensitive being, i.e. a "rational, mortal animal", that is to say a man, and he can be white and curly haired, can be a subject and receive other accidents. And while the substance, body, and animate being are identical in him according to number and essence, they are nevertheless different from one another according to their properties and must be determined on the basis of these with different definitions. One is proper to substance, another to the body or the other things, and one is called state of substance, another of the body or the other things.

---

[73] Ibid., pp. 146–47. The parts in italics are added by Cerulli to make it "possible to follow the thread of the argument through the highly intricate syntax peculiar to the style of the opuscula" (ibid., p. XXII).

In this way it is possible to attribute to individual things innumerable characteristics differing from one another in terms of properties while the essence remains identical. Why is it therefore any wonder that different properties should be found in God in terms of which the three persons can be distinguished while the divine essence remains one? In a man, who is substance and body at the same time, or the other individual things stated previously ... one is the property of the substance, another the property of the body and the other things, and another the property of the father and the son. In God, in the same way, even though the same essence is Father, Son and Holy Spirit, one is the property of the Father, whereby it generates, another the property of the Son, whereby it is generated, and another the property of the Holy Spirit, whereby it proceeds.[74]

The difference in the formulations is just as strong as the similarity between their content. Every essence, while remaining one and the same, has different properties and states. God can therefore be one in essence and trine in the relational identity between the different figures. The names are the persons and the persons are the names. While the use of these concepts is obviously not identical, there are deep similarities in the understanding of the problem. The investigation carried out appears to reveal definite similarities between the "Mikaelite" opuscula and the studies of European theologians, from St Augustine of Hippo to Thomas Aquinas, who reorganized the whole of previous theological speculation in his *Summa Theologiae*. In particular, the closest similarities appear to be with trails of investigation blazed by St Augustine and the medieval philosophers who followed in his footsteps. The results of a search for historical confirmation of this hypothesis prove disappointing, however, as no Augustinian models of thought appear to have found their way to Ethiopia. In the essay referred to above, Piovanelli offers another possible interpretation of the underlying rationale of the writings attributed by Cerulli to the Mikaelite heretics by pointing out that at the beginning of the 17th century, after consolidation of the doctrinal arguments put forward by the Christians of the different churches against the Muslims,

---

[74] M. Parodi, M. Rossini (eds.), *Fra le due rupi, La logica della trinità nella discussione tra Roscellino, Anselmo e Abelardo*, Milan, 2000, pp. 220-21.

"the incomprehensibility of God had become a classic theme."[75] The reason for this, in his view, lay in the difficulty of engaging in rational dialogue with Islamic theologians precisely on the question of the Trinity, in defending the assertion that three can be one and one can be three. In this connection, Piovanelli refers to the Jacobite Isa Ibn Zur'a (943-1008) and his speculations on the limitations of the senses and the intellect as regards comprehension of the divine. While this too is a possibility, doubts arise as to whether the authors of the opuscula would have continued to draw solely on this source some five hundred years later and whether not even the vaguest echoes had reached Ethiopia of the theological debate under way in Europe, with which contacts were now long established. As we have seen, Father Agostino himself attributed some of the originality of the "Mikaelite" opuscula to the influence of the Catholic missionaries. It should be pointed out in this connection that despite the frequent clashes between the Franciscan monastic movement and the Society of Jesus in European history, it is also true that in the great work of theological synthesis carried out by Thomas Aquinas, the influence of Augustine of Hippo is crucial for all the aspects regarding the divine mysteries and especially the mystery of the Trinity.

The Provenance of the Sole Manuscript

The above considerations as a whole prompted the present author to wonder about the provenance of the sole manuscript bearing witness to the "Mikaelite" opuscula. It was a great surprise to learn that it belonged to a certain Ṣägga Krəstos, described as a traveler by some and an adventurer by others, an Ethiopian who left traces of his presence in Cairo, Jerusalem, and other parts of Palestine as well as Rome, Turin, and Paris, where he died in 1638. He presented himself as heir to the Ethiopian throne and as persecuted by the king for dynastic reasons, but different versions exist of these claims and the identity of his alleged persecutor. There is no historical evidence of his participation in the debate with the Jesuits and the superior of the Dayr al-Muharraq monastery in Egypt reported him to the Franciscans in Cairo as an apostate who had abandoned the order of St John the Baptist. He was in constant, regular contact with friars of the Franciscan order in Cairo, Jerusalem, and Rome,

---

[75] Pierluigi Piovanelli, "Connaissance de Dieu et Sagesse Humaine en Ethiopie", op. cit., p. 207.

and converted to the Catholic faith in Nazareth in 1632. He lived in a Franciscan monastery in Rome too and unsuccessfully sought help to return to Ethiopia in the closing years of his life.[76]

What is striking about the life of this figure is his close contact with Franciscan circles. From the 13th century on, as is known, this monastic order was the greatest supporter of Augustinianism in the theological sphere as against Aristotelianism and Averroism and in opposition to the philosophical formulations of Scholasticism and, as from the 16th century, the Jesuit order. This is an important connection and one that inevitably prompts us to recall the great figures of medieval European philosophy belonging to the order: Bonaventure of Bagnoregio (1221-74), Roger Bacon (1214-92), Duns Scotus (1266-1308) and William of Ockham (1295/1300-1348). Practically all the themes discussed above in relation to the "Mikaelite" opuscula are to be found in the works of these philosophers, from the cognitive limitations of the senses and the intellect to the need to accept the unknowability of God. As we have seen, however, the sources for these could also have been Christian Arab thinkers like Isa Ibn Zur'a. Other characteristics that are more difficult to explain are also to be found in the opuscula, however, including the extraordinary attention to nature and its cycles as well as the behavior of animals like the leopard, spider, and chameleon, the subject of names, the interpretation of the Scriptures and its methods, proceeding by degrees, the idea clearly expressed in the *Safe Haven* that the search for God must proceed through study of the Scriptures and observation of the works of God, including nature. In the case of nature, as is known, many Franciscan philosophers were renowned scientists, including Roger Bacon. As regards the question of names, the most important point and one already discussed above, the formulations found in the first of the opuscula are directly related, as we have seen, to Abelard and his views on the Trinity. These formulations were then taken up by William of Ockham.

The question arises at this point of why there should be such a marked correspondence between the opuscula examined and the European traditions in terms both of subject matter and of solutions to the problems addressed. Why should these opuscula come as such a surprise to the reader in relation to the previous and coeval Ethiopian literature?

---

[76] For further information on Ṣägga Krəstos, see A. Martinez, "Ṣägga Krəstos," in Siegbert Uhlig (ed.), *Encyclopaedia Aethiopica*, vol. V, Wiesbaden 2014, pp. 503-04, and the extensive bibliography given there.

A number of doubts arise on consideration of the close contact between Ṣägga Krəstos and the Franciscan monastic order during his life, as outlined below.

- Ṣägga Krəstos moved to France in 1635 and died in 1638. The codex of the "Mikaelite" opuscula did not therefore enter the Colbert collection before 1635.
- The laws in favor of the Jesuit presence in Ethiopia had already been repealed in 1632.
- Ṣägga Krəstos is thought to have been born in 1608. He arrived in Cairo in 1632 as the self-proclaimed heir to the Ethiopian throne and a political refugee. His career as an "adventurer" therefore lasted only six years.
- Reflection on the origins of the "Mikaelite" manuscript reveals the surprising presence of many characteristics that apparently bear witness to European influence and make it seem "new" with respect to the Ethiopian cultural context. At the same time, the philosophical points of reference displayed establish links not only with the Jesuits but also with other thinkers that would then have been perceived in Europe not perhaps as their adversaries, because the old medieval disputes were now dying out, but certainly as occupying a different location on the map of Christian thought.
- Historians of the order suggest the possibility of a Franciscan presence in Ethiopia at the same time as the Jesuits.[77] While scholars have expressed doubts on this score, Franciscans were in any case present in Cairo as from 1620.
- The presence of Ethiopian monks in the Egyptian monasteries as from the 13th century at least is regarded as certain, and Ṣägga Krəstos may have been part of the monastic community of Dayr al-Muharraq.
- Ṣägga Krəstos is unlikely to have been the author of the manuscript in view of his youth and the eventful life he lived from 1632, when he was only 24, until his death in 1638. The possibility cannot be ruled out, however, that he had more mature companions during his life as an "adventurer" or that his wanderings in Egypt and Palestine

---

[77] See A. Martinez, "Franciscans," in Siegbert Uhlig (ed.), *Encyclopaedia Aethiopica*, vol. II, Wiesbaden 2005, pp. 578–79.

brought him into contact with other Ethiopian monks already connected with Franciscan monasteries.

- Following this train of thought, the present author read all the information available on the history of the sole manuscript from which the three "Mikaelite" opuscula are drawn.[78] This again revealed an important fact, namely that it also contains a letter published by Cerulli as *Consolazione dell'anima* (*Consolation of the Soul*) in the second volume of his *Scritti Teologici Etiopici dei Secoli XVI-XVII*.[79] The eminent scholar evidently discerned such differences not only between the letter and the opuscula but also between the three opuscula as to attribute them all to different authors. Comparison of the different texts does not, however, bear out this thesis conclusively due to the very marked stylistic similarities they all display, above all a taste for sophisticated expression, frequent use of metaphor, abundant quotation of the Scriptures, and great freedom in developing religious symbolism through metaphor. These are particular characteristics found to a lesser extent and degree of development in the other three tracts published by Cerulli in the second volume. This fact and the marked stylistic similarities suggest that the three "Mikaelite" opuscula and the letter could be the work of the same author. Evidence that this hypothesis is not far-fetched is indeed provided by Cerulli himself:

We have seen that in the single codex in Paris the *Consolation of the Soul* of Newaya Masqal follows the three opuscula of the Mikaelites published in the first volume of this collection of mine. The doubt may arise that this "open letter" to the Negus is also the work of a Mikaelite, not only because of its inclusion in the codex but also due to the similarity of the style, wearyingly overladen with rhetorical devices, to that of the Mikaelite opuscula, as well as the fact that Newaya Masqal presents himself as an exile in Egypt, where the small Mikaelite group were also exiles. It should be pointed out, however, that the

---

[78] The manuscript—Paris, Bibliothèque Nationale, Eth. 119—contains a note asserting the ownership of Ṣägga Krəstos and was certainly taken to Paris by him.

[79] Enrico Cerulli, *Scritti Teologici Etiopici dei secoli XVI-XVII – La Storia dei Quattro Concili ed altri opuscoli monofisiti*, op. cit., pp. 120-35.

"open letter" appears to make no reference to the Mikaelite doctrine but confines itself to defending the established monophysite doctrine of the Ethiopian Church.[80]

Cerulli attributes the peculiarities of the style of the three opuscula and the letter to a single model of Mikaelite writing. It is also possible, however, to see the same peculiarities as a hallmark so distinctive that it can be attributed to one highly characterized figure, namely Nəwayä Mäsqäl, identified by Cerulli on the basis of the following passage:

As regards my name, which has the Vessel below and the Cross on top,[81] because it opened its gates for the vile men of Babylon to enter, therefore have I placed it after the primogeniture[82] so that it might remain hidden in the ink, as those hide that are ugly of face among men with dress and superfluous greetings. Because of my baseness, of which I am ashamed. Let alone send any writing to you, I would not even feel worthy to bear writing by another's hand to present it to someone of lower rank than your officials. Your love, devoid of fallacy or rancor, has enabled me, however, to send this parchment in my stead to kiss the outer and inner curtains until it falls before the heels of my sovereign, weak in law, and rises from there to the mount of the (sovereign's) knees, which bend before the Crucified God his Master, and says (the parchment): May the Lord protect you as you deem sufficient and scatter your enemies. How are you? As for me, I have been no better than a swineherd but rejoice to hear that you have been well. I am, however, afflicted with grief because of your daughter,[83] who is like you and whom the hand of the wicked has assaulted. For this, may the Lord comfort you. Amen.[84]

---

[80] Ibid., p. XI.

[81] Transcription of the note by Cerulli: "L'Autore si chiamava dunque Newaya Masqal ('Vas Crucis') [The author was therefore named Newaya Masqal ('Vas Crucis')]."

[82] Probably an allusion to the fact that this passage is not placed at the beginning of the letter, where the author's name usually appears, but at the beginning of the second chapter.

[83] The Faith.

[84] Enrico Cerulli, *Scritti Teologici Etiopici dei secoli XVI-XVII – La Storia dei Quattro Concili ed altri opuscoli monofisiti*, op. cit., pp. 124-25.

But what are the distinguishing characteristics of this figure that appear to emerge from a reading of the different texts? He must have been a member of the clergy, as attested by his deep knowledge of theology, and also a sophisticated intellectual well acquainted with Qəne. By virtue of these various qualities, he must also have acquired a refined aesthetic and linguistic sensitivity. We do not know whether these characteristics could be attained through an education within the Ethiopian borders. Moreover, the polemical model developed in the "Mikaelite" opuscula is also highly sophisticated in that while the other anti-Catholic writings generally confined themselves to countering diaphysite with monophysite arguments, this author counters the Jesuits and their arguments with the unknowability of God and the ineffectiveness of human tools of knowledge, thus adopting an approach that radically undermined any assertion contrary to Ethiopian orthodoxy. The other important point to emerge is that Nəwayä Mäsqäl wrote his letter from Egypt. Ṣägga Krəstos therefore probably acquired or copied the manuscript during his stay in Cairo, as there is no evidence of the letter ever reaching the Ethiopian sovereign. As we know, however, Ṣägga Krəstos was in regular contact with the Franciscan community in Cairo.

Another Ambiguous Passage

While further difficulties already emerge from the above considerations as regards acceptance of the Gnostic interpretation of these opuscula,[85] progress toward our conclusions will be facilitated by examination of another passage that Cerulli interprets as Gnostic. The following is a brief extract:

> A man said to me, that I might learn about them: "The four *senses* that you bear, and which bear you too, treat them with moderation so that they do not go beyond their measure. If two *of them* refuse to be yoked by you in order to run *instead* like horses whose ropes have been cut and bits removed, or like wild animals that have smelled a corpse of which to eat their fill, or like a proud lion accustomed to the blood that pours from its

---

[85] The suggestion that they could be the work of followers of the Mikaelite heretics still remains valid, however.

prey, do not tire yourself by running to restrain them. But rather hide your strength in the place inside *your* weakness and appear powerless until desire is consumed to the limits of the corpse, *i.e.* of the land of *their* goal. After the carrion has been consumed, you will find them on their return to *your* vicinity grazing on ashes and licking the dirt of the house.[86]

This is the passage about "the four," interpreted by Cerulli as referring to the discipline of the senses[87] and by Father Agostino as referring to the arms and legs.[88] The latter interpretation appears unacceptable because it would make no sense in the logical development of the argument. As the author is speaking about the senses right up to this passage, the switch to the four limbs would be incomprehensible. Moreover, he immediately goes on to discuss the limitations of human intelligence, and is therefore examining man's cognitive faculties.

At the same time, it is strange that Cerulli's exposition of his interpretation should move so quickly from the evident gnoseological meaning, from the listing of rules or models of behavior to attain knowledge, to the moral meaning. Cerulli's reference to the senses "running wild"[89] appears to clash with the logical argument of the text and its avowed purpose to demonstrate the limitations of the human intellect, and we are therefore led to suspect that this is yet another challenging trap laid by the author. In our view, the author is speaking about the limitations of human intellect and the need to control the facile illusion that the senses can lead to knowledge of truth. He also indicates the other risk, however, of overly rigid

---

[86] Enrico Cerulli, *Scritti Teologici Etiopici dei Secoli XVI-XVII – Tre Opuscoli dei Mikaeliti*, op. cit., p. 139. The words in italics are additions made by Cerulli.

[87] Ibid., pp. 139-42. The author wishes to stress once again that the insertion of the word "senses" in italics in the first line is the work of Cerulli.

[88] Agostino Tedla, "A proposito di alcuni passi oscuri negli Scritti teologici etiopici pubblicati da E. Cerulli", op. cit., pp. 228-30.

[89] "Restraining the impetus of the senses is right and not only commendable but necessary as well. There is, however, spiritual profit to be derived also when the senses run wild, when their violence is not immediately curbed. Not closely bounded by reason and running free to their content, they will also run to their complete and bitter disillusionment. The disenchantment thus inevitably encountered and confessed will be of spiritual profit to the Mikaelite." Enrico Cerulli, *Scritti Teologici Etiopici dei secoli XVI-XVII – Tre opuscoli dei Mikaeliti*, op. cit., p. 139, note 2.

discipline leading to laziness of the senses and failure to pay attention to the limited powers they do offer. Given this risk, the author appears to suggest that it is better to leave the senses free to pursue their illusions of truth, as they will soon discover their limitations through experience and frustration. The importance and utility he attaches to the observation of nature is indeed demonstrated by his above-mentioned descriptions of natural cycles and animal behaviors. Within the framework of this explanation, the meaning of the phrase "If two of them refuse to be yoked by you" in the above quotation—interpreted by Father Agostino as a reference to the feet—is not clear. One possibility is that these "two" are sight and hearing, two of the senses mentioned in the pages previous to this passage, which certainly make a more significant contribution to the knowledge of truth than smell and taste.[90]

Doubts on the Gnostic Interpretation of the Opuscula and a New Dating

On the basis of the foregoing discussion, it appears possible to state that Cerulli's interpretation has lost much of its importance because the critical observations of Father Agostino and his alternative solution of the "riddles" as well as the hypothesis outlined here are capable of accounting for all the characteristics of these writings that may leave the reader surprised or incredulous on first reading.

At the same time, it is true that despite this analysis, some Gnosticizing elements still appear to be present in the tracts. We refer in particular to the figures of speech or comparisons that recall the concept of a "nebular" divinity, i.e. one that will absorb the individual souls into itself, as part of itself, at the end of time to create a whole no longer susceptible of division or differentiation. The individual souls will lose all memory of earthly life, all specific determination of gender, human history, and so on, and any other characteristic making them different and unique. Among the various allusions of this kind present in the opuscula, attention can be drawn to the particularly effective comparison drawn in the first

---

[90] The four senses discussed in the pages leading up to the passage in question are sight, hearing, smell and taste. No mention is made of touch.

between the persons of the Trinity and honey in a quotation from Athanasius of Alexandria:

> They (the persons of the Trinity) are neither comprehensible nor knowable as creatures are, neither comparable nor visible, just as honey is not visible while it is still with the things from which it is born, i.e. in the wide open countryside, on the trees and in the grass, distributed in the individual flowers, in the bitter and the sweet. But now come the tricksters to show us with their wisdom the corporeal form of the floral species in which the taste of the goodness of the Creator was mixed. But the wise bee instead, when it gathers the essences of the flowers through patient toil, from far and near, makes a body of those essences (i.e. honey) so that it may be visible. On the contrary, once the honey has been made, it is no longer possible for the bee to return it once again to its various essences. Such is divinity. While it is diffused everywhere, it cannot be seen, just as it is impossible to return the honey of which we have spoken to the individual flowers.[91]

The reference that comes immediately to mind is the Manichaean fragments of light dispersed in matter, which must be distilled in order to join together once again, travelling in the vessels of the sun and the moon with the king of light. Closer reflection suggests, however, that these metaphors too could fall within the conception of the divinity as "ineffable mystery," which moreover informs the long "journey in search of the knowledge of God" found in the first of the opuscula and published by Cerulli also in his *Letteratura Etiopica*.[92] This is an idea of divinity that is always expressed through metaphors of indiscernibility (like the nectar of the different flowers in honey), infinity, and incalculability. While these are unquestionably characteristics also of the primal Gnostic divinity, the conception had also become an integral part of the thinking of some schools of Christian mysticism.

Other apparently Gnosticizing characteristics, albeit of lesser importance, include the figure of the serpent in the symbolic narrative on erroneous interpretation of the scriptures in the *Ship of the Soul*,[93]

---

[91] Enrico Cerulli, *Scritti Teologici Etiopici dei secoli XVI-XVII – Tre opuscoli dei Mikaeliti*, op. cit., p. 95.

[92] Enrico Cerulli, *La Letteratura Etiopica*, Florence-Milan, 1968, pp. 147-49; also in *Scritti Teologici Etiopici dei secoli XVI-XVII – Tre opuscoli dei Mikaeliti*, op. cit., pp. 125-28.

[93] Enrico Cerulli, *Scritti Teologici Etiopici dei secoli XVI-XVII – Tre opuscoli dei Mikaeliti*, op. cit., p. 210.

which immediately recalls the identification of the serpent in Genesis with Christ in some Gnostic sects.[94] Anyone wishing to challenge this reference would do well to consider the ambiguous role of this serpent, which appears to act in full accord with the will of God (something that is moreover also suggested for "Evil" in the *Pseudo-Clementine Homilies*).

Another is found in the *Safe Haven*, which again presents the "figure" of Christ intent on concealing Himself and His work from Satan.[95] This figure, which we have already found in the *Ascension of Isaiah*, also appears in the opuscula contained in the second volume of Cerulli's *Scritti Teologici*. While it obviously suggests a dualistic conception of the world, such beliefs were in any case widely held by Egyptian Coptic Christians and may be no more than surviving remnants of ancient narratives of Manichaean origin.

On the whole, however, these are aspects of lesser importance. On the one hand, they prompt reflection on the Gnosticizing characteristics present, according to Cerulli, in Egyptian Coptic Christianity; on the other, they remind us that the *Exposition of the Divinity* is in any case an intentionally provocative text, as attested for example by the above-mentioned figure of the serpent and the marked ambiguities also with apparent sexual references.[96]

In our view, the foregoing considerations as a whole reveal the substantial coherence of the formulations expressed in the three "Mikaelite" opuscula and the letter. The fact, pointed out by Cerulli, that the letter expounds no unorthodox doctrines, could be explained by a difference in aim or in date of composition with respect to the opuscula. Cerulli dates the letter between 1603 and 1604, on the basis of the

---

[94] Birger A. Pearson, *Ancient Gnosticism*, op. cit. p. 119.

[95] "Il Porto Sicuro" in Enrico Cerulli, *Scritti Teologici Etiopici dei secoli XVI–XVII – Tre opuscoli dei Mikaeliti*, op. cit., p. 286.

[96] In addition to the metaphor of the raped girl in the passage discussed above, we also have the ambiguous meanings of "wind" in the cosmogony of mother earth and the fact that it appears to symbolize sin in the passage on the incarnation of the Word in the *Ship of the Soul* (Enrico Cerulli, *Scritti Teologici Etiopici dei secoli XVI–XVII – Tre opuscoli dei Mikaeliti*, op. cit., p. 195). It may be worth recalling here that the Gnostics interpreted the words "And the Spirit of God moved upon the face of the waters" at the beginning of Genesis as a reference to Sophia wandering over the waters in shame and repentance of her actions (see Birger A. Pearson, *Ancient Gnosticism*, op. cit., pp. 111-12).

historical references it contains, and the three opuscula at the end of the 16th century, during the period of debate within the Ethiopian Church prior to its union with the Roman Catholic Church (1607–32). In the absence of any evidence whatsoever and for the reasons put forward above, especially the radical opposition expressed to the Jesuit presence in Ethiopia and the violence of some of the accusations made, the present author thinks it more probable that the three opuscula were written in another country, perhaps in Cairo and possibly by someone in exile precisely because of his opposition to the Ethiopian ruler's conversion to Roman Catholicism. They would thus have been written with the aim of urging a return to the traditional religious heritage both through blandishments and through threats, as clearly emerges in the "prophetic" parts of the texts,[97] where Catholicism is likened to the whore of Babylon. Similar considerations lead Father Agostino to disagree with Cerulli and suggest 1630–32 as a probable date for the composition of the opuscula.[98]

The hypothesis put forward here is that the author of the opuscula already possessed a broader education than was available in Ethiopia or that his stay in Cairo and contact with the Franciscan community there made him familiar with the debate on the Trinity developed in Europe after the 11th century and especially the disputes between Anselm of Canterbury, Roscellinus of Compiègne and Peter Abelard. Explicit reference was indeed made during this debate to the theories of the Sabellian heretics, as shown by the following quotation from Roscellinus:

> If the ship of the Christian faith is therefore to proceed unharmed, slipping between the two rocks, the greatest care must be taken that it neither founders on the reef of Sabellian singularity, which holds that the Father became flesh and suffered, nor falls into the danger of Arian plurality, which diversifies substance with distinctions of prior-posterior and greater-lesser to the point of introducing a plurality of gods due to its extreme way of considering diversity.[99]

As we have seen above, Giyorgis of Sägla indicated the Sabellian as the first of the heresies to be refuted in his *Book of Mystery* (1424).

---

[97] Agostino Tedla, "A proposito di alcuni passi oscuri negli Scritti teologici etiopici pubblicati da E. Cerulli", op. cit., pp. 231–35.

[98] Ibid., p. 235.

[99] M. Parodi and M. Rossini (ed.), *Fra le due rupi*, op. cit., p. 96.

Finally, we have the possibility, put forward by Father Agostino, that the author of the opuscula was simply "influenced" by the Jesuit missionaries during the debates prior to the union of the Ethiopian and Catholic church, and that they bear witness to the penetration of new ideas and new models of theological speculation in Ethiopia.

The Attribution of the Opuscula to Mikaelite Heretics

The other hypothesis, left unexamined so far, is that the Mikaelites who opposed Zär'a Ya'əqob in 1400 and were condemned by him had defined their doctrinal positions in the light of knowledge of the European philosophical debate on the Trinity developed during the Middle Ages. The links discerned by various scholars between the Patriarchate of Alexandria and the Mikaelite heretics[100] certainly make this hypothesis impossible to rule out, but there is no supporting evidence due to the unfortunate lack of original Mikaelite sources. All the testimony available today comes from those who condemned the Mikaelites. Examination of these partisan sources reveals that the salient points of the dispute were as follows:

- Observance of the Sabbath
- The image of God and the interpretation of the "anthropomorphic" passages in the Scriptures
- The Trinity
- The eschatological idea of Christ returning before the end of the world to reign on earth for a thousand years in the "supper on Mount Zion"
- The Mikaelite rejection of some texts regarded as canonical
- The adoration of the Virgin

As shown by the examination already carried out, the first of these is wholly absent from the opuscula, which were clearly not concerned with this subject. It is mentioned, however, in the *Consolation of the Soul*, the letter included in the same manuscript as the opuscula, where the author protests against the Ethiopian sovereign's decision to abolish observance

---

[100] The question of whether this was a heretical movement or simply a number of individuals expressing non-orthodox idea, as Piovanelli suggests in the above-mentioned essay, is immaterial for our purposes.

of the Sabbath. If it were confirmed that the letter and the opuscula are the work of the same hand, as suggested above, then this would constitute evidence of the absence of any connection not only between the Mikaelites condemned in 1400 and these texts but also between their author and the Egyptian Coptic Church, whose opposition to observance of the Sabbath is a known fact. These are, however, obviously no more than hypotheses.

The second and third subjects listed above are instead specifically addressed in these texts, but while there appears to be perfect correspondence with the Mikaelite views for the former, the vagueness of the formulation for the latter is such that it remains unclear whether the views expressed in the dispute with Zär'a Ya'əqob were Sabellian or derived from the sophisticated meditations of St Augustine and Abelard on the unknowability of God and the use of human words to express the divine. While we would regard the latter as the view put forward in the opuscula, it is today impossible to establish the position of the Mikaelites who clashed with Zär'a Ya'əqob.

There is no mention of the eschatological idea of Christ's return and the supper on Mount Zion in the opuscula, which were again certainly not concerned with these subjects. The absence of any reference whatsoever could, however, also be interpreted as suggesting that the author did not share these eschatological expectations.

Finally, the last two subjects may have been used by Zär'a Ya'əqob as grounds for his condemnation of the Mikaelites. There was unquestionably widespread resistance in the Ethiopian Church to acceptance of the *Book of Mary's Miracles* as a canonical work, and the most outspoken opponents could thus have been accused of "Hebraism" and disrespect towards the Virgin.

At the same time, the rejection of various texts regarded as canonical, like the *Book of Enoch*, the *Book of Jubilees*, the *Book of the Maccabees* and the *Testament of the Lord*, which were moreover non-canonical for other Christian churches too, could also have been for reasons—of exegesis, for example[101]—other than the fact that they contained references to the

---

[101] To be understood here as examination of the dating and origin of the texts. One of the reasons for rejection of the *Book of Mary's Miracles*, for example, was awareness that this was born out of medieval narratives that generally had nothing to do with the Gospels or with any earlier and more authoritative narratives regarding Christ. Similar considerations may have been developed for other works, such as the *Book of Enoch* and the *Book of Jubilees*, which were clearly Jewish in origin despite the subsequent interpolation of Christian elements.

personification of the Trinity, as Zär'a Ya'əqob claimed. It is in any case certain that the opuscula published by Cerulli repeatedly refer to the Virgin in wholly unambiguous terms. At the same time, according to Cerulli, the opuscula also contain various references both to the *Book of Enoch* and to the *Book of the Maccabees*, albeit not to the other two texts rejected by the Mikaelites.[102]

While there are thus no grounds to rule out a remote connection between the author of the opuscula and the Mikaelite heretics, neither is there sufficient reason to assert its existence. In any case, if this line of descent did exist, it would have characteristics very different from the Sabellian ones indicated by Cerulli and instead attest to the influence of medieval European disputes about the Trinity on the Mikaelites in the 15th century, which is not chronologically impossible.[103] In this case, however, it would be necessary to assume that the Mikaelites abandoned their opposition to observance of the Sabbath after the year 1400.

These arguments as a whole lead the present author to regard as improbable any connection between the opuscula published by Cerulli in the first volume of his *Scritti Teologici Etiopici dei secoli XVI-XVII* and the Mikaelite heretics of the 15th century. Here we part company with Father Agostino, who writes as follows in the conclusions of his essay after discussing the "figure" and the "likeness" of God and the idea that this "figure" is one of the tools needed by man to distinguish the three Persons:

> For this reason it is very probable that the opuscula in question do belong to the sect of the Mikaelites, as Cerulli believes. The Mikaelites maintained the very same views as our author in fact and could therefore easily be accused of modalism through denial of what was generally regarded as the principle of the distinction of the persons in the Holy Trinity, as stated above. This identification does not, however, authorize us to accuse the doctrine put forward in the writings of our author of heresy.[104]

---

[102] Enrico Cerulli, *Scritti Teologici Etiopici dei secoli XVI-XVII – Tre opuscoli dei Mikaeliti*, op. cit., p. 323.

[103] Peter Abelard was born in 1079 and died in 1142.

[104] Agostino Tedla, "A proposito di alcuni passi oscuri negli Scritti teologici etiopici pubblicati da E. Cerulli", op. cit., p. 241.

But who could this Nəwayä Mäsqäl have been? As a sophisticated intellectual, close enough to the ruler of Ethiopia to address him by letter in respectful but not obsequious terms, well versed in Qəne and aesthetics, and keenly aware of linguistic questions, he cannot have been someone never mentioned in the chronicles. We would venture to suggest that he may have been the Nəway—a hypocoristic form of Nəwayä Mäsqäl (or Krəstos)—mentioned in the abridged chronicle.[105] Täklä Śəllase, the royal chronicler and a convinced supporter of the Catholic party, was already principal secretary to the Ethiopian sovereign around 1612. He died in 1638. He appears to have been the leader, together with a certain Abib, of a group of priests renowned for their practice of Qəne, which included the Nəway we refer to here.

In conclusion, as shown also by the many uncertainties pointed out and the numerous hypotheses formulated with a view to painting a full picture, the "Mikaelite" opuscula published by Cerulli can be regarded as still retaining their enigmatic character for the reader nearly four centuries after their composition.

---

[105] D. Toubkis, "Täklä Śəllase" in Siegbert Uhlig (a cura di), *Encyclopaedia Aethiopica*, vol. IV, Wiesbaden 2010, pp. 843-844: p. 843.

BIBLIOGRAPHY OF WORKS CITED

This study is the initial, incomplete fruit of a broader investigation that is still under way. It is not easy to distinguish within this sphere between the works strictly relevant to the present study and those relevant instead to the ongoing investigations. For this reason, the following bibliography lists only a few works of general reference and those mentioned or specifically referred to during the study. The works are listed by the last name of the author or editor in alphabetical order.

Works of General Reference

Willis Barnstone and Marvin Meyer (eds.), *Essential Gnostic Scriptures*, Boston & London, 2010.

Marcello Craveri (ed.), *I Vangeli Apocrifi*, Turin, 2005.

Ambrogio Donini, *Storia del Cristianesimo*, Milan, 1975.

Mircea Eliade, *Trattato di Storia delle Religioni*, Turin, 2008.

Giovanni Filoramo, *Veggenti Profeti Gnostici*, Brescia, 2005.

Hans Jonas, *Lo Gnosticismo*, Turin, 1991.

Jacques-Paul Migne (ed.), *Dictionnaire des Apocryphes: Ou, Collection de tous le livres Apocryphes relatives à l'Ancien et au Nouveau Testament*, Paris, 1858.

Birger A. Pearson, *Ancient Gnosticism – Traditions and Literature*, Minneapolis, 2007.

Kurt Rudolph, *La Gnosi*, Brescia, 2000.

Paolo Sacchi (ed.), *Apocrifi dell'Antico Testamento*, Turin, 1981.

Siegbert Uhlig (ed.), *Encyclopaedia Aethiopica*, Wiesbaden, 2003–2014.

Other Works

St Augustine of Hippo, *La Trinità*, sito internet: "*http://www.augustinus.it/italiano/index.htm*"

Barbara Baert, *A Heritage of Holy Wood*, Leiden-Boston, 2004.

Antonio Battista and Bellarmino Bagatti, *La Caverna dei Tesori*, Jerusalem, 1980.

Antonio Battista and Bellarmino Bagatti, *Il Combattimento di Adamo*, Jerusalem, 1982.

Alessandro Bausi, *Il Qälemənṭos Etiopico. La rivelazione di Pietro a Clemente. I libri 3–7*, Naples, 1992.

Angela Bianchini (ed.), *Romanzi medievali d'amore e d'avventura*, Milan, 1981.

Bonaventura da Bagnoregio, *Itinerario della Mente in Dio*, Milan, 1996.

Rosanna Budelli (ed.), *Il Sigillo di Salomone. In tre manoscritti di magia copta in lingua araba*, Milan, 2014.

Ernest A. Wallis Budge, *The Queen of Sheba and her only son Menelik*, London 1932.

Ernest A. Wallis Budge, *Baralam and Yewasef – Being the Ethiopic Version of the Christianized Recension of the Buddist Legend of the Buddha and the Bodhisattva*, Cambridge, 1923.

Ernest A. Wallis Budge, *One Hundred and Ten Miracles of Our Lady Mary*, Oxford, 1933.

Ernest A. Wallis Budge, *The Ethiopian Book of the Dead – Ləfafä ṣədəq*, London, 1929.

Alberto Camplani (ed.), *Scritti Ermetici in Copto*, Brescia, 2000,

A. Caquot, "Aperçu préliminaire sur le *Mashafa Tefut* de Gechen Amba," in *Annales d'Ethiopie*, 1955, vol. 1, no. 1, pp. 89–108.

Enrico Cerulli, *Il Libro etiopico dei Miracoli di Maria e le sue fonti nelle letterature del Medio Evo latino*, Rome, 1958.

Enrico Cerulli, *La Letteratura Etiopica*, Florence-Milan, 1968.

Enrico Cerulli, *Scritti Teologici Etiopici dei secoli XVI-XVII – Tre opuscoli dei Mikaeliti*, Città del Vaticano, 1958.

Enrico Cerulli *Scritti Teologici Etiopici dei secoli XVI-XVII – La Storia dei Quattro Concili ed altri opuscoli monofisiti*, Città del Vaticano, 1960.

Gérard Colin, *Alexandre le Grand, héros chrétien en Ethiopie. Histoire d'Alexandre (Zênâ Eskender)*, Leuven, 2007.

Jean Daniélou, *La Teologia del Giudeo-Cristianesimo*, Bologna, 1964.

Jean Doresse, "Survivance d'Ecrits Gnostiques dans la Litterature Gueze," in *Proceedings of the Third International Conference of Ethiopian Studies*, Addis Ababa, 1970.

Maria Beatrice Durante Mangoni (ed.), *Erma - Il Pastore*, Bologna, 2003.

Helen C. Evans with Brandie Ratliff, *Byzantium and Islam. Age of Transition 7th-9th Century*, New York, 2012.

Sara Fani, "Magic, traditional medicine and theurgy in Arabo-Islamic manuscripts of the Horn of Africa: a brief note on their description," in *Essays in Ethiopian Manuscript Studies - Proceedings of the International Conference Manuscripts and Texts, Languages and Contexts: The Transmission of Knowledge in the Horn of*

Africa, Hamburg 17–19 July 2014, edited by Alessandro Bausi, Alessandro Gori and Denis Nosnitsin, Wiesbaden, 2015.

Eugenio Garin, *Il Ritorno dei Filosofi Antichi*, Naples, 1983.

Eugenio Garin, *Lo Zodiaco della Vita. La Polemica sull'Astrologia dal Trecento al Cinquecento*, Rome-Bari, 1976.

S. Grébaut, "Les Trois Dernièrs Traités du Livre de Mystères du Ciel et de la Terre," in *Patrologia Orientalis*, vol. 6, 1911.

S. Grébaut, "Littérature éthiopienne pseudo-clémentine. Texte et traduction du mystère du jugement des pécheurs," in *Revue de l'Orient Chrétien* 12 (1907), pp. 285–97, 380–92, and 13 (1908), pp. 166–80 and 314–20, and "Littérature éthiopienne pseudo-clémentine. Texte et traduction du traité La seconde venue du Christ et la résurrections des morts," in *Revue de l'Orient Chrétien* 15 (1910), pp. 198–214, 307–23, 425–39.

A. Giambelluca Kossava, C. Leonardi, L. Perrone, E. Norelli, P. Bettiolo (eds.), *Ascensio Isaiae. Textus*, Turnhout, 1995 (Corpus Christianorum. Series Apocryphorum 7).

G. Lusini, "Naufragio e conservazione di testi cristiani antichi: il contributo della tradizione etiopica," in *Annali dell'Università di Naples "L'Orientale"*, 69 (2009).

G. Lusini, "Origine e significato della presenza di Alessandro Magno nella letteratura etiopica," in *Rassegna di Studi Etiopici* 38 (1994).

Gianfrancesco Lusini, "Tradizione Origeniana in Etiopia," in *Origeniana Octava. Papers of the 8th International Origen Congress*, vol. II, Leuven, 2003.

Solomon Caesar Malan, *The Book of Adam and Eve, also called the conflict of Adam and Eve with Satan, a book of the early Eastern Church, translated from the Ethiopic, with notes from the Kufale, Talmud, Midrashim, and other Eastern works*, Edinburgh, 1882.

Paolo Marrassini, "L'Apocalisse di Pietro," in *Etiopia e oltre. Studi in onore di Lanfranco Ricci*, Naples, 1994.

Lorenzo Mazzoni (ed.), Kəbrä nägäśt – *La Bibbia Segreta del Rastafari*, Milan, 2013.

Jacques Mercier, *Le Roi Salomon et les maîtres du regard: art et médecine en Ethiopie*, Paris, 1994.

M. Parodi e M. Rossini (ed.), *Fra le due rupi, La logica della trinità nella discussione tra Roscellino, Anselmo e Abelardo*, Milan, 2000.

J. Perruchon, "Le Livre des Mystères du Ciel et de la Terre," in *Patrologia Orientalis*, Tome I, Fascicule 1, 1903.

Alberto Pincherle, *Introduzione al Cristianesimo Antico*, Bari, 1974.

Pierluigi Piovanelli, "Connaissance de Dieu et Sagenne Humaine en Ethiopie," in *Le Museon* 117, Leuven, 2004.

Pierluigi Piovanelli, "Les Aventures des Apocryphes en Ethiopie," in *Apocrypha. Revue Internationale des Littératures Apocryphes*, 4, Turnhout, 1993.

James B. Pritchard (ed.), *Solomon & Sheba*, London, 1974.

Anne Regourd, "Le Kitab al-Mandal al-Sulaymani, un ouvrage d'exorcisme yéménite postérieur au Ve/XIe s.?," in R. Gyselen (ed.) *Démons et merveilles d'Orient*, Res Orientales 13, Bures sur Yvette: Groupe pour l'étude de la civilization du Moyen-Orient, 2001.

S. Ronchey – P. Cesaretti (ed.), *Storia di Barlaam e Ioasaf. La vita bizantina del Buddha*, Turin, 2012.

Paolo A. Rossi, *Picatrix. Dalla versione latina del Ghayat al-hakim*, Milan, 2011.

David T. Runia, *Filone di Alessandria nella prima letteratura cristiana*, Milan, 1999.

Gershom Scholem, *La Kabbalah e il suo Simbolismo*, Turin, 1960.

Taddesse Tamrat, *Church and State in Ethiopia 1270–1527*, Oxford, 1972.

Agostino Tedla, "A proposito di alcuni passi oscuri negli Scritti teologici etiopici pubblicati da E. Cerulli," in *Proceedings of the Third International Conference of Ethiopian Studies*, Addis Ababa, 1970.

E.J. Van Donzel, *ʾƎnbaqom – Anqāṣā amin – La Porte de la Foi*, Leiden, 1969.

Jessie L. Weston, *From Ritual to Romance*, New York, 1957.

INDEX OF NAMES

Page numbers followed by 'n' refer to notes.

During the compilation of this index, the question arose of whether to include all the names of the Gnostic emanations. Given their sheer number and the limited usefulness of items like Foreknowledge or Selfbegotten, which are both names and definitions, it was decided to exclude all those not also present in other religions, philosophical conceptions or historical narratives of a more or less mythicized nature. Sophia, Hermes Trismegistus and Seth are thus included, for example, as figures taken up by certain Gnostic sects when already known in other contexts. It was also decided not to include minor entities personified in Gnosticism or other religions or philosophies, e.g. planets, angels and devils. Movements like Catharism are also excluded.

In addition to the names of people and places, the index also includes the titles of the works cited in the text.

Abel, 4, 71
Abelard, Peter, 147, 228, 231, 240, 242, 243n103
Abib, 244
Abraham, 71, 144, 147, 213n48, 218
Abu Maa'shir, 178
Acts of the Apostles, 1, 15, 81n87, 89
Acts of Thomas, 76, 81, 81n87, 89
Adam, 3–5, 20, 34, 54–59, 55, 56, 71–73, 76, 87, 91–93, 109, 144, 152n199, 169, 171, 174, 180

Addis Ababa, 24, 65
Adrami (son of Solomon), 72, 73
Adulis, xi, xii, 29, 105
Africa, 15, 21
Aksum, viii, x, xi, xii, 69, 70, 74n82
Al Kindi, 178
al-Buni, Ahmad, 66
Alexander the Great, 85–90
Alexandria, xii, 12–14, 16, 21, 33, 85, 105, 128, 146, 149, 151, 170, 172, 178, 182, 185, 226, 238, 241
Algeria, 21
Al-Nur al-asna fi sarh al-asma' al-husna ("The most brilliant light on the explanation of the most

INDEX OF NAMES

beautiful Names of God"), 65–66
'Amdä Səyon (Ethiopian king), 53, 69
Amélineau, Edouard, 70
Andärta, 69
Anne (St Anne, mother of the Virgin Mary), 170n211
Anqäṣä Amin (see *Gate of Faith*)
Anselm, St Anselm, 240
Apocalypse of Peter, 54
Apocryphon of John, 3
Apostolic Letters, 1
Arabia, 15
Arabian Nights, 86, 177
Aristotle, 112
Armenia, 21
Ascension of Isaiah, 34, 39–43, 150, 167, 171, 239
Asclepius, 5
Asia Minor, 21
'Aṣqa (Ethiopian heretic), 127, 185
Athanasius of Alexandria, 16, 149, 238
Augustine, St Augustine of Hippo, 21, 147, 148, 227–230, 242

Babel, 77, 78
Babylon, 19, 21, 204, 234, 240
Bacon, Roger, 231
Baert, Barbara, 86n100
Bagatti, Bellarmino, 90nn108–110
Balkans, 21
Bandlet of Righteousness (*Ləfafä ṣədəq*), 53, 96–120, 96n124, 125, 163, 175, 179–180
Barlaam and Josaphat, 53, 94–96, 176
Barnstone, Willis, 14n9, 33n28, 48n46
Bärtälomewos (Metropolitan of Ethiopia), 127, 185
Bäṣälotä Mika'el (Ethiopian abbot), 84
Battista, Antonio, 90nn108–110
Bausi, Alessandro, xiiin6, 54n54, 61, 66n71
Bethlehem, 42
Beylot, Robert, 69, 70, 174n216
Bezold, Carl, 70
Bible, 5, 9, 13, 16, 33, 35n31, 48, 67, 172
Bonaventure (St Bonaventure), 227, 227n68, 231
Book of Enoch, 11–12, 19, 34–39, 44, 85, 122, 153, 166–167, 242, 242n101, 243
Book of Jubilees, 167, 168, 242, 242n101
Book of Life, 98
Book of Mary's Miracles, 175, 186, 242, 242n101
Book of Mysteries of Heaven and Earth, 53, 153
Book of Mystery, 24, 186, 240
Book of the Dead, 31, 102, 103
Buddha, 20, 94, 96n123
Budelli, Rosanna, 63n67, 65n70
Budge, Ernest A. Wallis, 67, 70, 72n80, 81nn86–87, 89n106, 95n118, 96n122,n124, 98, 98n127, 100n129, 102, 102n132, 103, 105n134, 106, 111
Byzantium, 51n47, 68

Cain, 4, 71
Cairo, 70n77, 230, 232, 235, 240
Caligula, 13
Callisthenes of Olynthus (Pseudo-Callisthenes), 85
Camplani, Alberto, 30n26
Caquot, A., 174n213

INDEX OF NAMES

Caucasus, 19
Cave of Treasures, 90
Cerulli, Enrico, ii, iii, xiiin8,
    23–26, 23n14, 24n16, 33, 70, 71,
    86–87, 87n101, 96, 127–152,
    128n152, 129n154, 130n157,
    131nn158,159,161, 132n162,
    136nn167–168, 138nn172,174,
    140n178, 142n182, 147n191,
    149nn193–194, 150nn195,197,
    169n208, 170n210, 185–244,
    186nn1,3, 188–189nn6–7,
    193nn8,9,12, 194n13, 197n18,
    199n23, 202n29, 204–205nn33–
    35, 207n39, 211n46, 216n52,
    218n53, 220n56, 222nn59–60,
    225n63, 226n65, 227nn66,69,72,
    228n73, 233n79, 234nn81,84,
    236nn86,87,89, 238nn91–93,
    239nn95–96, 243n102
Cesaretti, P., 96n122
China, 21
*Christian Romance of Alexander
    (Zena Əskəndər)*, 53, 85, 86,
    89–90, 172, 177, 180
Clement (Christian saint, the
    second pope according to some
    traditions), 54, 59
Colbert, Jean-Baptiste, 232
Colin, Gérard, 85n98, 87n102,
    88n104, 138n173, 207n40
Combat of Adam, 53, 90–94, 91n111,
    172, 174, 177, 179
*Consolazione dell'Anima
    (Consolation of the Soul)*, 233,
    241
Constantine (Roman emperor),
    16–17, 175n218

Constantinople, 16, 96, 176
Conti Rossini, Carlo, vii, 24
Convivio, 136n169, 198n20
Corpus Hermeticum, 82
Craveri, Marcello, 245
Cyprus, 15
Cyriacus of Behnesā, 189
Daniélou, Jean, 167–168
Dante Alighieri, 136, 198
David, 42, 70, 72, 73
Dayr al Muharraq, 230, 232
De Trinitate (On the Trinity),
    227, 227n67
*Describing how the Kingdom of
    David was Transferred from
    Jerusalem to Ethiopia*, 70
Dieci Questioni (Ten Questions),
    138n174, 169, 207n42
Diocletian (Roman emperor), 21
Doresse, Jean, iii, 24, 24n15, 25
Duns Scotus, 231
Durante Mangoni, Maria Beatrice,
    45n43

Egypt, vii, 13–17, 21, 27, 29, 29n25,
    33, 51–53, 62, 63, 65, 70, 77–78,
    81, 82, 85, 90, 103–105, 118, 123,
    161, 169–170, 173, 176, 178, 179,
    182, 230, 232–233, 235
'Ənbaqom, 51n47
*Encyclical epistle of Athanasius of
    Alexandria*, 16, 149, 238
Enoch (biblical patriarch), 34–35, 61
Esau, 71
Esdras (2 Esdras), 167
Ethiopia, i–v, vii–xiii, 11, 17, 23–27,
    29–30, 33–34, 39, 48, 51–54, 60,
    62–63, 65, 67–70, 73, 80, 90, 92,

98, 100, 105, 111, 118–120, 123–124, 127, 128, 128n153, 130, 139, 146, 152, 153, 161–163, 165–168, 170–171, 173–188, 202–206, 208, 224–227, 229–235, 240–242, 244
Evans, Helen C., 51n47
Eve, 4, 15, 20, 33–34, 55–56, 59, 91–92, 152n199, 171, 174, 180
Ewosṭatewos (founder of the Eustacian movement), 128n153, 186n2
Exposition of the Divinity (*Fəkkare mäläkot*), 25, 130, 131, 150, 188, 189, 193, 198, 202, 207, 208, 210, 220, 224, 239

Fani, Sara, 63n66, 66, 66n71, 67n74
Fəkkare mäläkot (see *Exposition of the Divinity*)
Foucault, Michel, 71n79

Gäbrə'el (metropolitan of Ethiopia), 128, 185
Garin, Eugenio, 178n222, 178n223
Gate of Faith (*Anqäṣä Amin*), 51n47
Gaul, 21
Gelasius (pope), 43
Genesis, vii, 34, 40, 43, 61, 150, 150n198, 169, 172–174, 239
Georgia, 94
Gəšän Amba (Gechen Amba), 174
Giyorgis (Eustacian monk), 129, 186
Giyorgis of Sägla, 128, 143, 182, 185, 186, 240
Goliath
Gori, Alessandro, 66n71
Gospel of John, 82
Gospel of Thomas, 19, 81, 82, 82n90,
83n91, 88, 138n173
Gospel of Truth, 8n5, 76
Grebaut, Sylvain, 54n53, 56n55, 84, 84n95
Greece, 5, 13, 21, 161n201
Gregory (St Gregory Thaumaturgus), 143, 218
Guide to the Guide, 63
Gunda, Gunde, 48
Gyselen, R., 63n66

Hegel, Georg Wilhelm Friedrich, 75
Heraclius (Byzantine emperor), 86, 86n100
Hermas, 43, 44
Hermes Trismegistus, 5, 30, 117, 178
Hezekiah, 40
Hymn of the Pearl, 19, 76, 81, 81n87, 83, 84
Hypostasis of the Archon, 33

India, xii, 19, 76, 94, 96n123
Iran, 19
Isa Ibn Zur'a, 230, 231
Isaac, 71, 143–144, 147, 218, 228
Isaiah (biblical prophet), 39, 40, 144, 219
Ishmael, 71
Israel, 12, 67–68, 72, 74n83, 80, 124, 173, 174
Italy, i, 21, 120

Jacob, 71, 143, 144, 147, 218, 228
Jacobus da Varagine, 94
Jeroboam (son of Solomon), 68
Jerusalem, 12, 70, 86, 230
Jesse, 72
Jesus Christ, 20, 39, 41, 82

INDEX OF NAMES

Joachim, 72
John (St John the Evangelist), 230
John, son of Zebedee (St John the Apostle), 3
Jonas, Hans, 79n85, 87n103
Josab, 40
Joseph (husband of the Virgin Mary), 42
Judas, 14
Judas Iscariot, 14, 123
Judas Thomas (St Thomas the Apostle), 76, 82n90, 171
Justinian (Roman emperor), 16

Kəbrä nägäśt, 53, 62n64, 67–84, 68, 69n75, 70n78, 72n80, 74n83, 123, 169, 170, 173, 174n216, 175, 175n218, 176, 177
Kitab al-Mandal al-Sulaymani, 63n66
Kitab bahga al-tarf fi 'ilm al-harf ("The book of the joy of the glance into the science of the letters"), 65
Kitab fi 'ilm al-arqam wa-l-awfaq ("The book on the science of number and of the magic squares"), 65
Komsat (folower of Alexander the Great), 87, 88

Ləfafä ṣədəq (see *Bandlet of Righteousness*)
Licopolis, 21
Life of St Anne, 84, 170
Lusini, Gianfrancesco, iv, vii, 60, 60n58, 85, 85nn98–99, 92, 92n115, 129n156, 187n5

Maishan, 77
Makədda (see Sheba)
Malan, Solomon Caesar, 91, 91n111, 174n214
Manasseh, 39
Mani, 19, 20–21
Märbäbtä Sälomon (see *Net of Solomon*)
Marrassini, Paolo, 54n52, 69, 70, 70n78
Mary (Virgin Mary), 42, 74, 89, 96, 98, 100, 105, 118, 119, 120, 125, 140, 200, 223
Mäṣhafä Bərhan, 127, 128, 129, 185, 186
Mäṣhafä Tefut (*Mashafa Tefut*), 174n213
Mazzoni, Lorenzo, 247
Media, 19
Mediterranean, i, viii, 13, 14, 53, 94, 111, 162, 178
Mənilək I (Ethiopian king), 67, 68, 76, 80, 81, 81n86, 175
Mercier, Jacques, v, 63, 105, 153, 153n200, 161–162, 163
Mesopotamia, 76, 82
Meyer, Marvin, 14n9, 33n28, 48n46, 83n91, 111n140, 138n173, 207n40
Migne, Jacques-Paul, 62n63
Mika'el (metropolitan of Ethiopia), 84, 128, 185
Mirror of the Intellect, 205, 206, 220, 222, 223
Moses, 110, 172, 172n218
Muslama al-Magritti, 111
Mystery of the Judgment of Sinners, 54

INDEX OF NAMES

Nag Hammadi, iii, 17, 17n12, 25
Nasr al-Din Muhammad b. 'Abdallah Ibn Qurqmas, 65
Nave dell'Anima (Ship of the Soul), 130n157
Nazareth, 231
Net of Solomon (Märbäbtä Sälomon), 63
Nəway, 244
Nəwayä Mäsqäl, 234, 235, 244
Noah, 72, 74, 213
Norelli, Enrico, 247
Nosnitsin, Denis, 66n71
On the Origin of the World, 33, 33n28, 169n207
Origen, 16, 60–61, 91–94, 123, 171–173, 176, 181, 183

Palestine, 12, 230, 232
Paracelsus, 111
Paris, 230, 233
Parthia, 19, 78
Paul (St Paul of Tarsus), 15, 19, 20, 144, 219
Pearson, Birger A., 1, 1n1, 26, 26n21, 33, 33n27, 34, 81, 81n88, 82, 138n175, 150n196, 169, 169n207, 208, 208n43, 214n49, 239n94
Perez, 72
Perruchon J., 84, 84n94
Persia, 15, 19, 94, 111n140, 161
Peter (St Peter the Apostle), 2, 54, 59, 189
Philo of Alexandria, 12–14, 172
Picatrix, 111–118, 112n141, 113, 119, 120, 178, 178n222, 179
Pico della Mirandola, 111
Piovanelli, Pierluigi, ii, xiin5, 25, 25n17, 26, 26n24, 39n38, 131n160, 137n171, 138, 139, 193, 193n11, 199n22, 206–207, 207nn38,41, 208, 229–230, 230n75, 241n100
Plato, 10–11, 30, 75, 83, 170–171, 172
Pliny, 217
Porto Sicuro (Safe Haven), 130, 130n157, 150, 150n197, 188, 188n6, 231, 239, 239n95
Prayer of Redemption, 98
Prayer of Salvation, 98
Pritchard, James B., 162n202
Psalms, 64–65, 64n69
Pseudo-Clementine Homilies, 150, 167n205, 214, 239

Qälemənṭos, 53, 54–61, 54n53, 171–172, 174, 177
Qumran, 12
Quran, 62, 86

Ratliff, Brandie, 51n47
Red Sea, viii, xi, 29, 51, 51n48
Regourd, Anne, 63n66
Reuben, 71
Revelation (Book of Revelation), 84, 204
Ricci, Lanfranco, ixn2, 54n52, 69
Rodinson, Maxime, 166
Rohoboam (see Jeroboam)
Romance of Alexander, 53, 85, 86, 89–90, 172, 177, 180
Rome, v, 15, 21, 43, 48, 230–231
Ronchey, S., 96n122

INDEX OF NAMES

Roscellinus of Compiègne, 240
Rossi, Paolo A., 112n141, 148n192, 229n74, 240n99
Runia, David T., 171

Sacchi, Paolo, 245
Ṣägga Krəstos, 230, 231n76, 232, 233n78, 235
Sälama "the Translator" (metropolitan of Ethiopia), 52, 53
Samarkand, 21
Sams al-ma'arif al-Kubra ("The big sun of knowledge"), 66
Sarbug, 77, 78
Šäwa, 53
Scholem, Gershom, 109n135, 110, 119, 178n221
Seal of Solomon (Egyptian), 63–64, 96, 100, 102, 111, 118, 179
Seal of Solomon (Ethiopian), 63, 163
Second Coming of Christ and the Resurrection of the Dead, 54
Seth (biblical patriarch), 3, 4–5, 14, 43
Sheba (Queen Sheba of Ethiopia, Makədda), 67, 69, 70, 80, 81n86, 173, 175, 175n219
Shem (biblical patriarch), 20
Shepherd of Hermas, 34, 43–48, 167
Silk Road, 21
Simon Magus, 1, 2
Solomon (biblical king), 62–63, 62n61, 67–71, 80, 81n86, 104, 124, 124n151, 161, 173, 174, 178
Sophia (Wisdom), 3–5, 10, 34, 43, 81, 169
Spain, 21, 111
Storia dei Quattro Concili (*Mazgaba Haymanot* or *Treasure/Treasury of Faith*), 169, 222, 223, 224
Sudan, xii, 161
Syria, 15, 21, 39, 82

Taddesse Tamrat, 52, 53, 53n50
Täklä Śəllase, 244, 244n105
Tamrin (merchant at the service of the Queen of Sheba), 67
Tana (Lake Tana), 60, 92
Tarmiza (wife of Noah), 72
Tedla Agostino (Father), 24, 24n16, 131, 131n159, 134, 136n168, 137, 141n179, 146n189, 183, 193, 196, 197n16, 198, 201n25, 204n32, 214n50, 220n55, 226n65, 227n71, 236n88, 240n97, 243n104
Təgray, 70
Testament of Solomon, 53, 62–67, 96, 102, 119, 163, 177, 179, 182
Theonas of Alexandria (Egyptian bishop), 16
Theophilus (Egyptian bishop), 16
Thomas (St Thomas the Apostle), see Judas Thomas
Toth (Egyptian god), 30
Tripartite Tractate, 172
Turin, 230

Uhlig, Siegbert, 23n13, 62n60, 69n75, 70n78, 129n156, 187n5, 231–232nn76–77, 244n105
Uzbekistan, 21

Valentinian I (Roman emperor), 21
Valentinus, 16, 30, 88
Van Donzel, E.J., 51n47

Weil, G., 62n63

Weston, Jessie L., 166n203
William of Ockham, 231

Ya'əbikä Egzi', 69
Ya'əqob (Abuna), 52
Yəshaq (Ethiopian king, brother of Zär'a Ya'əqob), 120, 127, 162, 185
Yəshaq (Ethiopian monk, regarded by some scholars as another name of Zosimas), 84
Yoḥannəs (bishop of Ethiopia), 128, 185

Zagwe, 51–52, 69
Zämika'el (Ethiopian heretic), 127–130, 185–188
Zär'a Ya'əqob (Ethiopian king), 26–27, 39, 53, 70, 98, 100, 119, 120, 124, 125, 127–128, 128n153, 129, 130, 138, 151, 162, 173–176, 179, 185–186, 188, 207, 241–243
Zena Əskəndər (see *Christian Romance of Alexander*)
Zoroaster, 5, 20
Zosimas, see Yəshaq

www.ingramcontent.com/pod-product-compliance
Lightning Source LLC
Chambersburg PA
CBHW030530230426
43665CB00010B/835